Goodbye Lizzie Borden

Lizzie Borden, *circa* 1890

Goodbye
Lizzie Borden

ROBERT SULLIVAN

THE STEPHEN GREENE PRESS

BRATTLEBORO, VERMONT

This book has been produced in the United States of America, designed by R. L. Dothard Associates, and composed, printed, and bound by The Colonial Press.

It is published by The Stephen Greene Press, Brattleboro, Vermont 05301.

Library of Congress Cataloging in Publication Data

Sullivan, Robert, 1916–

  Goodbye Lizzie Borden.

  Bibliography: p.
  1. Borden, Lizzie Andrew, 1860–1927. 2. Borden, Abby Durfee (Gray) 1828–1892. 3. Borden, Andrew Jackson, 1822–1892. I. Title.
KF223.B6S9   345'.73'02523   73-86037
ISBN 0-8289-0203-8

74 75 76 77 78 79 9 8 7 6 5 4 3 2 1

CONTENTS

LIST OF ILLUSTRATIONS

For Billie and Sally

The Fascination:

A PREFACE

CURRENTLY, as this is written, there are eighteen thousand murders committed annually in the United States. This shocking statistic means that every half-hour of every average day someone somewhere in this country falls victim to the most aggravated heinousness, to that ultimate crime—murder.

It is perplexing that the American public, swimming as it is in a sea of contemporary violence, still finds the trial of Lizzie Borden in the early 1890's the most continually absorbing case in the annals of this nation's homicides. Many sensational murder trials of the twentieth century have received extensive press notice, and a few have been given saturation news coverage. It is unlikely, however, that any capital crime has held such a firm purchase on public attention and so completely engrossed the nation's press as did the savage butchery of Andrew Jackson Borden and his wife, Abby, in Fall River, Massachusetts, in 1892, and the trial of their daughter Lizzie in nearby New Bedford the following year.

Lexicographers define parricide as the murder of one who stands in a specially sacred relation, as that of a parent. Despite the frightening number of murders, parricide is not a common crime in America; double parricide is rare here; and double parricide with the contextual ramifications of the Borden killings may be unique. For the slaughter on that sultry August morning occurred in the staid household of a "first family," and the person brought to trial was a dominant and well-to-do spinster, not a deranged juvenile gone berserk against domestic oppression. Perhaps this singularity—coupled with what the peerless William Roughead, a Scot, and in all likelihood the greatest writer in the English language on notable murders, called the "sheer cold-drawn horror of 'the Borden home' "—contributes much to the sustained public interest in the case, and explains why attention has been aroused periodically, from decade to decade, from generation to generation, for four score years.

Throughout this time the memory of the murders, the memory of the principals, and the memory of the deadly hatchet, simply will not erode from the American consciousness. This enduring public obsession is fed by the whimsical and numerically inaccurate jingle which, in celebrating the crime and its characters, has become this country's best-known quatrain:

> *Lizzie Borden took an axe*
> *And gave her mother forty whacks;*
> *And when she saw what she had done,*
> *She gave her father forty-one.*

This little rhyme, with its measured pulsation, is as popularly recited today as it was at the turn of the century, and has done much to make the incomparable Lizzie Borden a part of the nation's folklore.

But there have been many other contributions to the legend of Lizzie, and they range from the sound and sensible to the silly and senseless, from the factual to the fanciful, from the realistic to the ridiculous. Since the 1893 verdict to the present day there have appeared thousands of articles in every imaginable sort of publication; at least six full-length books; a ballet, several plays on the stage and one on television; and, as this is written, a motion picture is said to be in production—and all telling the sad saga of the murders and the trial. In addition, there has been a mass of spin-offs both literary and theatrical, works which are, on their face, fiction, but which bear a strikingly recognizable reference or resemblance to facts in the Borden story.

The approaches and conclusions of all this material vary widely and are marked by inaccuracy and disparity. Among the books alone, one, written in 1937, implies that the prosecution's case failed by reason of being poorly structured and poorly presented, but presses the author's view of Lizzie's categorical guilt. Another, written twenty years later, postulates the author's conviction of Lizzie's absolute innocence. A third assumes her guilt but attributes her murderous hand to a type of epileptic seizure first detected and diagnosed by the author of the book seventy-five years after the killings and forty years after Lizzie's death.

Like any other member of the public interested in our American criminal history, initially I experienced the confusion compounded by this welter of reportage, which is so notably marked by its lack of unanimity as to what actually happened at the Borden home the morning of 4 August 1892, and as to what actually transpired in the New Bedford courthouse in June 1893 when Lizzie Andrew Borden was placed at the bar to be tried for the ferocious murders of her father and stepmother.

Later, after serving a number of years as a justice of the Massachusetts Superior Court, the tribunal before which Lizzie was tried for her life some eighty years ago, I turned to the official verbatim transcript of all the testimony at her trial: because the actual evidence adduced at the trial is the only accurate disclosure of the circumstances surrounding the deaths of the victims and the fate of the defendant, it would seem therefore to be the only completely satisfactory source in resolving the Borden case.

I then examined this record as any professional in the law would do, and the result is this book.

Parenthetically, the nearly two thousand pages of the trial transcript are fascinating—more so than all the conjectures. Any member of the public can share the fascination by examining the entire official record in the form of microtext at the Boston Public Library, or elsewhere.

Meanwhile it has been attempted within the pages that follow to exhume and reproduce faithfully the facts surrounding the murders and the events leading to the trial. In addition, the conduct of the trial has been to some extent analyzed and dissected. An effort to perform an autopsy has been undertaken here, if you will, an autopsy of a murder trial held in 1893.

It has been my earnest purpose to present the facts and the trial testimony of the witnesses with as much accuracy and objectivity as it is possible to do. As to the conduct of the Borden trial, special care has been taken to opine only when the opinion lies within my own area of sophistication, and then only when the opinion is clearly indicated and marked as such.

The Bordens
and the Town

ALL PERSONS who had any intimate connection with the Borden case, which was tried four score years ago, are now long dead—dead all but one: the niece and namesake of the first victim of the murderer's hatchet, Abby Borden. She is Mrs. Abby Potter, and at this writing she is living in Providence, Rhode Island.

Ninety years old in 1973, this lady is, or appears to be, perfectly healthy, intelligent, and extremely articulate. For eighty years she has lived with her memories of the case and now, philosophically, constantly—even compulsively—she talks of Fall River in 1892, of the Bordens, of the murders and the trial. To Mrs. Potter there is no mystery surrounding the deaths by violence of Andrew J. Borden and Abby, his wife: Lizzie Borden killed them; Lizzie Borden slaughtered them; there is no note of equivocation in Mrs. Potter's conversation—Lizzie was guilty; and that is, or was, that.

I first met Abby Borden Whitehead Potter on the Memorial Day weekend of 1972. Her nephew, George Whitehead, had called me to say that his aunt understood I had been working on the Borden case and that she was anxious to talk with me. Recognizing the Whitehead name for its close family connection with the woman slain so long ago, I called Mrs. Potter and then traveled with tape recorder and camera to see her at her home in Providence. Astonishingly, Mrs. Potter had never before been interviewed by anyone who has written about the murders and the trial. Her story, her views, and her knowledge of the case—which is in some measure firsthand and in part family lore—have never before been publicly disclosed.

When she greeted me, I was struck by her vigor, and later, completely at ease, Mrs. Potter talked and answered questions for several hours as we sat at her kitchen table with the tape recorder in front of her. In her pleasant New England accent she described for me the Fall River scene in 1892, and vividly she brought onstage for my benefit all the characters of the

4

grisly drama enacted that sweltering August morning—her aunt, Abby Borden; Andrew Borden; Emma Borden, Lizzie Borden's sister; Bridget Sullivan, the maid; and, of course, Lizzie. Mrs. Potter made them all live again.

Later we drove together from Providence to Fall River, and there without hesitation she directed me to each place of significance in her account of the Borden tragedy. From the former home on Fourth Street of Mrs. Potter's mother—Sarah Whitehead, Abby Borden's younger sister, who was called "Bertie"—we drove to Andrew J. Borden's house near by on Second Street; then we crossed the city to the fashionable residential area to see the fine house Lizzie bought after the trial and named "Maplecroft"; and, last, on to the inconceivable arrangement of family graves, planned by Lizzie, in the Oak Grove Cemetery. Throughout the tour Mrs. Potter discussed the Fall River of her childhood, and the murders and the trial, and their effect on the lives of those involved. The earnest way she spoke made me feel that Mrs. Potter wished sincerely for all the truths to be known, wished that, for once, for all and finally, the clouds of fiction which for decades have surrounded the Borden case could be dispelled forever.

Partly based upon Mrs. Potter's recollections, partly upon my own experiences in Fall River, and partly upon a wide variety of geographical and genealogical source material, here follows a description of the backdrop against which the ghastly events of the Borden murders were unfolded.

In 1958 I presided at the long winter session of the Bristol County Superior Court sitting in Fall River. It was a winter too harsh for commuting from my home outside Boston, so I elected to live in Fall River throughout the entire session of the court. Thus I came to know the city, and to enjoy it. I liked its people, who are courteous and friendly, albeit with a pleasantly reserved manner native to this part of the country.

Fall River looks not at all like the typical mill town, for parts of it are scenic, almost beautiful. The city proper is located on what might be called a plateau, with a series of abrupt slopes rising from the Taunton River and Mount Hope Bay, which form its westerly boundary. "The Hill," as the prime residential section is called, commands a magnificent view over the bay and the river, and the stately late-Victorian homes there look solid enough to last another century or more.

To the east, Fall River is bounded by two large lakes—called ponds in the traditionally low-key Yankee way—North Watuppa Pond and South Watuppa Pond, and together they are about seven miles long and nearly one mile wide. From these lakes to Mount Hope Bay courses the Quequechan River, which, descending one hundred twenty-seven feet in a length of less than half a mile, gives the city the name of Fall River.

The stream bisects the town from east to west, running directly through it and immediately beneath the central business district. Obviously the great mills of the last century were built along the river's banks to utilize the tremendous surge of waterpower it generated as it raced to the bay.

On the north lies an expanse of gently rolling country, and on the south is Stafford Pond and the Rhode Island state line; Portsmouth, Rhode Island, where the original Bordens first settled, is only a very few miles south of Fall River. Historically, the precise location of the Massachusetts-Rhode Island line at the southerly end of Fall River has been a source of dispute between the two states almost since the area was settled. Be that as it may, like the people of New Bedford, Massachusetts, ten miles to the east, the people of Fall River seem to have a greater affinity toward Providence, the capital city of Rhode Island, just to their west, than they do toward Boston, the capital of the Commonwealth of Massachusetts but nearly fifty miles to the north.

Water transportation from Mount Hope Bay into Narragansett Bay and the Atlantic, coupled with waterpower provided by the swiftly flowing river, accounted in large measure for the rapid growth of Fall River in the 1800's. However, in the latter half of the century Fall River grew and prospered too fast, too soon, for the twentieth century brought the almost complete shift of the textile industry to the Southern states, and this, plus local labor troubles and the slump in cotton manufacturing after World War I, resulted in urban economic decay. Thus in later years Fall River was left with pleasant memories of prosperous days past and the unpleasant realities of unemployment lines and ugly, deserted factories and mills ringing its southern perimeter.

But the beauty of Fall River was largely unspoiled when the Bordens owned it. Yes, owned it. And not in the colloquial but in the literal sense, for the history of Lizzie Borden's family was in major part the history of Fall River. Lizzie was the ninth generation in her paternal line of Bordens to live in or near what is now Fall River, and an overview of her genealogy demonstrates how important Fall River was to the Bordens and how important the Bordens were to Fall River. Historic and economic considerations aside, at the time of the murders the Bordens were leading citizens by virtue of sheer numbers: the City Directory for 1892 lists one hundred twenty-six Borden heads of families within the city limits.

The progenitor of this powerful clan was John Borden, who arrived with his family in Portsmouth, Rhode Island, in 1638, three years after arriving in Boston from his native Kent, in England. In that same year Anne Hutchinson and her small band of followers, called Antinomians, had been banished from the Massachusetts Bay Colony for heresy and had settled Portsmouth. Although there exists no complete list of the few followers of Anne Hutchinson, John Borden was almost certainly one of the Antinomians, since he appears as an original landholder of Portsmouth in 1638, the year of its settlement.

When he died, he left a substantial estate and a son, also John, born in 1640, who became a very important—and colorful—figure in this part of New England in the seventeenth century. Unsuccessful in negotiating for peace with King Philip, the Indian leader with whom he had traded and become very friendly, the next highlight of his career came in 1684 when he refused to pay taxes on land he owned that was assessed by both Bristol and Plymouth counties. He was arrested and jailed in Bristol County, not far from where his descendant was to be confined to await trial for murder some two centuries later.

At the age of seventy he owned all the land now known as the West End of Fall River and he settled his two sons there; one of them was Richard Borden, third generation of Lizzie's paternal genealogical line. In time, Richard and his brother became involved in a dispute over water rights with the only other property owner in the Fall River area; the matter was finally resolved when the Borden brothers bought the additional vast holdings for seven hundred forty dollars. Thus with this purchase, together with their own inheritance, in the year 1714 the Bordens owned all of what is now Fall River, and a great deal more land across the Taunton River comprising the present site of the towns of Swansea and Somerset, Massachusetts.

In the fourth generation, Thomas Borden, son of Richard, built his home upon land near what is now the southerly boundary of Fall River, and less than a mile south of where later would be built a dwelling designated as 92 Second Street. His son—the fifth generation of Lizzie's paternal line and called Richard for his grandfather—constructed and operated a sawmill on the Quequechan River until it was burned to the ground by a landing party of British soldiers at the height of the American Revolution.

Richard's son, also named Richard, was born in Fall River in 1750. He was one of the eighteen settlers, nine of whom were Bordens, to whom the Massachusetts legislature granted township rights in 1803, when Richard's son Abraham, Lizzie Borden's grandfather, was five years old.

It was with Abraham that Lizzie's branch of the family began to fail to measure up to other Borden cousins who engaged in more profitable businesses with more social cachet. A fisherman and fishmonger, he was nevertheless prudent enough to retain the real estate and water rights which he had inherited from his father and which, with a very modest monetary inheritance, he passed on to his son Andrew Jackson Borden, the male victim of this strange case. In 1854, when Fall River received its first city charter from the legislature of the Commonwealth, Andrew Borden was then thirty-two years old and a successful undertaker.

At the high noon of the nineteenth century, Fall River began to prosper. The potential of the waterpower inherent in the waterways was enormous; great financial investments were sought and made, new inventions spurred the rapid growth of the textile industry; foundries, factories, mills sprang up, and hordes of immigrant labor poured into the area and were exploited to serve them. In a short span of time Fall River became the third largest city in Massachusetts. One of its proudest boasts was the Fall River Steamship Line, the "old Fall River Line" which for ninety years was to provide transportation for goods and passengers from Boston to New York. The New Haven Railroad, and later the Old Colony Railroad, ran a fast train from Boston directly to the wharf on the bay at the very heart of the city of Fall River, where goods and passengers were put aboard a steamship for the eight- or nine-hour sail through inland waterways to New York harbor and thence to the world beyond. The line, heartbeat of the city's industry, survived Fall River's bankruptcy in the early 1930's, but itself finally expired in 1937.

Its other boast—though one of less widespread fame—was the great chimney of the Fall River Iron Works, in 1892 the tallest chimney in the United States. Dominating the city skyline, it rose to the incredible, the almost preposterous, height of three hundred fifty feet. It was the focal point of the complex of mills which nearly encircled the southern section of the town, and during every shift added an incalculable amount of pollutants to the smog-laden air in its vicinity.

Fall River in this its heyday was a busy, bustling city of seventy-seven thousand people, whose livelihoods were actually controlled by a relatively few families—the Buffintons, Grays, Durfees, Chases, Braytons, and, of course, the Bordens. Members of these families dominated the professions, business and finance. A glance at the names of the directors of the forty-four milling corporations and the banks of the city in 1892 reveals that the same names appear time and again; there was an unparalleled system of interlocking directorates. The scions of the earliest arrivals held the reins of the economy of Fall River and they held them tightly, all, no doubt, because their progenitors had had the wisdom to retain water rights from generation to generation.

Quite naturally, there was a Borden on very nearly every important corporate board. Not the least of these was Andrew J. Borden, who by 1892 had converted his inheritance and his early undertaking business into a financial standing—and a string of titles—as impressive as that of any of his relatives. He was president of the Union Savings Bank, director of the First National Bank, director of the Durfee Safe Deposit and Trust Company, director of the Globe Yarn Mill Company, director of Troy Cotton and Woolen Manufacturing Company, and director of the Merchants Manufacturing Company. Yes, clearly the Bordens were important to Fall River, its birth, its growth, its early maturity. It is said, however, that the Bordens took from Fall River but gave back little. There is a great Borden mill in Fall River; there are the Borden business block, several Borden banks, even a Borden Street in the central part of the city. But on my visits over recent years I saw no Borden Park, no Borden Library.

If the business and financial structure of Fall River in 1892 was hierarchical, the social stratification was more so. Paraphrasing the twentieth-century wit who described old Boston society in terms of the Lowells and the Cabots, in Fall River the Durfees and the Braytons spoke only to the Bordens, and the Bordens spoke only to God. Of the rest, nearly half the city's population was foreign-born—English, French Canadian, Irish and Portuguese. These were, in the contemporary course of things, mill and factory workers; very often their wives were also employed in the industries or as domestic help.

The residential arrangement of the city was not so clearly structured. True, the millworkers lived mainly near the city's core, while in the northerly part of town was The Hill, the area of fine homes and lovely views, with its streets laid out in a gridwork pattern, intersecting at right angles in a gracious and orderly manner. But then there was the southerly section, which also contained some residences, but which could not in 1892 be fairly described as residential. Here was the business district, the stores, the Court House—for Fall River is one of three shire towns for Bristol County—the City Hall, some churches and schools; here the street pattern was irregular, with streets angling into one another and running closely together, creating a cramped, uneven pattern. Immediately south of it and west of it, and in effect ringing it, were the huge mills. Thus the southerly residential section, such as it was, was pressed by the business district and the industrial area, and there were incursions of business and industry into it. The result was that the southern part of the city was not a fashionable place to live—far from it. The streets, short as they were, were heavily traveled, and the proximity of the factories and the great iron works created an environmental problem.

Yet it was here that Andrew J. Borden lived in 1892 with his wife and his two daughters. No impressive estate on the heights for Andrew: his house was at 92 Second Street, several hundred yards from City Hall, from his banking interests, from his real estate holdings in the business district, in the shadow of the tall chimney of the Iron Works three short streets away. Unfashionable perhaps, and inexpensive, but solid, this was to be the scene of the horror that shocked North America and made headlines across the Atlantic. This was the home of Lizzie Borden in Fall River, Massachusetts.

"Aunt Abby's house looks just the same, but everything around it is so different," said Abby Potter as, on 30 May 1972, she stood with me looking at the residence that had become famous across the nation as 92 Second Street.

Arriving in Fall River from Mrs. Potter's present home in Providence, we had first visited the former Whitehead place, only two short city blocks behind the Bordens'. Mrs. Potter was delighted to find that 45 Fourth Street was in remarkably good condition, for the attractive small dwelling was where she had been born and raised and where her mother, Mrs. Whitehead, had been born, raised, married and lived her entire life. This property is doubly interesting because the matter of its ownership had significant bearing on the murders.

We then went around a corner to the former Borden house some three hundred yards away, and it was while standing here, in what once was Andrew Borden's yard, that Mrs. Potter pointed out to me the changes that had taken place in the neighborhood since the days of her childhood. Gone is the large, square, cupola-topped home of the Bordens' close neighbor to the north, a widow named Adelaide B. Churchill; it was still known in Mrs. Churchill's day as the "old Mayor Buffinton house" because Fall River's first mayor had lived there in the mid-1800's. To the south of No. 92 lived Mrs. Caroline Kelly, the wife of a doctor, but today their Cape Cod-style house has been remodeled for business in such a way as to make it unrecognizable as the dwelling it was in 1892.

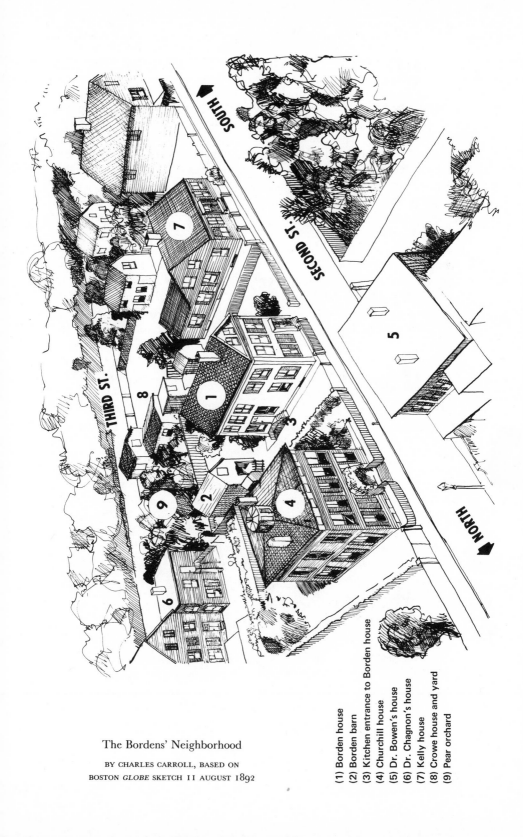

The Bordens' Neighborhood

BY CHARLES CARROLL, BASED ON
BOSTON *GLOBE* SKETCH 11 AUGUST 1892

(1) Borden house
(2) Borden barn
(3) Kitchen entrance to Borden house
(4) Churchill house
(5) Dr. Bowen's house
(6) Dr. Chagnon's house
(7) Kelly house
(8) Crowe house and yard
(9) Pear orchard

On Third Street, directly behind the Borden property, was a small pear orchard that occupied the equivalent of a house lot. North of the orchard, and fronting on Third Street, was the house in which lived a Doctor Chagnon with his wife, Mrs. Marienne Chagnon, and daughter, Miss Martha Chagnon. South of the pear orchard on Third Street was the property of John Crowe, who conducted there a business in stonemasonry. From the back of these three premises the rear of the Borden place could be seen to some extent. The pear orchard has long since disappeared. And gone too is the house of Seabury W. Bowen, M.D., the Bordens' family doctor, who lived diagonally to the west of them across Second Street: now its site is a paved public parking area.

A former neighbor who had moved a short distance away at the time of the murders was Miss Alice Russell; she had become friendly with the Borden sisters when she lived in the house later acquired by the Kellys, and their relationship was maintained after she went to live in a little house tucked in the middle of the block between Third and Fourth streets. Thirteen hundred feet from No. 92 north along Second Street was the Central Police Station; a livery stable was somewhat beyond Andrew Borden's house to the south.

Equally as she was to bring to life the *dramatis personae* of the Borden case did Mrs. Potter pare away the intervening years and give me a detailed

No. 92 Second Street, in Late Autumn 1892
COURTESY OF THE FALL RIVER HISTORICAL SOCIETY

view of these landmarks as they existed in 1892. Then we turned to examine the premises of what had been No. 92 itself.

In part from Mrs. Potter's recollections, in part from sketches published in the Boston *Globe* shortly after the murders and during the trial, nearly a year later, and in part from my measurements of the interior of the house, I have concluded that, though the dwelling proper remains very much the same, the lot on which it sits has been altered almost completely.

At the time of the murders the Borden property consisted of a plot with rather narrow street frontage but extending deep to the back, a proportionately narrow, rectangular house set back from the street fifteen feet and with a yard around its other sides, and a small barn to the rear of, but not in line with, the house. Standing some twenty-five feet north and east from the house toward the angle formed by the fences of the Churchill property and the pear orchard, the barn was used, if it was used at all, for storage, since Andrew Borden had not kept a horse for about a year. Inside the barn was a water tap; up a ladderlike stair was the former hayloft, which was lit at either end by a window—one toward the pear orchard, and the other overlooking the stretch of yard leading to Second Street; entrance to the barn was on the Second Street end, and close by the barn door was a covered well. In the Borden back yard was a small grape arbor and a few pear trees.

A handsome picket fence traversed the Borden lot along the sidewalk on Second Street, broken by two gates: one opened on to the short walk leading to the front entrance of the house; the other, several yards along the fence toward Mrs. Churchill's, opened on to a longer walk that led to the kitchen entrance at the rear of the house on the north side, and thence to the back yard. These two gates were the only entrances to the Borden lot, which was enclosed on the remaining three sides by an uninterrupted fence; the back fence separating the Borden property from the pear orchard was topped with barbed wire.

But gone now are the trim fence, the barn, the well, the grape arbor, the pear trees. The present owner of the property operates a printing business there, and he has erected a plant which covers the entire east and south portions of the lot, as well as the northeast portion where the barn and the well once stood. The buildings are constructed not more than two feet from the exterior wall of the house on the south and east sides. The house itself, however, appears relatively unchanged and, despite an air-conditioner jutting incongruously from a downstairs window, looks much as it did in photographs spread over the front pages of newspapers throughout the Northeast in 1892. The Borden home in 1892 and today stands on a

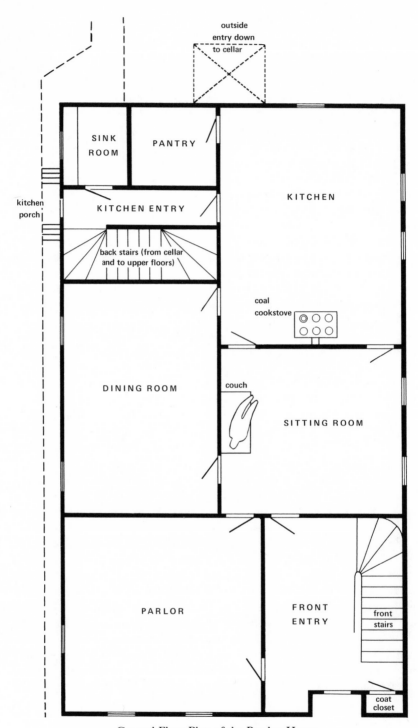

Ground-Floor Plan of the Borden Home

BY CHARLES CARROLL, BASED ON OFFICIAL TESTIMONY, AND PORTER

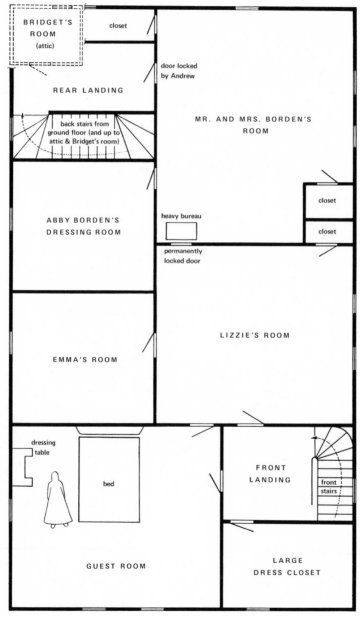

BRIDGET'S ROOM (attic)

closet

door locked by Andrew

REAR LANDING

back stairs from ground floor (and up to attic & Bridget's room)

MR. AND MRS. BORDEN'S ROOM

closet

closet

ABBY BORDEN'S DRESSING ROOM

heavy bureau

permanently locked door

LIZZIE'S ROOM

EMMA'S ROOM

dressing table

bed

FRONT LANDING

front stairs

GUEST ROOM

LARGE DRESS CLOSET

Upstairs-Floor Plan of the Borden Home

BY CHARLES CARROLL, AFTER PORTER

stone foundation rising several feet above ground. Its front door is on the right side of the house as you face it from Second Street, and its back entrance is at the rear of the house, on the side which faces the former Churchill home. This side, or rear, door provided easy access to the barn and well, and to the back yard. At the back end of the house there was a door leading into the cellar.

In 1871, twenty-one years before his murder, Andrew Borden had purchased this property. It had originally been a two-family home with a five-room apartment on each floor; with difficulty, Borden had converted it to a single dwelling. This fact accounts for the structural plans of each of the two floors being nearly identical and accounts for the unusual arrangement of rooms on the second floor.

On each floor the complete absence of passageways made it necessary to pass through one or more rooms to reach the back of the house from the front. This fact had evidentiary importance at the trial of Lizzie Borden.

When I examined and measured the interior of the house, I had in hand copies of the plans of the ground floor and the second floor which had been prepared in 1892 for use at the murder trial and which had been introduced into evidence by the prosecution and marked as exhibits by the Court. Clearly there had been no substantial structural alterations made on the interior of the Borden house since the time of the preparation of the plans.

Naturally, however, the décor had been changed and a bathroom had long since been installed. In 1892 the only washing facilities in the house were a faucet in a sinkroom located just inside the kitchen door and a tap in a laundry room in the cellar. The only toilet in the house was a water closet in the cellar. Thus the family ablutions were performed in the sink which also served the kitchen, or in a washtub in the cellar laundry room, or in portable basins in the upstairs bedrooms. Also in the cellar was a coal furnace, since the house had natural-draft central heat. Near the furnace were a chopping block and hand axe and the usual supplies of wood to be split for kindling fires in the furnace and in the coal-burning cookstove in the kitchen.

As one entered the front door from Second Street, there was a large hall. Immediately to the right of the door was a small coat closet; also on the right side of the hall was a curving flight of stairs leading up to the bedroom floor. From this hall one could go straight into the sitting room, and thence through to the kitchen. Or, from this front entry, one could take a rather zigzag route to the kitchen by turning left into the more formal parlor, going through doors set at right angles in the corner of the sitting room to reach the dining room, and from there go into the kitchen. In addition to the sinkroom and pantry, the back hall next to the kitchen held back stairs which led up to the second floor and down to the cellar.

From the front entry one reached the bedroom floor by going up the front stairs, at the top of which was a landing. To the left, above the parlor, was a guest room. Doors from both the guest room and the landing led to Lizzie's room, which was directly above the sitting room. In Lizzie's room was the only entrance to Emma's smaller bedroom. Beyond Lizzie's room was a large bedroom used by Mr. and Mrs. Borden, whose dressing room was directly behind Emma's room. There was a connecting door between Lizzie's room and that of the elder Bordens, but on 4 August 1892—and for a long time previously—this door was locked and blocked with heavy furniture. As a result, the only means of access to and from the bedroom and anteroom used by Mr. and Mrs. Borden was by means of the back stairway leading from the kitchen entry on the first floor; in addition, Andrew Borden locked his bedroom door at the top of these stairs whenever he and his wife were out of the room, though he left the key on the sitting-room mantelpiece. Access to the elder Bordens' room was to be a significant piece of evidence at the trial, as was the fact that it had become family practice to keep locked all outside doors on the ground floor—even on the briefest errand to the yard around the house—as well as those to the second-floor bedrooms.

Under the pitched roof was an attic where Bridget Sullivan, the maid, slept in a partitioned space or room at the rear of the house, and which could be reached only by the back stairway.

In these less than elegant but more than adequate surroundings lived Andrew Jackson Borden and his family in August of 1892. Borden, then seventy years old, was a dour, tight-fisted man. Unpretentious in his tastes and in his habits, he was temperate, tidy, reserved, and by some considered brusque in manner to the point of being unfriendly. Tall and lean, his hair was thinning and white, and he wore closely cropped sideburns and chin whiskers which circled his face like a frame. His eyes, set closely together, were dark; his nose was aquiline, but his firmly—almost grimly—set mouth was the feature which most clearly reflected his personality. By all accounts there was about Andrew J. Borden an aura almost totally lacking in warmth. And it was this personality which pervaded the home atmosphere of 92 Second Street at the time of the murders, and had done so for more than twenty years before that.

In 1845 Andrew had married his first wife, Sarah J. Morse, and from this marriage two children were born who survived, Emma Lenora, born in 1849, and Lizzie Andrew, born in 1860. When Sarah Morse Borden died in 1862, Andrew was a widower with two daughters: Emma, almost thirteen years old, and Lizzie, aged two.

Two years after the death of his first wife, and some twenty-seven years before the murders, Andrew married his second wife, Abby Durfee Gray, a spinster, daughter of Oliver Gray of Fourth Street, Fall River.

Andrew's new father-in-law was a tin-peddler who sold sundries, china, linen and household goods from a pushcart in the Fall River streets—certainly a respectable occupation, but equally certainly one not likely to advance the social position of Andrew's branch of the Borden family, despite his new wife's probable—though apparently distant—connection with the prominent Durfee and Gray families mentioned earlier. Gray had fathered two daughters thirty-five years apart in age—Abby, the second Mrs. Borden, who at the time of her marriage to Andrew was thirty-seven years old, and her half-sister, Sarah, later Sarah Gray Whitehead, who at the time of her sister's marriage was a one-year-old infant. Sarah Gray Whitehead was the mother of Mrs. Abby Potter, who accompanied this writer to the neighborhood of the murders in 1972 and limned the figures of the principal actors in the tragedy.

It is appropriate to note here that the two daughters of Oliver Gray, Abby and Sarah, because of the wide difference in age, shared a close mother-daughter relationship rather than a sisterly one. Throughout her life and until her hideously gruesome death, Abby Durfee Gray Borden and Sarah Gray Whitehead were inseparable. Rebuffed in her home by her stepdaughters, childless herself, Abby Borden quite naturally lavished her maternal affection and attention upon Sarah, her sister, her junior by thirty-six years. Therefore for long before the murders, Sarah Whitehead was Abby Borden's sole female friend and constant companion.

In 1892 when she was murdered, Abby was nearly sixty-four years old. She was short and very stout, weighing about two hundred pounds. Shy, timid, reportedly of a generous and kindly disposition, Abby was easy to please, even anxious to please, but she had consistently failed in achieving a reasonably cordial relationship with her two stepdaughters, Emma and Lizzie Borden.

However unhappy Abby Borden was in No. 92, she was much loved in the Whitehead house near by on Fourth Street where lived her half-sister and her nephew, George, and the little niece, Abby Borden Whitehead who was named for her. There were almost daily visits between the two

Mrs. Abby Durfee Gray Borden

Andrew Jackson Borden

homes. Mrs. Abby Potter recalls those visits and the little gifts which her aunt brought to the far less prosperous Whiteheads; especially she recalls her aunt's freshly baked mince pies, into which Mrs. Borden had sprinkled rosewater to make them more tempting to taste and smell.

Andrew Borden's elder daughter, Emma, was forty-two and unmarried at the time of the murders. Although she was ten years senior to Lizzie, she was completely dominated by her. Emma deferred to Lizzie, stood in her shadow—her whole attitude toward her younger sister was one of complete obeisance. Unlike Lizzie, Emma was small in stature, almost frail, with somewhat sharp features about her thin face. She had the shy, drab, quiet, self-effacing personality of a middle-aged spinster of the nineteenth century.

Lizzie Borden was thirty-two at the time of the murders. No great beauty was Lizzie, but on the other hand she was not without a redeeming feature. Her reddish hair was slightly crimped in the fashion of the day, parted exactly in the center and drawn into a high bun behind her head; her cheeks were full; her large, light eyes were by far her most attractive feature. Whether or not her mouth, as it appears in some photographs, was habitually set with a determination that characterized her father's expression is impossible to say; nevertheless, every known portrait of her reflects utter composure. From all contemporary reports—including Mrs. Potter's—she had her father's abrupt manner, his shrewd business acumen, and, like him, an unfortunate inability to engender warm friendships.

Before her birth Andrew had hoped for a son and, perhaps in some small way to compensate for his disappointment, he had given Lizzie his name as her middle name. Lizzie Andrew Borden's legal name was just that. After her trial she began calling herself Lizbeth Andrews Borden, although her will probated in 1927 was signed with both signatures, and the new name appears on her gravestone. The point of using the thinly disguised pseudonym is elusive, except that perhaps she felt it was more dramatic, more befitting the heroine of America's most famous murder trial; perhaps she also thought it more fashionable.

For Lizzzie had always been ambitious socially, and her father's frugality, her family branch's alliance with a modest tin-peddler, and her home on Second Street instead of on The Hill must all have been sources of some discontent. At any rate, well before the murders she had directed herself toward advancement in *le monde* of Fall River. There had been the grand tour of Europe in 1890, when Lizzie had accompanied another lady of refinement, another Miss Borden, remotely related, to see the world

Lizzie Borden, *circa* 1892

COURTESY OF THE FALL RIVER HISTORICAL SOCIETY

capitals, as was the fashion among New England's elite in the nineteenth century. This is by no means to say that Lizzie was a social butterfly, although, as a member of the Central Congregational Church, she was active in the Christian Endeavor Society and the missionary committee, and taught a Sunday-school class; she also belonged to the Woman's Christian Temperance Union. These unimpeachable activities, coupled no doubt with her family's standing, earned her the regard of the two ministers, the Reverends W. Walter Jubb and E. A. Buck.

It was fairly common knowledge, however, that Lizzie—and to a somewhat lesser extent, Emma—did not get on well with her stepmother. It appears that even in their tender years, the two stepdaughters maintained at least a cool reserve toward the mild-mannered Abby. Typifying this was this excerpt from Lizzie Borden's statement made at the inquest a few days after her father and stepmother were butchered. The District Attorney's questions were directed to Lizzie to establish her relationship with the murdered Mrs. Borden:

Q. Were you always cordial with your stepmother?

A. That depends upon one's idea of cordiality. Yes.

Q. Was it cordial according to your idea of cordiality?

A. Yes, I did not regard her as my mother, though she came there when I was young. I decline to say whether my relations between her and myself were those of mother and daughter or not. I called her Mrs. Borden and sometimes mother. I stopped calling her mother after the affair [to be described below] regarding her half-sister [Mrs. White-head].

Q. Why did you leave off calling her mother?

A. Because I wanted to.

Q. Have you any other answer to give me?

A. No, sir. I always went to my sister. She was older than I was.

Every known account of the Borden case concedes that Andrew Borden's unusual generosity to Abby's family, the Whiteheads, provoked Lizzie's resentment, and therefore was an important factor in the background of the Borden case. Andrew's rare benefaction, not at all in keeping with his well-known frugality, was this: When Sarah and Abby's father, Oliver Gray, died, the interest in the Fourth Street home was divided four ways—one-fourth to the widow, Mrs. Gray; one-fourth to Mrs. Priscilla Fish, a daughter by Gray who does not otherwise enter this story; one-fourth to Sarah Gray Whitehead; and one-fourth to Abby Durfee Gray Borden. Abby gave her one-fourth to her young half-sister, Sarah, and, some five years before the murders, Andrew Borden bought the Widow Gray's portion and gave it to Sarah Whitehead. So strong were the expressions of Lizzie's and Emma's reaction to their father's unusual largess (". . . we thought what he did for her [Abby Borden's] people, he ought to do for his own," Lizzie would say at the inquest) that he compensated his daughters with a gift of real estate of much greater value—and which, for reasons never made explicit, he bought back from them several weeks before he was killed.

If the resentment which Lizzie Borden admittedly harbored for her stepmother did not begin with the incident of the Whitehead house, by all accounts her ill will definitely reached a high plateau on that occasion. Two stories told me by Mrs. Potter—and to my knowledge never before published—amplify the various reports from disinterested persons concerning Lizzie's feelings toward her father's wife.

The first describes an incident apparently recounted by Abby Borden on one of her visits to her sister's home, and these are Mrs. Potter's words as recorded on tape for me in 1972:

Lizzie Borden had company and my aunt had a tabby cat and the cat was trained so that it would touch the latch—you know, it was [sic] latches in those days—she'd touch the latch and the door would open. So the cat went in where Lizzie was entertaining and she took it out and shut the door again, and it came back so this is what she told Aunt Abby and Abby told my mother . . . Lizzie Borden finally excused herself and went downstairs—took the cat downstairs—and put the carcass on the chopping block and chopped its head off. My aunt . . . for days wondered where the cat was—all she talked about. Finally Lizzie said, "You go downstairs and you'll find your cat." My aunt did.

The second incident Mrs. Potter related was that, after the murders and after the trial, Lizzie sent to Mrs. Whitehead all the personal effects of the murdered Abby, including Abby's wedding picture. Perhaps Lizzie did this to rid herself of unpleasant reminders; perhaps it was a final salute of hostility, of total rejection; perhaps it was a gesture of remorse. Whatever her motives, they remain inscrutable. Mrs. Potter still has this picture of her Aunt Abby, prominently displayed in her modest Providence apartment. It shows Mrs. Borden in her wedding gown, not at all the stout woman she was to become after twenty-eight years of marriage to Andrew, but as a slender woman with a somewhat cherubic face, half smiling and with a twinkle in her eye.

The only other permanent member of the Borden household was the maid, Bridget Sullivan, an unmarried Irish girl. At the time of the murders Bridget was twenty-six years old. She had come to this country in 1886, arriving in Fall River in 1889. She had been hired by Andrew Borden to wash, iron, cook and sweep. It is important to note that her duties did not extend to caring for any of the bedrooms, except for her own small attic room at the rear of the house. A photograph of Bridget shows her to be a tall and well-developed young woman with dark hair braided tightly to her head, her pretty face wearing a pleasant, shy and trusting expression. Bridget was industrious, reasonably intelligent, quite articulate, tractable and submissive. She was also inclined to be somewhat excitable and apprehensive during the course of the trial.

Interestingly, Lizzie Borden at all times—and Emma occasionally, too—called Bridget "Maggie," after Bridget's predecessor, who had been named Maggie. Nothing in the evidence indicates why Lizzie chose to do so, and under some pressure later at the trial Bridget denied that she resented the practice, which would usually be construed as a disregard for the young maidservant's feelings. Obviously Lizzie's habit led to some confusion, carried over to later pages in this book where testimony is given verbatim; but all references to "Maggie" in fact have application to Bridget Sullivan.

Miss Alice Russell, a good friend of the Borden family, who had occupied the Kelly house next door before moving to another house around the corner from No. 92 on Borden Street, was a frequent visitor to the Borden home. Miss Russell was a spinster, a good deal older than Lizzie and Emma Borden; nevertheless she appears to have been their closest friend, so close, in fact, that she was the first person Lizzie sent for—aside from the doctor—after the discovery of Andrew Borden's hacked and lifeless body. And it was Alice Russell, the night before the murders, to whom Lizzie confided fears that nameless enemies might try to harm her father.

Another regular visitor to the house on Second Street was John Vinnicum Morse, brother of Andrew Borden's first wife, Sarah Morse Borden, and thus the uncle of Lizzie and Emma. Morse was sixty-nine years old, and had lived a large part of his life in the Middle West where he had been a reasonably prosperous farmer in Iowa. In 1889 he returned to his native New England and for three years had resided in nearby South Dartmouth, Massachusetts. He was semi-retired.

From time to time Morse was accustomed to pay an overnight visit with Andrew Borden when business and a desire to see other of his relatives brought him to Fall River. Such an occasion arose the first week of August 1892, and he had arrived unannounced at the Borden house on Wednesday, 3 August, at about 1:30 in the afternoon. He would sleep that evening in the Borden guest room, arise Thursday morning, breakfast, and leave the house at 8:45 to see the family of a sister who also lived in Fall River. He would be at all times material on the following day, absent from the Borden premises.

Also absent was Emma. Nearly two weeks earlier—on 23 July—she had gone to pay an extended visit to a friend, a Mrs. Brownell, in Fairhaven, Massachusetts, about fifteen miles away. Lizzie had accompanied her part of the way, going to New Bedford and then to Marion, on Buzzards Bay, for several days, returning home via Fairhaven on the 30th. Emma would arrive back, summoned by a telegram announcing the deaths of her father and stepmother, the evening of 4 August.

Day of Horror

ON THURSDAY MORNING, 4 August 1892, Bridget Sullivan arose, left her oppressively hot attic room, and came down the back stairs into the Borden kitchen to begin her daily chores. Already at 6:15 A.M. the newly risen sun was blazing hot, signaling that the severe heat wave which had prostrated Fall River for three days was continuing.

As Bridget built the fire in the kitchen range, she felt ill. Beginning late Tuesday night, the elder Bordens had been acutely nauseated, and during Wednesday Lizzie also complained of feeling sick. However, only Mrs. Borden had sought medical attention: she had called Dr. Bowen from across the street to treat her, but he had considered her condition unremarkable, concluding that her discomfort was the result of eating meat that had spoiled in the intense heat. It was to be learned later at the trial that Lizzie Borden had, in conversation with others, attributed the sickness in the family to unfit baker's bread or to some unknown person having poisoned the milk as it stood on the back porch after being delivered by the farmer at dawn. Be that as it may, Bridget Sullivan felt nauseated as she unlocked the back door and took in the milk can from the back steps on Thursday morning.

To reach the back steps it was necessary for Bridget to unlock both the wooden door and the screen door. She then rehooked the screen door but left the back door unlocked and open, as was her custom in the summer months to help dissipate heat from the coal cookstove in the kitchen.

Shortly before seven o'clock Mrs. Borden came downstairs, wearing a cotton housedress. Her husband appeared a few minutes later, went directly to the back yard to empty his slop pail outside, and unlocked the barn. John Morse then joined them in the kitchen; he had spent the night in the guest bedroom over the parlor. With Mrs. Borden, he and Andrew went into the dining room shortly after seven o'clock for a breakfast of warmed-over mutton broth, bananas, bread, johnnycake and coffee. Many witticisms have been expended on this hot-weather menu over the years since the Borden case; yet it is perhaps likely that the breakfast, involving

25

meat soup, was stressed during subsequent investigations because of the suspected food-poisoning already mentioned.

Lizzie was not present at the breakfast table. However, since family relationships were such that the daughters preferred to eat by themselves rather than with their father and stepmother, her absence on this occasion was not at all unusual. After breakfast Mrs. Borden rang for Bridget to clear the table while she, her husband, and Morse went into the sitting room together.

About 8:45 John Morse left to walk to 4 Weybosset Street, about a mile and a half away, to visit a niece and nephew. He departed by the back door. Andrew Borden hooked the screen again after him, according to the household practice, and, after cleaning his teeth at the sink, went upstairs to finish dressing before going out himself.

Her uncle had just gone when Lizzie came to the kitchen, indicated a disinclination to eat breakfast, and poured and sipped a cup of coffee. Bridget, who had started washing the dishes, was overtaken by another spell of illness and hurried out to the back yard to vomit; as she re-entered the house around ten minutes later she automatically locked the screen door.

Andrew Borden had left the house by the time Bridget returned to the kitchen. According to his established routine, he walked to the financial district, a few blocks away, for his daily check on his multifold business interests. In the meantime Mrs. Borden had made up the bed in the guest room where Morse had slept the night before and had returned to the dining room to dust. She then remarked to Bridget that she was going back up to the guest room to place two fresh cases on the pillows there, and she directed Bridget to wash the first-floor windows, both inside and out.

Lizzie by this time had finished her coffee and left the kitchen. It was never established where Lizzie was at this moment, but she was not within the purview of Bridget Sullivan. Abby Borden left the dining room and ascended the front stairs to the second floor. The time was 9:30 A.M. She was never seen alive again.

Having finished cleaning up the kitchen, Bridget prepared to wash windows. She first went from room to room, closing the windows on the inside; she saw no one in any of the downstairs rooms. Then she collected her equipment from the cellar washroom and, unlocking the screen door, went down the back steps. At this point Lizzie appeared in the back entry and started to rehook the screen. Bridget dissuaded her—she would be "out around," she said, "and getting fresh water from the barn." Lizzie left the entryway, and Bridget commenced her task.

She began by washing the sitting-room windows, which were located at the center of the south side of the house next to the Kellys' yard, the farthest point from the back door. While there, she chatted briefly with the servant girl from the Kellys', who was also working outside. She then washed the parlor windows on the front of the house and those on the northerly side, toward Mrs. Churchill's, continuing around the exterior of the house. She had a clear view into each room as she worked her way around the house, and she made numerous trips to the barn for fresh water: at no time did she see anyone within the downstairs rooms, nor did she see anyone in the yard or at the back entrance.

The outside part of her job finished, Bridget re-entered the house through the still unlocked screen door. She hooked the screen behind her and, following her earlier order, began with the sitting room to wash the windows inside.

Meanwhile, Andrew Borden was going his rounds in the Fall River business district. All his movements that morning prior to his return home were accounted for. After leaving his house Borden went first to the Union Savings Bank, of which he was president; here he spoke with Abraham G. Hart, the bank's treasurer, and left. He then went to the National Union Bank, where he met with the cashier, John T. Burrill, discussed business, and left. He proceeded to the First National Bank of Fall River and spoke briefly with Andrew Cook, one of the bank's officers. From there he went immediately to the nearby shop of Jonathan Clegg, a hatter and haberdasher who was also one of Borden's tenants; he parted company with Clegg but was next seen by a carpenter working in Clegg's store, a man named Joseph Shortsleeves. Shortsleeves saw Borden pick up an old, badly broken lock from the floor and put it into his pocket, giving no reason for doing so, although Shortsleeves apparently put the act down to Borden's well-known parsimony. Borden then left about 10:35, heading toward Second Street and home. At approximately 10:40 he was seen at his front door by Mrs. Kelly, his next-door neighbor, who said she noted the time as she was hurrying to keep a dental appointment. At that time Borden was using his keys on his front door with some apparent difficulty.

Within the house and from the sitting room, Bridget, still washing windows, heard Borden fumbling at the lock and went to the door. The door was double locked and bolted. Bridget had some difficulty moving the bolt back and muttered a mild expletive, clicking her tongue. At that very moment Lizzie was noticed standing at the top of the stairway on the second-floor landing; because of the room arrangement on the bedroom floor, Lizzie could have come only from her own room or from the guest room. And, as Bridget struggled with the door, Lizzie laughed. Then Bridget managed to get the door open, and Andrew Borden strode into the hall.

While her father was still in the entry Lizzie came down the stairs and asked for the day's mail. She then informed her father in Bridget's presence:

"Mrs. Borden has gone out—she had a note from somebody who is sick."

Andrew Borden received this information and then, still somewhat wan from his nausea of the previous day, he took his bedroom key from the sitting-room mantel where he customarily kept it and went up the back stairs to his room.

About 10:50 he came down the back stairs into the kitchen. He then passed through the dining room, where Bridget had resumed washing windows, and passed into the sitting room.

Along the north wall of the sitting room was a mahogany-framed, upholstered couch, with tufted and well-padded arms at either end and several decorative cushions upon it. Andrew stretched out on the couch in a semiprone position with both his feet upon the floor to take a nap. He never awoke.

During this short period Lizzie had joined Bridget in the dining room, setting up an ironing board on the table there. She was ironing handkerchiefs as Bridget finished the last of the windows. She asked Bridget, "Maggie, are you going out this afternoon?"

Bridget replied, "I don't know, I might and I might not. I don't feel very well."

Lizzie's response repeated the information she had earlier given her father and Bridget. "If you go out, be sure to lock the door, for Mrs. Borden has gone out on a sick call, and I might go out too."

Puzzled, Bridget asked, "Who is sick, Miss Lizzie?"

Lizzie replied, "I don't know; she had a note this morning. It must be someone in town."

As Bridget left the dining room and went to the kitchen, Lizzie stopped ironing to say: "There is a cheap sale of dress goods at Sargent's today at eight cents a yard."

To which Bridget replied, "I am going to have one."

Then, tired, and still not feeling well, Bridget went up the back stairs to her third-floor room and lay, fully clothed, on her bed. The City Hall clock struck 11:00.

At about 11:10 Bridget, still in her attic room, was startled to hear Lizzie cry out: "Maggie, come down!"

"What's the matter?"

"Come down quick! Father's dead! Somebody's come in and killed him!"

When Bridget hurried down the stairs she found Lizzie standing at the back door. As Bridget headed toward the sitting room, Lizzie stopped her, saying: "Don't go in there. Go over and get the doctor. Run!"

Bridget raced across the street to Dr. Bowen's house, only to discover that he was out. She blurted out the news of the tragedy to the doctor's wife and then ran back to the house and to Lizzie. She then asked Lizzie where she was when the murder occurred. Lizzie responded:

"I was in the yard and heard a groan, and came in and the screen door was wide open."

Lizzie then dispatched Bridget to summon Miss Russell, saying that she did not want to be alone in the house. Meanwhile Mrs. Churchill, from her kitchen window overlooking the Bordens' back entrance, saw Bridget's comings and goings and noticed that Lizzie, standing just inside the screen door, appeared in distress. She called across to her, learned that Andrew Borden was dead, and immediately went to Lizzie's aid. She looked briefly into the sitting room, saw Andrew Borden's body, and asked, "Where were you when it happened?"

In the barn, Lizzie told her, on an errand.

"Where is your mother?"

But Lizzie did not know: she said Abby Borden had received a note calling her to see someone who was sick. When she added that Bridget was unable to reach Dr. Bowen, Mrs. Churchill volunteered to fetch a doctor; she went outside, found her handyman, and sent him to the livery stable near by to telephone for help; a passer-by learned from the man that there was trouble at the Borden house, and himself called the Central Police Station, which was only some four hundred yards away from No. 92. The telephone message was logged by the police at 11:15.

Within only a couple of minutes of Mrs. Churchill's return to the Borden kitchen, Dr. Bowen arrived and Bridget hurried in from notifying Miss Russell. He viewed briefly the body of his neighbor and obtained a sheet to cover it. Following this considerate action, Bridget, concerned for Mrs. Borden, said to Lizzie, "If I knew where Mrs. Whitehead was, I would go and see if Mrs. Borden was there and tell her that Mr. Borden was very sick."

And Lizzie answered her:

"Maggie, I am almost positive I heard her coming in. Go upstairs and see."

Bridget refused to go to the second floor alone, so Mrs. Churchill offered to go up with her. The two ascended the front stairs together, and before they reached the landing they were able to see Mrs. Borden lying on the floor of the guest room, on the far side of, and partially hidden by, the bed. The door to the room was open, and when Bridget had reached a point on the stairs where the guest-room floor was at eye level, she saw Mrs. Borden. Mrs. Churchill rushed past her into the room, viewed the obviously dead body of her neighbor, and then returned downstairs, gasping, "There is another one!"

Meanwhile, Alice Russell had arrived, and Dr. Bowen, having rushed out to telegraph Emma and returned, had been examining Andrew Borden's corpse in the sitting room. It was partly on its right side on the sofa. The feet, still in their congress shoes, were resting on the floor; his coat had been carefully rolled over the arm of the sofa. Borden's head was bent slightly to the right, but his face was almost unrecognizable as human: one eye had been cut in half and protruded in a ghastly manner, his nose had been severed, and there were eleven distinct cuts within a relatively small area extending from the eye and nose to the ear. Fresh blood was still seeping from the wounds, which were so severe that the first of the eleven blows must have killed him, the doctor concluded.

There were blood spots on the floor, on the wall over the sofa, on a picture hanging on the wall but, Bowen said, there was "nothing to indicate the slaughter that had taken place." The clothing on the body was not at all disturbed, nor was there any injury other than to the face.

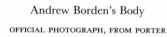

Andrew Borden's Body

OFFICIAL PHOTOGRAPH, FROM PORTER

Obviously the wounds had been inflicted by a sharp, heavy weapon; equally obviously, Borden had been struck from above the head and by blows delivered vertically while he slept.

When Dr. Bowen went upstairs to examine Mrs. Borden's body, he found that her head had been crushed by nineteen axe or hatchet wounds in the back of the head. In addition, there was one wound at the back of the neck, and a misdirected or poorly aimed blow had cut a great and grotesque flap from the back of the scalp.

The blood on and about Mrs. Borden's body was dark and congealed.

So far, the foregoing were the activities of the household of 92 Second Street, and its habitués, from six o'clock in the morning to approximately 11:40 A.M., half an hour after Andrew Borden's lifeless body was discovered on the sitting-room couch. We turn now to the reactions of Fall River officialdom and outsiders.

It was John Cunningham, the local newsdealer, who telephoned word of Andrew Borden's death to the Central Police Station. Rufus B. Hilliard, the City Marshal, received the call himself at 11:15 A.M., and he immediately dispatched Officer George W. Allen to the Borden house.

As he had been directed to do, Allen ran the four hundred-odd yards to the scene of the tragedy. He found the front door locked and bolted, so he ran around to the rear and entered through the back door. Not pausing, he was directed into the sitting room where he was confronted by the hideous mask of Andrew Borden's face.

Acting swiftly, Allen ran from the house, deputized a passer-by, one Charles Sawyer, to stand guard at the rear door, and again ran at top speed back to the stationhouse for assistance.

Much has been written about the fact that on the day of the Borden murders the entire police force of Fall River was at Rocky Point, Rhode Island, attending the department's annual picnic and clambake. The outing was indeed held that day, but the entire force was by no means present: an adequate complement had remained on duty. Thus the police picnic did in no way hamper the immediate investigation of the Borden murders.

Within minutes of Allen's return to the station to report, Officers Wixon, Mullaly and Devine arrived at the Borden house, and they were followed almost immediately by Deputy Marshal John Fleet, Inspector William H. Medley, and Officer Charles Wilson; Sergeant (soon to become Captain) Philip H. Harrington arrived shortly thereafter.

It was in the midst of these official arrivals that John Vinnicum Morse strolled into the side yard of 92 Second Street, fresh from a pleasant visit with his relatives across town. As other members of the household had done earlier in the day, he picked up some ripe fruit from under the pear tree and ate it. While he was fortifying himself against midday dinner, presumably nearly an hour away, he was informed of the tragedy by the man posted at the back door, and promptly went inside. From then on John Morse apparently milled around sporadically, occasionally speaking with the police about his actions that morning.

Meanwhile each of the officers present viewed the bodies of Andrew Borden and his wife, each saw that the blood around and upon the body of Mrs. Borden was dark and coagulated, and the blood around and upon her husband's body was red, wet and fresh; all reached the obvious conclusion that Mrs. Borden had died some substantial period of time before her husband. Then the officers fanned out to make a preliminary search of the premises and, in the course of this search, each of them had an opportunity to converse with the persons in the house, and especially with Lizzie Borden.

By the nature of things, these conversations with Lizzie took place at various times and lasted for varying lengths of time. The object of the preliminary search was to discover if an intruder was hiding on the premises. Knowing nothing, or very little, at this time about the circumstances surrounding the killings, the police were understandably in no position to search for specific clues.

In the kitchen, while such initial investigation was going on, Lizzie was being ministered to by Miss Russell and Mrs. Churchill. They hovered about her, murmuring expressions of sympathy and attempting offices for her comfort, despite the fact that her composure seemed absolute. She rose from her chair in the kitchen, passed through a portion of the sitting room where her father's corpse lay upon the couch, ascended the front stairs, passed the bedroom where her stepmother's corpse lay, and went into her own bedroom. There she changed her costume, donning a pink wrapper or housecoat; she then allowed a select few to wait upon her in her room—Dr. Bowen, Miss Russell, and, shortly thereafter, the Reverend E. A. Buck.

Apparently without emotion, Lizzie told Miss Russell, "When it is necessary, I should like to have Undertaker Winwood."

As an aside, but an important one, it is well to note here that this marks the first appearance of the Reverend Mr. Buck in the story of Lizzie's travail. He and his colleague, the Reverend W. Walker Jubb, were

Guest Bedroom as Seen from the Landing (*above*)

Abby Borden's Body

hereafter constantly at Lizzie Borden's side at every publicized appearance which she was to make until after her acquittal. Whether the two clergymen had insatiable appetites for personal publicity it is impossible to determine. The cold, hard fact is, however, that the newspaper accounts of the assiduous attentions of the Reverend Messrs. Buck and Jubb were so frequent as to be almost sickening; nonetheless, they were very effective in presenting Lizzie's public image favorably. Mr. Buck was even present when Lizzie was questioned by police from time to time later in the course of the day.

Returning from a professional house call, Dr. William A. Dolan, Medical Examiner for Bristol County, was passing the Borden house and noticed the flurry of activity there. It was then 11:45 A.M. He entered the house and talked to Lizzie in her room and, among other things, Lizzie said that Mrs. Borden had received a note to go see someone who was sick. She also said she did not know where the note was and that Mrs. Borden had probably burned it in the kitchen stove.

Parenthetically, one of the great mysteries of the Borden case was, and remains, that Sarah Whitehead, beloved half-sister of Abby Borden, was never inquired of at any time in the police investigation of the murders. Indeed, only Bridget, and she during the first frenzy following the discovery of Andrew's murder, thought it would be logical to ask if Mrs. Whitehead knew where Abby could have gone. Also, by all accounts—including Mrs. Potter's when I discussed the murders with her—Abby Borden had few if any friends other than Mrs. Whitehead, and none other than Mrs. Whitehead would be likely to write a note to Mrs. Borden in the event of sickness. And still further, when the note from the "sick friend" was supposed to have been sent, Sarah Whitehead was hale and hearty and was, in fact, that day on the sail to Rocky Point to attend the police clambake, about which so much has been written. All in all, it is incredible that a thorough examination of the total transcript reveals that Sarah Whitehead was never called to the witness stand by the prosecution. A distressing footnote was supplied by Mrs. Abby Potter, who told me:

"On the morning of 4 August, the day of the murders, my mother [Mrs. Sarah Whitehead], planning to attend the policemen's annual picnic at Rocky Point, was making arrangements for the care of my younger brother and myself: George was to go to [another aunt's house], and I was to spend the day with Aunt Abby at 92 Second Street. At the last moment there was a change in plans, and I was sent with my brother to [my other aunt's] house, which was next door to the home of Marshal Hilliard in another section of Fall River.

"In the late afternoon, while I was helping Aunt Lucy wash windows, Marshal Hilliard returned home, and, standing in the yard, informed Aunt Lucy of Aunt Abby's murder. The shock of the news was so great that Aunt Lucy dropped the window on my hand."

Of all the questionings of Lizzie during these hours, Deputy Marshal Fleet's apparently were the most detailed. Since by her own account Lizzie had been active around the house every minute of the morning except for a brief errand to the barn loft after her father's return, he perhaps felt that she would be the person most able to throw light on the comings and goings of the family.

During her interrupted sessions with Fleet and other officers she mentioned the workaday events of the household: that her stepmother had received a note to go on a sick call; that her ironing remained unfinished because the flatirons needed reheating on the kitchen stove, and so, after her father's return, she had gone to the barn loft to hunt up some metal to use for sinkers on a prospective fishing trip; that she discovered her father's death on returning to the house; and that at no time during the morning did she see any stranger on the Borden premises.

Inspector Medley, after hearing Lizzie's account of her actions after her father's return, had gone directly to the barn loft. This was shortly after noon, or about one hour after Andrew Borden died. Medley found the loft to be insufferably hot, so much so that it was almost impossible to breathe there with comfort. Most significantly, the floor of the loft was thickly and completely covered with hay dust and ordinary dust, and this coating was absolutely free of footprints or marks of any kind. Medley placed his hand upon the hayloft floor and a clearly defined impression appeared. Shortly afterward another police officer, Sergeant (later Captain) Philip Harrington, went up to the loft and made the same observations concerning the heat and the lack of footprints on the dusty floor.

Police searched the premises, including the barn. In the cellar they found two hatchets, two axes—all four with handles—and a chopping block. There was also found a hatchet head, with part of a freshly broken handle still in the eye. This partially handleless hatchet was completely dusted with ashes, and lay in a wooden box a few feet from a pile of ashes on the cellar floor.

With Dr. Bowen, Dr. Dolan had examined the bodies and, pursuant to his statutory duties as medical examiner, he took possession of whatever evidence had been discovered.

He then left the Borden house and a few hours later returned. At three o'clock he caused the bodies of Mr. and Mrs. Borden to be moved into the dining room, where he conducted the first of two autopsies on each body. The gruesome task was performed on the dining room table. As an aid to establishing the time span between the deaths, the stomach of each of the victims was removed and tied at either end to retain the contents of the organ, and was then placed in an individual container. These containers, together with the hatchets, he gave to the police with instructions to send them to Edward S. Wood, M.D., professor of chemistry at Harvard Medical School.

By now the police had discounted the idea of an intruder. That there was a substantial time span between the deaths of the two victims was obvious to them, and this fact militated against any theory that an intruder could have concealed himself in the house for that length of time. Nothing was missing from the personal effects of the deceased, nor, as far as could be determined, from the premises; hence the theory of robbery as a motive for the killings was foreclosed.

Nevertheless, the power and the prestige of the Borden name caused the police officers to proceed cautiously: how could anyone from the staid household on Second Street play a participatory rôle in this so heinous an event? They did not wish to believe it, but the likelihood was hard to avoid. Whether the police relished it or not—and they did not—on Thursday afternoon, within a few hours of the murders, Lizzie Andrew Borden had become Police Suspect Number One.

Thursday night, in standard operating procedure, police officers were stationed around No. 92 to guard it from the curious, who had begun to gather on Second Street shortly after news of the murders had become common knowledge. The dread household included Lizzie and Emma— who had returned in the evening from Fairhaven; Miss Russell—she had agreed to remain with the sisters for several days; and, presumably, John Morse—he was in and out of the Borden house the next day, and there is no record that he opted to sleep at his other relatives' home across town. The only member of the household who was absent was Bridget Sullivan: professedly terrified that the unknown murderer would seek further victims, she was escorted to the home of a neighbor, where, for several nights, she slept with the maidservant. She was never to return to the Borden house again.

As the night wore on, there were no lamps lit in the guest room, where the iron-nerved Uncle John Morse was sleeping; nor in Emma's or Lizzie's rooms, nor in the victims' bedroom, where Alice Russell was; nor in the dining room, where still lay the bodies of Andrew and Abby Borden, awaiting removal by the undertaker the following morning, their blood-drenched clothes having been rolled up and placed in the cellar washroom.

Then, in the early morning hours after midnight, Miss Russell and Lizzie were seen by the officer on duty outside the rear of the house. He watched through the rear cellar window as the two women descended the back stairs into the cellar, Lizzie carrying a slop pail, Miss Russell holding a light. As the officer viewed this eerie tableau from the yard, Miss Russell, holding the lamp, remained in view of the officer who was peering through the cellar window, but Lizzie disappeared farther into the cellar and was lost from his sight. This episode, although reported, was not inquired into at the time, presumably because the police felt that the presence of the water closet in the cellar made any inquiry altogether indelicate.

The evening of Friday, 5 August, the Fall River *Herald* carried prominently the following notice:

$5,000.

Reward

The above Reward will be paid to any

one who may secure the

ARREST AND CONVICTION

of the person or persons who occasioned the

death of

MR. ANDREW J. BORDEN AND HIS WIFE

EMMA J. BORDEN

LIZZIE A. BORDEN

The advertisement climaxed a day during which the police of Fall River pursued all sorts of rumors and suggestions that poured into the stationhouse. The most dramatic of these led to the revelation of actions by Lizzie Borden on 3 August, the day before the murders. This disclosure was one of considerable significance in the trial of the Borden case. The police were quite properly reluctant to mention the evidence, but the Fall River *Globe* published a featured article headlined WHAT DID LIZZIE WANT OF POISON? and relating the story of one Eli Bence, pharmacist, who said he knew Lizzie by sight and on Wednesday, the day before her parents died, had refused to sell her prussic acid, a deadly poison.

By this time the city of Fall River was completely mesmerized by the

Borden case. Business ceased, groups of people gathered on sidewalks, in public places. No other subject was discussed—it seemed that each person had a theory of the murders and who had committed them. Waves of excitement swept the crowds gathered on Second Street every time the door of No. 92 was opened. Police were assigned to control the crowd outside the house and officers stood at the door, allowing only a few friends to enter. John Morse, who had eluded notice when he departed to post a letter, required a police escort back to the house to keep sensation-seekers at bay.

Already newsmen from leading papers in Providence, Boston, and New York were arriving by train and by boat, and naturally they all went immediately to the Second Street house, but had to be content with peering through the windows and attempting to sift a scintilla of real news from an avalanche of wild rumors and senseless theories. The Borden sisters' munificent reward had magically transformed every citizen of Fall River into a detective who was searching for, or inventing, leads, clues and suspects of every kind and nature. In addition, a New York newspaper published a reward of $500.00 for the production of the note which Mrs. Borden was supposed to have received on the morning of the murders, and the Fall River newspapers urged the public to come forward with information about the note, its sender, or the messenger who supposedly had delivered it to the Borden house.

Meanwhile, Marshal Hilliard, placing on duty his entire complement of one hundred twenty-five officers, had his difficulties. Rumors that a mad killer was loose in the city required a show of police force on the streets to calm the frightened and unsettled citizens, and hundreds of leads, some sensible, some senseless and absurd, flooded the stationhouse, and the Marshal attempted to pursue as many as possible with the officers he could make available for the purpose.

Nor were the officials of Fall River and Bristol County, and the amateur sleuths and inevitable cranks, the only persons questioning events immediately surrounding the murders. Sometime early in the weekend—exactly when has never been recorded—a Pinkerton detective from Boston, one O. M. Hanscom, was retained by the Bordens' family lawyer to make independent inquiries. He discussed random points with police officers, he was at the house during a further and exhaustive search for clues on Saturday, he was also there on Sunday morning and Monday. Thereafter he fades from the scene—and the case.

By the time of the double funeral on Saturday, excitement in the city was at fever pitch. However, those keeping morbid watch on Second Street were denied full satisfaction, for at 10:00 A.M. the service for Andrew and Abby Borden was held privately in the sitting room of No. 92, with very few persons allowed to attend. Little Abby Whitehead was there, with her mother, Sarah Whitehead, and her grandmother, Mrs. Oliver Gray. Only those three came to mourn Abby Borden; the rest of the assemblage was made up of business associates and relatives of Andrew Borden. Mrs. Abby Borden Whitehead Potter remembers the occasion, remembers the sadness and shock which she, even as a child of nine, felt at the loss of her kindly aunt. Here is how she described the funeral scene eighty-one years after it took place:

"The two black caskets were in the Borden sitting room side by side. Andrew Borden's casket was completely closed but Abby's was not: it was half open—or open to about the waist—so that Mrs. Borden's face and upper body were on view. On one casket was placed an olive branch, on the other a sheaf of wheat. There were no flowers in the room. The funeral ceremony consisted of a reading from the Scriptures and the recitation of a series of prayers."

While this solemn rite was taking place, hundreds of people crowded the street outside the Borden house, and were kept in control by a detail of police. Hundreds more lined Fall River curb-sides, waiting for a glimpse of the funeral cortège as it traveled to the cemetery located on the other side of the city.

The pallbearers for Andrew Borden, according to contemporary newspaper accounts, were businessmen: Abraham G. Hart, cashier of the Union Savings Bank; George W. Dean; Jerome C. Borden; Richard B. Borden, treasurer of Troy Mills; James M. Osborne; and a namesake, Andrew Borden, treasurer of Merchant's Mills. The pallbearers for Abby Borden were also business connections of her husband's: James C. Eddy; Henry S. Buffinton; John H. Boone—all names that appeared time and time again in the directory of Fall River's leading businesses in 1892.

The two hearses and eleven hacks awaited the end of the services at the curb of 92 Second Street. The principal mourners were of course Emma and Lizzie, and the first to leave the house was Lizzie, leaning upon the arm of Undertaker Winwood.

At the graveside, the Reverend Mr. Buck of the Central Congregational Church read the traditional passage from the New Testament beginning, "I am the Resurrection and the Life"; then the pastor of Andrew Borden's church intoned a prayer which ended with a request for spiritual guidance for the investigators of justice to deliver them from mistake. There may have been a message meant here not entirely for celestial reception.

Unbeknown to the mourners, however, the bodies were not then interred. After the carriages had left the cemetery, the caskets were placed again in a receiving vault. An official telegram had arrived at the graveside directing Undertaker Winwood to do so: a second and more thorough autopsy was to be performed.

By pre-arrangement, late Saturday afternoon after the funeral John W. Coughlin, M.D., who was Mayor of Fall River, with Marshal Hilliard, District Attorney Hosea Knowlton and County Medical Examiner William Dolan held a meeting at the Mellen House, the city's finest hotel. It was by now obvious that some definitive action must be taken by the city and county officials to allay the unrest that was gripping Fall River concerning the evidence so far discovered by the police. Mayor Coughlin and Marshal Hilliard were delegated to go to the Bordens' to offer the household further police protection. There they talked with the sisters and John Morse and cautioned them, especially Lizzie, against going into the streets, referring obliquely to her uncle's harassment by the crowd the day before. In the course of the visit the physician-mayor suggested to Lizzie, really in response to her pressing inquiry, that she was suspected of the crimes.

This was a serious blunder made by Mayor Coughlin, because it would afford Lizzie's attorney at her trial, in June 1893, to make an arguable case for the exclusion of her statements made on oath at the inquest scarcely a week after the murders. This point will be discussed in context later and at length. It is enough to say here, however, that there is no indication that Lizzie was seriously disturbed by the Mayor's comment: she retired as usual, as did Emma and Miss Russell.

On Sunday morning Alice Russell prepared breakfast for the Borden sisters and herself. There was then no one else in the house, although Hanscom, the private detective, and John Morse were about the premises from time to time, and the police were still on guard outside. In the kitchen after breakfast Miss Russell saw Lizzie at the stove with what appeared to be a skirt in her hand, and, when Emma asked her sister what she was doing, Lizzie said she was going to burn "the old thing, it's all covered with paint." Shortly thereafter Alice Russell saw her again ripping a garment and placing a remnant of it in a kitchen cupboard. Still later, on Monday, her friend told Lizzie that she had spoken to Hanscom, the Pinkerton man, and added: "I'm afraid, Lizzie, the worst thing you could have done was to burn that dress. I have been asked about your dresses."

"Oh, what made you let me do it?" Lizzie asked Alice Russell—"why didn't you tell me?"

It was also on 7 August, the day of the dress-burning, that the Reverend W. Walker Jubb issued the first of his many offensive defenses of Lizzie Borden: he devoted his entire sermon at the Central Congregational Church to the Borden murders and their effect upon the community. It did little to alleviate the fears of a mad killer loose in the city that the seemingly omnipresent clergyman called from his pulpit for divine guidance for the police officials in searching out the murderer. "Save us from blasting a life at once innocent and blameless," he cried, warning the press against blackening forever a pure and holy life. And he ended with a dramatic salute: "God help and comfort her, poor, stricken girl!"

But even the Reverend Jubb's best efforts were not good enough. They did not forestall the inevitable, for Monday there was widespread public comment throughout the city that the police had found no substantial clue of any kind outside the Borden premises, and the finger of suspicion pointed incriminatingly at only one person—Lizzie Andrew Borden.

The intense public excitement grew rapidly during the day, then peaked when it was learned that at last, after five days of uncertainty and insecurity, at long last there would be official action. Judge Josiah C. Blaisdell, presiding Justice of the Second District Court of Bristol County, had called for an inquest to begin the next day, Tuesday, 9 August 1892, at the Fall River jailhouse.

The Anatomy

of Accusation

CHARLES MACKLIN, eighteenth-century London playwright and Shakespearean actor, was as famous for his turbulent private life as he was for his magnificent interpretation of the rôle of Shylock. Litigious by nature, his violent temper and abrasive personality soon made his appearances in the courts of London as frequent as his appearances on the stages of Covent Garden and Drury Lane. In each lawsuit he represented himself—sometimes successfully, other times less so. His legal education consisted of his thousands of performances in *The Merchant of Venice*, and he was convinced that play-acting and the trial of cases were kindred arts.

In despair after one of his many defeats at the Assizes he wrote, "The law is a hocus-pocus science and the glorious uncertainty of it is that it is of more use to the professors than to the justice of it."

Many laymen today share Macklin's view that the law, as a science, is cleverly designed to confound the nonprofessional. However, after thirty-seven years of serving "the jealous mistress"—as Oliver Wendell Holmes, Jr., dubbed the pursuit of the law—it is easy for me to disagree with Macklin.

In the Anglo-American world the lengthy and seemingly complicated procedures surrounding the preparation and trial of a criminal case are designed to guard zealously the rights of one who is criminally accused, and this dominating principle obtained in the circumstances surrounding the Borden case.

The legalistic events leading to the arrest of Lizzie Borden for the double murders and continuing through the trial and acquittal in 1893, do, in no substantial way, differ from the procedures pursued in Massachusetts today. Stripped of their technical and somewhat archaic nomenclature and reduced to their basics, these procedures are, actually, not too difficult for the layman to understand. Therefore, by way of an informal syllabus, here follows a description of the nature and purpose of the three legal proceedings which took place prior to the trial of Lizzie Borden: the inquest, the preliminary hearing, and the grand jury hearing.

THE INQUEST

The preliminary inquest in Massachusetts is a legacy from the old English law and is basically investigative. In seventeenth-century England the Courts of Assizes traveled circuit, and transportation difficulties and a shortage of judges made judicial sittings in rural and remote counties infrequent.

If a violent death occurred between judicial sittings, as was most often the case, it was necessary to have a method of recording and memorializing all facts and circumstances surrounding the death in order that they would be available at the next Court sitting. For this purpose there was adopted a device called "a coroner's jury," a body of responsible local persons charged with the duty of immediate inquiry and recording of facts surrounding violent or mysterious deaths. Later, for much the same reasons, a coroner's-jury procedure was adopted in Massachusetts in its earliest days.

In 1850 the "coroner's jury statute" was amended to allow the conduct of hearings in absolute secrecy in order to avoid pre-trial publicity which might later prove to be prejudicial to a defendant.

The Massachusetts legislature took this action immediately after, and as a result of, the celebrated Parkman-Webster murder trial. Within weeks of Professor Webster's hanging following conviction for the murder of Doctor Parkman, the legislature voiced grave concern about early and widespread publicity given to Webster's rôle in the disappearance of Doctor Parkman. This publicity was precipitated by "leaks" to the press from the coroner's jury hearings, which traditionally were secret. Many felt even in 1850 that publicity of this kind could, and indeed did, prejudice Professor Webster's defense.

The next step in the evolution of the inquest occurred in 1877 when the "coroner's-jury" statute was revised and the duties of the coroner and his jury were transferred to a judicial officer; in such proceedings this was the judge of the nearest district, or lower, court. The revision of the Act required that these district court judges hold hearings forthwith when a mysterious violent death was discovered. At the conclusion of the hearings the judge filed a report certifying: (1) the name of the deceased and how and when the death occurred, and (2) if indicated by the disclosures of witnesses, the name of the person or persons causing the death. It also established the office of Medical Examiner in each of the counties, required autopsies, and set out the specific procedures for the district court judge to follow.

Interestingly, this revised statute of 1877, in full force and effect at the time of the Borden killings, strongly suggested but did not absolutely require complete secrecy of hearings. It was changed in no substantial way until 1969, when the Massachusetts Supreme Judicial Court in the case of *Edward M. Kennedy v James A. Boyle, as he is Justice of the District Court of Dukes County* ruled that inquests must be closed to the public and to the news media; that witnesses could be advised by counsel when testifying; and, with some minor qualifications, that the district court judge's report and all inquest documents must remain impounded. The salutory basis for this ruling was that excessive news coverage, generated by the prosecution at a one-sided, or *ex parte,* hearing before a trial, would or could violate the two principles inherent in the American concept of trial by jury—that jurors selected must be impartial, and that the eventual trial jury's verdict must be based solely upon evidence adduced at the trial.

Thus in the Senator Kennedy case in 1969 the Supreme Judicial Court in effect ruled that inquests must be absolutely secret.

However, the 1877 Act in effect at the time of the Borden murders had contained this less than mandatory, indeed almost precatory, language: "The court or trial justice shall thereupon hold an inquest which may be private." In practice, though, all inquests before and after 1893 were held in private, but clearly the language of the statute did not absolutely require this secrecy.

Pursuant to this statute and from 9 August through 11 August 1892—from Tuesday through Thursday—an inquest was held at the Fall River Police Station. It was conducted by Judge Josiah C. Blaisdell, presiding judge of the Second District Court of Bristol County, Fall River District. By this time the horror of the two murders, the prominence of the victims, and the shroud of mystery which engulfed the tragedy had made the Borden case a matter of much more than regional concern.

All during the inquest, each day hundreds of curious surrounded the grim walls of the police station to see the comings and goings of the prime suspect and other witnesses, and representatives of the press from all the newspapers of the Eastern cities raced through and around the crowds hoping for a hint, a suggestion, even a rumor of what was going on inside the jail at the hearing. Impenetrable secrecy was preserved.

On Wednesday, 10 August, the district attorney's office issued a short and wholly unsatisfying bulletin: "Inquest continued at 10:00 today. Witnesses examined were Lizzie Borden, Dr. S. W. Bowen, Adelaide B. Churchill, Hiram C. Harrington, John V. Morse, and Emma Borden. Nothing developed for publication."

Thursday, 11 August, exactly one week after the murders, was to be the last day of Judge Blaisdell's inquest. As the inquest was about to adjourn for the day there occurred a series of comings and goings bizarre enough to satisfy every news-hungry reporter and to saturate the press with headline stories sensational enough to rivet the attention of the entire nation.

While the inquest was in progress, Medical Examiner William Dolan of Bristol County, with the medical examiner imported from Boston and two other physicians, performed a second autopsy upon the bodies of Andrew Borden and Abby Borden. As already mentioned, following religious observances the family and friends had departed from the cemetery, but burial had not thereupon taken place; the bodies were held pending a more complete autopsy than the hurried dissection performed in the dining room of the Second Street home on the day of the murders.

Now, as a result of this second autopsy, conducted 11 August at the Oak Grove Cemetery, came word that the medical experts had discovered a wound on Mrs. Borden's back. Not noticed before, it was just above and between the shoulder blades and was very deep. Next the corpses had been decapitated and all tissue removed, exposing the bare skulls ripped and smashed by the murderer's slashing blade.

As the evening progressed, there was a growing excitement generated by activity which was immediately followed by the return of Marshal Hilliard to the jail to confront Lizzie Borden at the scene of the inquest. Addressing Lizzie, Marshal Hilliard said: "I have here a warrant for your arrest, for the murder of Andrew J. Borden. Do you wish it read?" Upon advice of her counsel, Andrew Jennings, to waive the reading of the warrant, Lizzie said, "You need not read it."

Thus was Lizzie Borden arrested by a warrant issued by Judge Blaisdell. The newspaper-reading public was shocked. Public sentiment was sharply divided: some felt relieved and assured that at last the authorities had acted properly and forcefully; others were crushed and appalled that law enforcement officials would dare accuse the daughter of one of the most prominent families in southeastern Massachusetts: they considered the arrest an outrage.

The press across the country cried the news, and the interest, if not the reaction, was shared by the public in Britain. On 12 August 1892 a number of London journals featured a telegraphed report by Reuter's news agency of Lizzie's arrest the preceding day. Headed SHOCKING PARRICIDE IN AMERICA, the stories began, "A terrible crime is believed to have been committed in Fall River, Massachusetts . . ." and continued with a précis of events that included incidents which will be discussed in

proper context in later chapters here. Curiously, the London evening *Echo*
carried on the same page a report of the opening day of testimony against
Dr. Thomas Neill Cream—often described by British writers as "an
American doctor" because he had practiced medicine and been impris-
oned for a time in Illinois—for the systematic killing by strychnine of a
number of London prostitutes.

Following the arrest, no inquest report was filed by Judge Blaisdell.
Although it appeared that the hearings had not been completed, even the
defendant's lawyer, Jennings, conceded that the issuance of the arrest
warrant by Judge Blaisdell properly terminated the inquest proceedings.

The first phase of the case was now over, and Lizzie was held in custody
for her father's murder. Oddly, the warrant charging Lizzie mentioned
only the murder of Andrew Borden; at this time no warrant was issued or
served which concerned itself with the murder of her stepmother. It was
only as a result of the grand jury's findings on 2 December 1892 that she
would be charged with Abby Borden's murder, as well as with the double
murder of both parents.

For a thorough understanding of Lizzie Borden's jury trial and verdict
ten months later it is extremely important to note that at the inquest, *and
only at the inquest,* did the defendant herself testify. The entire testimony at
the hearings held by Judge Blaisdell at the Fall River jail were recorded
by one Annie White, stenographer. Not only because of their content
would these stenographic notes create a problem of paramount importance
in the murder trial of Lizzie Borden ten months later.

Judge Blaisdell's assiduous efforts to shroud his inquiry proceedings in
complete secrecy were very effective. No hint or suggestion of the contents
of the stenographer's notes of Lizzie's testimony came to the attention of
the public during the pendency of the inquest. At the preliminary hearing,
which followed the inquest, the notes were read but they were not then
published.

⚬⚬⚬

"Arraignment" in Massachusetts and elsewhere means that the defendant
is brought before the Court merely for the purpose of entering a formal
plea to a charge.

Having been held in custody from the time of her arrest late Thursday
on the formal charge of murdering her father, Lizzie Andrew Borden was
arraigned the following morning, 12 August 1892, before Judge Blaisdell
at the Fall River District Court.

A heavy summer rain failed to deter the tremendous crowd gathered around the courthouse and courthouse steps. Here is how a contemporary newsman described the day of arraignment:

Miss Lizzie A. Borden was to be arraigned in the Second District Court, on Friday morning. By 9 o'clock a crowd of people thronged the streets and stood in a drenching rain to await the opening of the door of the room in which the court held its sittings. It was not a well-dressed crowd, nor was there anybody in it from the acquaintance circle of the Borden family in Fall River. Soon after 9 o'clock, a hack rolled up to the side door and Emma Borden and John V. Morse alighted and went up the stairs. They were not admitted at once to the matron's room.

The Reverend E. A. Buck

FROM PORTER

Reverend E. A. Buck was already present and was at the time engaged in conversation with the prisoner. Judge Blaisdell passed up the stairs, while Miss Emma was waiting to see her sister, and entered the courtroom. Mr. Jennings, Lizzie Borden's attorney, also arrived. The District Attorney was already in the courtroom, and soon the Marshal brought in his large book of complaints and took his seat at the desk. The door of the matron's room opened, and Mr. Jennings, Miss Emma Borden and Mr. Morse met the prisoner. All retired within the room. A few moments later Mr. Jennings came out and entered the courtroom. He at once secured a blank sheet of legal cap and began to write. The City Marshal approached him, and Mr. Jennings nodded an assent to an inquiry if the prisoner could now be brought in.

Lizzie Borden entered the room immediately after on the arm of

Reverend Mr. Buck. She was dressed in a dark blue suit and her hat was black with red flowers on the front. She was escorted to a chair.

The Court ordered the Clerk to read the warrant.

"You needn't read it," said Mr. Jennings, her attorney, "the prisoner pleads not guilty."

"The prisoner must plead in person," said Judge Blaisdell. At a sign from City Marshal Hilliard the prisoner arose in her seat.

"What is your plea?" asked the Clerk.

"Not guilty," said the girl, and then, having said this indistinctly and the Clerk repeating his question, she answered the same thing in a louder voice and with a very clearly cut emphasis on the word "Not."

Since murder in Massachusetts was not a bailable offense in 1892, after her arraignment Lizzie was led off to Taunton Jail—Taunton also being a shire town of Bristol County—which offered facilities appropriate for housing a female prisoner. Preliminary hearing on the charge of murdering her father was set for Monday, 22 August 1892, ten days after arraignment.

THE PRELIMINARY HEARING

The preliminary trial, or hearing—in Massachusetts now called a "probable-cause hearing"—is a hybrid criminal proceeding held in the District, or lower, courts of the state to determine if there is probable cause for charging a defendant with a crime which is beyond the jurisdiction of the District Court.

In Massachusetts, the district, or lower, courts have criminal jurisdiction which extends only to misdemeanors and to the few felonies which carry a maximum sentence of imprisonment in the state prison for five years or less; all more serious crimes must be heard by the Superior Court. Quite obviously, therefore, murder is beyond the jurisdiction of a district court. Accordingly, in August of 1892 it became the responsibility of District Court Judge Josiah C. Blaisdell of Fall River to determine whether there was probable cause for believing that the defendant, Lizzie Borden, was guilty of the murder of her father, Andrew J. Borden, as charged in the warrant.

If Judge Blaisdell found probable cause to believe Lizzie Borden guilty of murder, he would be obliged to hold, or "bind over," the defendant for the Superior Court, for the grand jury. It is important to note here that there is *no* requirement in the Constitution of the Commonwealth, in

Massachusetts statutes, or in case law that there be a probable-cause hearing prior to an indictment.

In practice, the probable-cause proceedings weed out the most frivolous and contrived criminal charges, for a finding of "no probable cause" by a district court judge usually, although not necessarily, terminates the matter he has considered. In the great majority of cases, the district court judge hears only enough evidence to convince himself that there is probable cause to believe the defendant guilty and then sets bail, if any is required, and the defendant is bound over for the next grand jury sitting.

The real importance of a probable-cause hearing, however, is that it allows the defendant the opportunity for early discovery. "Discovery" is legal jargon meaning "disclosure of the extent and kind of evidence in the possession of the prosecution and likely to be used against the defendant in the subsequent trial." To be forewarned is to be forearmed.

Unlike a grand jury investigation, the defendant has a right to be present at a probable-cause hearing and to be represented by counsel; and, naturally, defense counsel has the right to cross-examine witnesses for the prosecution. Normally the amount of evidence received by the district court judge is a discretionary matter resting with him. By suspending the inquest unfinished, and at the same time ordering a probable-cause, or preliminary, hearing, to take place forthwith, Judge Blaisdell had accomplished an odd and interesting judicial switch. He had doffed his hat as presiding officer at the inquest and donned his hat as presiding judge at the preliminary hearing. This action, perhaps harmless, did have about it some overtones of lack of objectivity. Lizzie's attorney, Andrew Jennings, immediately filed a motion asking Judge Blaisdell to recuse himself on the grounds that he had already heard testimony on the same matter at the inquest held in secret. Judge Blaisdell refused to recuse himself. The press criticized his failure to disqualify himself, and the headline-hunting Reverend Mr. Jubb blasted him from the pulpit as "indecent and uncivilized."

Judge Blaisdell's proper but awkward handling of this matter set off the first salvo of the artillery of propaganda which was to beat back the prosecution of Lizzie Borden—beat it back as surely as the Russian guns repulsed the charge of the Light Cavalry Brigade at Balaklava nearly forty years earlier.

On 22 August, therefore, Lizzie was duly transported from Taunton Jail to her probable-cause hearing in Fall River. There she was lodged in the private quarters of police matron Hannah Reagan in the Central Police Station, since the jail in the building lacked suitable amenities; and there,

Lizzie's Arrival for the Preliminary Hearing 22 August 1892

FROM PORTER

in Mrs. Reagan's room, occurred an incident fraught with dramatic possibilities and which will be described in context in the account of her trial by jury. In the meantime her arrival in her home town set off such a wave of excitement and attracted such huge crowds that a near riot was barely averted, and the feverish atmosphere was not allayed by the fact that her case was continued until Thursday, 25 August, to allow the prosecution to present certain evidence not yet available. On that date, however, the preliminary hearing before Judge Blaisdell did begin, and it lasted for six trial days.

Andrew Jennings, perhaps sensing that he was now in a case beyond his professional depth, called for assistance, and his choice fell upon Colonel Melvin O. Adams of Boston, a former Assistant District Attorney for Suffolk County.

Adams, acting as attorney for Lizzie at the hearing, cross-examined each of the twenty-two prosecution witnesses who were called to the stand by District Attorney Knowlton. They included, but were not limited to, Medical Examiner William Dolan, John V. Morse, Bridget Sullivan, Mrs. Adelaide B. Churchill, Miss Alice M. Russell, Deputy Marshal John Fleet, and Edward S. Wood, M.D., Harvard Medical School professor of chemistry. Since all the witnesses but one were to testify at the actual trial on the merits in the Superior Court, and since their testimony in that court would be virtually unchanged from their testimony given before Judge Blaisdell at this preliminary hearing, it shall be digested later in the account of the actual trial.

The preliminary hearing did provide Adams and Jennings, Lizzie's attorneys, with unlimited opportunity for discovery by direct and cross-examination of the government witnesses. Judge Blaisdell forced the prosecution to unfurl its entire case before he made his determination that he believed Lizzie Borden was probably guilty of the murder of Andrew J. Borden, her father, and bound her over for the grand jury, without bail.

During this determination of probable cause, Lizzie of course did not testify, but on 28 August Knowlton read to Judge Blaisdell from the stenographic notes of Annie White, the stenographer who had recorded Lizzie's interrogation by Knowlton at the secret inquest earlier that month.

These notes represent *the only statement of any nature or kind ever made by Lizzie Borden with regard to the murders of her father and her stepmother.* The effort to introduce these stenographic notes was to become a pivotal evidentiary point in the Superior Court trial of Lizzie Borden in June 1893.

Perhaps, taken out of context, the stenographic notes of Lizzie's inquest statements were too confusing or too vague for newspaper readers' consumption in August of 1892; perhaps the press felt a responsibility to keep Lizzie's statements from the public until the jury for her trial had been selected, and had been "locked up," or isolated. For whatever reason, Lizzie's testimony was not published until the actual trial was in progress: on 11 June 1893 in the Providence *Journal*, and the following day, 12 June, in the New Bedford *Standard*. At that time the trial jury was of course locked up and not allowed to read newspapers. This testimony as published appears in full as Appendix I of this book.

With the reading of Lizzie's inquest statements the proceeding for determination of probable cause ended, for Judge Blaisdell felt then that he had heard enough incriminating evidence to believe Lizzie Borden probably guilty of the two parricides. Tearfully, the elderly judge pronounced Lizzie's probable guilt and bound her over, without bail, for

Courtroom Drawing of the Borden Sisters at the Preliminary Hearing,
Containing a Rare Representation of Emma (*right*)

FROM THE *ILLUSTRATED AMERICAN*

the next sitting of the Grand Jury of Bristol County. Lizzie was led from the courtroom, and her anguished friends and supporters wept openly as she was returned to the county jail in Taunton.

THE GRAND JURY HEARING

Few terms in common usage are so little understood or so often misunderstood as is the legal term "grand jury." This misconception is in part due to the fact that the terminology itself is somewhat misleading.

The modifying word "grand" does not, in this context, imply pre-eminence, grandeur, or magnificence; it is simply the French word for "large," just as "petit" is the French word for "small." Thus the term "grand jury" merely distinguishes that body from a petit, or trial, jury, since a grand jury has twenty-three members and a petit jury—more properly called a trial jury—has but twelve members. Both juries are drawn by lottery from lists of those qualified to vote, and are summoned in precisely the same manner. Accordingly, both bodies represent a cross-section of the community, both bodies having their share of the young, the old; the rich, the poor; the black, the white; the energetic, the lazy; the wise and the dull. The functions of the two bodies differ, however, and the proper administration of justice requires that these respective functions be separate the one from the other.

In Massachusetts the grand jury is, and always was, merely an informing and accusatory body: it does *not* hear criminal cases on the merits; it does *not* determine guilt or innocence, for such determination is the function and the prerogative of the petit, or trial, jury. Hence the grand jury hears only the evidence presented by the prosecution in support of the charge and, in general, never hears evidence from the defense in exculpation. The trial jury, on the other hand, hears evidence from both sides, weighs this evidence, and determines the case upon its merits, and determines the guilt or innocence of the person criminally accused. In short, the function of the grand jury is a preliminary one, to make a formal accusation or not; the function of the trial jury is final and dispositive, for it determines the merits of the accusation, and thus the guilt or innocence of the accused.

A grand jury in Massachusetts may consist of not more than twenty-three nor less than thirteen persons. An indictment—the formal written accusation—must be voted by at least twelve grand jurors, regardless of the number present at the time of voting the indictment. Thus a majority vote is always assured. This vote is unlike that of a trial jury, where unanimity is required to establish guilt.

In general, the procedure before a grand jury is, in a sense, informal. No judge presides, the grand jurors elect their own foreman, and he administers oaths to witnesses who appear. During the proceedings the prosecutor's duty is merely to present the case, and to advise the grand jury concerning the law; the prosecutor must not express his own opinion or influence the grand jury in their deliberations in any way. Hearsay and other legally inadmissible evidence is heard and may be considered. Among the cases the grand jury hears are those which have originated in the District Court and are before the grand jury as a result of being bound over from a probable-cause hearing, as was the case of Lizzie Borden.

Secrecy is the keynote of grand jury deliberations and this secrecy extends to the vote given in any case, to the evidence introduced, to the testimony of the witnesses, and to the questions put by the grand jurors, as well as their talk and communications with each other. Disclosure of any of these facts is punishable by law, and a grand juror cannot be compelled to break his oath of secrecy even in a court of law.

Historically, Massachusetts accepted the grand jury as a legacy from the English common law, and the procedure was little changed between colonial days and 1892, and has been virtually unchanged from the date of Lizzie Borden's time until today. Certainly the grand jury system is a remarkable institution and it remains deeply imbedded in the laws of Massachusetts. Twenty-six of the United States and, ironically, England in 1933, have abolished the grand jury. In the Commonwealth the grand jury is and always has been considered a bulwark of individual liberty, a protection against false, frivolous, damaging accusations being publicly made, a protection against overzealous prosecutors and other despotic public officials—a protection, if you will, against tyranny.

The grand jury for the County of Bristol was assembled 7 November 1892 to deliberate upon criminal matters, complaints and accusations made in that county. The last week of the sitting was given over to the consideration of Lizzie Borden's case.

For most of the week, Bristol County District Attorney Hosea M. Knowlton presented his evidence and then, presumably having finished his presentation to the grand jury, he did an astonishing thing. He notified Andrew J. Jennings, attorney for Lizzie Borden, that Jennings would be allowed to present to the grand jury evidence for the defense. This was a gesture to my knowledge unheard of in Massachusetts if not in Anglo-American jurisprudence, before or, for that matter, since the indictment of Lizzie Borden.

As has already been pointed out, it is not and was not the function of the grand jury to weigh both sides of the case and determine guilt or innocence. That is the exclusive responsibility of the trial jury, the petit jury. The grand jury's duty and responsibility was and is only to weigh the evidence of the prosecution to satisfy themselves that there is enough evidence to warrant a trial by a petit jury to determine the issue of guilt or innocence.

District Attorney Knowlton's artful action struck at the very heart of the basic principle under which the grand jury operates, and has operated, for centuries. By inviting evidence in Lizzie's defense, he was giving her the opportunity for a trial on the merits of the case to be held in complete secrecy before the grand jury: he was, in effect, converting the grand jury into a petit jury, a trial jury, by allowing her lawyer to present evidence for the defendant.

On 21 November 1892 the grand jury adjourned without taking any action. No indictments were returned against Lizzie, and there was no return endorsed "No true bill" to indicate that the grand jury had rejected or ignored the accusations.

The newspapers of the country carried these amazing and puzzling events on their front pages. Professionals in the law were completely dumfounded. District Attorney Knowlton's disingenuous attempt to demonstrate complete fairness, if that were his motive in making his offer to Lizzie's attorney, seemed to have backfired.

Then on 1 December 1892 the grand jury reconvened and heard one witness, Miss Alice Russell, who had already testified before them but who had apparently forgotten or omitted something. The next day three indictments were returned against Lizzie Borden: one charged her with the murder of her father, a second charged her with the murder of her stepmother, and the third charged her with the murder of both.

It was reported by a contemporary newspaperman that of the twenty-one grand jurors voting, twenty voted for the indictment, one voted against it. The disclosure of this vote was, of course, in itself a criminal offense.

Immediately after the indictments were returned against Lizzie, there was another great burst of publicity and another wave of excitement which swept the nation. Lizzie was returned to the Taunton jail.

On 8 May 1893 she appeared briefly for her arraignment in the Superior Court, which was sitting in New Bedford. In the preceding five months the flush of public interest in the case had, to some extent, waned, and newspaper coverage regarding the murders, and the defendant, became spasmodic. Several personal interviews with Lizzie, either real or fanciful, appeared, but the cold fact was that nothing newsworthy was occurring; Lizzie Borden merely sat in her cell at the Taunton jail awaiting her arraignment.

On the appointed day Lizzie appeared briefly before Judge J. W. Hammond of the Superior Court to be arraigned upon the three indictments. In a firm voice she pleaded "Not guilty" to each of them, and trial was set for 5 June 1893 in New Bedford.

By contrast with the tremendous public attention which was later focused on her trial, Lizzie Borden's arraignment went relatively unnoticed. On 8 May she was again remanded to the Taunton jail to await trial for her life four weeks later.

Juris Personae

IN THE MONTH following Lizzie's arraignment, and while she sat, seemingly imperturbable, in Taunton Jail awaiting the determination of her fate, there occurred a startling and unexpected chain of events which was to have an immeasurable impact on the outcome of her trial for murder. I refer to the selection of the three-judge panel to preside at the June trial; the arrival on the scene of William H. Moody to assist Hosea M. Knowlton in the prosecution of the case; and finally—and most significantly—the re-alignment of Lizzie Borden's battery of defense attorneys.

In 1893, as it is today, the Superior Court of Massachusetts was a state-wide, circuit court. It had then, and it has now, regularly scheduled sittings in each of the fourteen counties of the Commonwealth. At the time of the Borden trial there were thirteen Justices of the Superior Court; all of them, then as now, were appointed by the Governor of the state "for life or for good behavior."

At its founding in 1859, the Superior Court had been given jurisdiction to hear capital cases, but that jurisdiction was almost immediately withdrawn and revested in the state's highest court, the Supreme Judicial Court. Then, in 1891, the Superior Court, by an act of the state legislature, re-acquired jurisdiction of capital cases. Previously all such cases were heard by a quorum of the Supreme Court; the 1891 legislation required a panel of three Superior Court judges to preside at the trial of a capital case. Therefore if the trial of Lizzie Borden was not the first murder case presided over by Superior Court Justices, certainly it was one of the first. The panel selected by Chief Justice Mason was composed of the Chief Justice himself, Associate Justice Caleb Blodgett, and Associate Justice Justin Dewey.

A Civil War veteran, fifty-seven years old, Chief Justice Albert Mason had served in the Massachusetts legislature representing a Plymouth County district. He had practiced law in Plymouth and at the same time had maintained a law office in Boston; when he was appointed as an Associate Justice of the Superior Court in 1882, he moved his family to Brookline. He became Chief Justice in 1890.

The Presiding Judges
at the Borden Trial:

Chief Justice Albert Mason
(*above, left*)

FROM PORTER

Justice Caleb Blodgett
(*above, right*)

FROM THE WILLARD COLLECTION

Justice Justin Dewey (*left*)

FROM JONES AND RENO

Judge Mason was heavy-set, of medium height, and wore a flowing white beard. Beneath a crown of thinning white hair, his sad eyes gave to his face a benign, almost sympathetic expression. He was married and the father of three daughters all in the approximate age bracket of Lizzie Borden.

The senior of the two Associate Justices chosen for the Borden trial was Caleb Blodgett of Boston, who had been appointed to the Superior Court in 1882. He was a graduate of Dartmouth College, and had practiced law in Boston, specializing in the law of bankruptcy, before his appointment to the bench. Judge Blodgett also wore a full white beard. He was partially bald, and his prominent, outthrust jaw, accentuated by his beard, gave him the caricatured appearance of a New Hampshire farmer—which in fact he had been before undertaking the study of law.

Except for his participation in the Borden case, Judge Blodgett's judicial career seems to have been unremarkable. In the early 1900's there were published several large tomes containing biographical sketches of the many members of the Massachusetts Bench and Bar of the preceding century. Each of the authors of these memorials seems to be attempting to outdo the others in his application of the Latin *de mortuis nil nisi bonum,* which, loosely translated, means "let nothing but good be spoken of the dead," for nearly every entry is replete with flattering superlatives. One or more of the phrases "most scholarly," "extremely profound," "very learned," and "wise" are used to describe nearly every Massachusetts lawyer and judge who had lived and died in the century just past. Judge Blodgett, however, is modestly described as "genial and unaffected in manner."

By far the best remembered of the three judges who presided at the Borden trial was the judge with the least judicial experience, the junior Associate Justice, who was Justin Dewey of Springfield. Born in Alford, a small town in western Massachusetts near the New York boundary, he had graduated from Williams College; he then studied in, and subsequently practiced law in, the office of an outstanding lawyer in that section of the state who bore the strikingly New England name of Increase Sumner. Like Chief Justice Mason, Judge Dewey had served in the legislature, and he was later elected a state senator. He was a handsome man, with white hair and beard, an aquiline nose and deep-set, piercing eyes. He was married and the father of three daughters, all in their late twenties.

In 1886 Judge Dewey had been appointed to the Superior Court by the then Governor, George D. Robinson, and shortly after his service on the bench began he and his family had moved to Springfield. Interestingly, a portrait of Judge Dewey and a portrait of Governor Robinson hang in the courtroom of the Hampden County Superior Court in Springfield—interestingly, because George D. Robinson was also to be a principal in the Borden trial.

It must be said with regret that Judge Dewey's best-remembered judicial acts were his participation in the Borden case, and his charge to the jury, both of which provoked a deluge of criticism from the press and from professionals in the law.

Until the trial of Lizzie Borden, it had been the accepted practice that the Attorney General of the Commonwealth would prosecute all capital cases, regardless of where within the state the trial was held. However, as her trial date approached and spokesmen for liberal women's-rights pressure groups, for conservative religious groups of all denominations, and for the area's textile-manufacturing "establishment" grew more clamorous in Lizzie's behalf, being the prosecutor of a well-connected—though possibly self-made—female orphan began to seem a less than politic rôle to play, and Arthur E. Pillsbury, Attorney General of Massachusetts, realized this. Asserting that his health would not permit his participation in a strenuous trial, Pillsbury directed District Attorney Knowlton of Fall River, a less astute but more ambitious politician, to conduct the prosecution as his proxy. Pillsbury also directed William H. Moody, the District Attorney for the Eastern District, Essex County, to assist Knowlton in the preparation and the trial of the case.

Hosea M. Knowlton, a graduate of Tufts College and Harvard Law School, was forty-five years old in 1893. He had served in both branches of the state legislature prior to his election, four years before the trial, to the office of District Attorney for the Southern District, including Bristol County. A few months after the trial ended he would be elected to replace Pillsbury as the state's Attorney General.

A short, stocky, bustling man with an air of haste and impatience, Knowlton's questioning of witnesses reflected his personality traits. Although his prosecution of the case appeared to be earnest and persistent, one who examines the transcript of the record professionally cannot avoid the unhappy conclusion that, despite his display of energy, Knowlton actually approached the trial, and even the probable-cause hearing that preceded the grand jury indictment, with a lack of zeal.

The late Edmund Pearson, writer of a number of popular accounts of famous murder cases, salutes Knowlton as a "courageous public official" in the dedication of his book devoted to the Borden trial. Pearson was a friend of Knowlton's son and thus became privy to some of the District Attorney's correspondence years after the trial had ended. One copy of a letter which Knowlton wrote to Pillsbury and which Pearson presents is hardly supportive of Pearson's evaluation of courage:

Hon. A. E. Pillsbury, Attorney General

My Dear Sir:

I have thought more about the Lizzie Borden case since I talked with you, and think perhaps that it may be well to write to you, as I shall not be able to meet you probably until Thursday, possibly Wednesday, afternoon.

Personally I would like very much to get rid of the trial of the case, and feel that my feelings in that direction may have influenced my better judgment; I feel this all the more upon your not unexpected announcement that the burden of the trial would come upon me . . .

Yours truly,

Hosea M. Knowlton

If this is the pre-trial statement of a courageous public prosecutor, then I do not know the meaning of words.

Although this language is the most specific indication of Knowlton's attitude toward the trial, it is by no means the only one. Beginning with his fastidiously proper but unnecessarily dilatory and protracted preliminary proceedings before Judge Blaisdell, and ending with his inappropriate words of congratulation to Lizzie uttered in open court after the jury's verdict of acquittal, there appears a clear pattern of reluctance and lethargy which District Attorney Knowlton pursued, yet carefully concealed, throughout the Borden trial. This pattern underlies the entire record.

In sharp contrast, Knowlton's co-prosecutor, William H. Moody, was to hold the prosecution team together, for to the professional in the law it is clear that Moody was easily the most competent lawyer participating in the Borden trial. His professional superiority was apparent in his questioning of witnesses, and in the sound arguments he advanced when addressing the Court concerning questions of admissibility of evidence.

A graduate of Harvard College, where he had known Theodore Roosevelt, Moody had prepared for his profession in the law office of Richard H. Dana, better remembered as the author of *Two Years Before the Mast* than as the able lawyer which he was. Moody had been elected District Attorney of Essex County three years before Attorney General

Attorneys for the Commonwealth:

Hosea M. Knowlton (*above*)
William H. Moody

Pillsbury assigned him to work with Knowlton on the trial of Lizzie Borden.

Partly as a result of the national prominence Moody gained by his remarkably capable performance 5–20 June 1893 in the New Bedford courtroom, he was elected to the Congress of the United States in 1895. He was twice re-elected by the time Theodore Roosevelt became President and named Congressman Moody to his cabinet, first as Secretary of the Navy and later as Attorney General of the United States. He served with distinction in both cabinet posts, and in 1906 Roosevelt appointed him Justice of the Supreme Court of the United States. Moody, a lifelong bachelor, often escorted the President's younger daughter, Alice, to Washington social affairs; years later she asked Moody to be her father's biographer, but Moody, by then old and in ill health, could not undertake a project so protracted.

So far have been presented the Bench and prosecution; now we turn to Lizzie Borden's battery of defense counsel. The most significant and curious re-alignment of the trial personnel occurred in the ranks of Lizzie Borden's defense team, and shortly before she was placed at the bar.

Lizzie initially, from the very day of the murders, had been advised, and later represented, by Andrew J. Jennings, who practiced law in Fall River and had been her father's lawyer. Jennings was a leader of the local attorneys. Like Knowlton, whom he was to succeed as District Attorney the year after Lizzie was acquitted, Andrew Jennings was short, thickly set, with a brusque, almost antagonistic, air of importance. He lived a long life and was one of Fall River's most prominent citizens. A taciturn man, Jennings never spoke of the Borden case at any time after the trial. His daughter, Mrs. Dwight Waring of Fall River, a charming lady of advanced years when I talked with her in 1973, told me that throughout his lifetime her father had never allowed the trial to be a topic of conversation in his household. I might add that Mrs. Waring herself, although very obliging in discussing her father's distinguished career at the Bristol County Bar, seemed to be somewhat reluctant to talk about Lizzie Borden, or her trial, or her life and behavior after the trial. It seemed to me that Mrs. Waring looked upon the whole Borden matter as something unpleasant that should be forgotten and laid to rest. Perhaps she was right.

Jennings's partner, James M. Morton, had been appointed to the Supreme Judicial Court of Massachusetts three years before the Borden trial, and Jennings was assisted by a young associate, Arthur S. Philipps, who later was to write his *History of Fall River*. Philipps's contribution to the

Borden case was confined to investigation and preparation, and he played no significant rôle in the courtroom. Because he no longer had the experienced Morton as a partner, Jennings, able though he himself was, had, prior to the preliminary hearing, retained Melvin O. Adams of Boston to assist him. Perhaps Jennings felt that undertaking a case of this magnitude with only a young associate was too great a burden for him to shoulder alone; at any rate, he made a wise choice. Adams—who was not a member of the famous Boston family—was a Dartmouth College graduate who had studied law with Jennings at Boston University Law School, and went on to establish a fine reputation in the Boston area as an outstanding trial lawyer, specializing in criminal cases. He had served as an Assistant District Attorney in Suffolk County (Boston) before resigning to devote his time to private trial practice.

A very handsome man of medium build, Adams wore a waxed moustache and was always elegantly dressed; his wit and his urbane manner somehow helped him establish a rapport with jurors, and he was to provide the only incident of frivolity at the Borden trial. But Adams's wit was a professional tool: he was a skilled, experienced criminal-trial lawyer who had a long and prosperous career at the bar. In later years he was president of the locally famous narrow-gauge Boston, Revere Beach & Lynn Railroad.

Amazingly, this experienced, skillful combination of Adams and Jennings, shortly before the trial and at about the time the judges' panel had been selected, announced that a third attorney was to join them as head of the defense team and actually to try the case. He was George D. Robinson of Chicopee, in western Massachusetts.

Rarely in Massachusetts even today do lawyers from the western part of the state try jury cases in the eastern part, and almost as rarely do lawyers from the eastern part of Massachusetts try jury cases in the western counties. But George D. Robinson had been Governor of Massachusetts for three one-year terms between 1884 and 1887, so at least he was known by name to the average citizen in Bristol County.

Moreover, George D. Robinson certainly was well known to the other legal participants at the trial of Lizzie Borden. In 1892 he had acted as co-counsel with District Attorney William H. Moody and another lawyer representing the City of Haverhill in an eminent-domain case involving the city's acquisition of the privately owned water company providing water to the city. The city paid the water company $637,000 for its assets and paid to its attorneys, former Governor Robinson and District Attorney Moody and another, a legal fee of $22,000. The eminent-domain case was

Attorneys for the Defense:

Andrew J. Jennings
(*above, left*)

Melvin O. Adams (*above, right*)

George D. Robinson

determined 17 October 1892, and the giant fee of $22,000 was divided between Moody and Robinson and the third attorney just before the Borden trial began.

Furthermore, during his years of service in the state legislature he had served on the select judiciary committee with the then senator from Plymouth County, Chief Justice Albert Mason, presiding judge at the Borden trial.

But by far Robinson's strongest connection derived from the fact that judges in Massachusetts are appointed for life by the Governor; and in 1886 George D. Robinson, then Governor, had appointed Justice Dewey to the Superior Court.

Despite his prominence, a study of the official trial transcript indicates to this writer that Robinson was not an experienced trial lawyer when contrasted with his co-counsel Jennings and, more particularly, Adams. This is not to say that Robinson was not able, articulate and shrewd in his trial technique; but it is clear that he lacked the final polish that comes only with years of experience at the trial bar. This is understandable when one considers Robinson's curriculum vitae. He had first studied medicine, then became a school teacher and served as the principal of Chicopee High School. He did not begin to study law until he was in his early thirties, and after being admitted to the bar at the age of thirty-three, he entered politics. Robinson served in the state legislature, three terms in the Congress of the United States, and three terms as Governor of Massachusetts. Thereupon he retired from public life and re-entered the practice of law only six years before the Borden case was tried.

Carnival Time
in Old New Bedford

BY THE DAY before Lizzie's trial began, a carnival-like atmosphere had settled over southeastern Massachusetts. In Fall River and in New Bedford ordinary business was immobilized, people gathered on the sidewalks and in public places, and everywhere the sole topic of conversation was the imminent trial of Lizzie Borden. Western Union and Postal Telegraph had installed thirty temporary lines serving New Bedford for the use of newspapermen, and thus, on the wings of the press, the tension and anticipation spread to Boston, Providence and New York, then with amazing rapidity throughout the nation. This was no ordinary murder trial. This was the trial of a socially prominent woman accused of double parricide, parricides committed in a most gruesome and bestial manner.

The hotels and lodging houses of New Bedford were full to overflowing with correspondents from the leading newspapers in the nation. Today's giant domestic wire services as we know them did not exist in 1893, and the few loosely organized associations which then existed were ineffective, their membership limited, the scope of their coverage narrow. The fact is that in 1893 newspapers battled individually and with fierce rivalry for news, just as they competed viciously for the sale of advertising space. This sharp competition for news and the almost complete absence of source centralization often led to rash and reckless reporting. This was the era of "the scoop" in then current newspaper parlance, the beginning of the era of yellow journalism, a time in our history generally marked by inaccurate and sometimes totally irresponsible news coverage.

In the ten months from the shocking murders on 4 August 1892 to the trial of Lizzie Borden in June of 1893, little had happened to engross the nation's press. Even the Presidential election of November 1892 had been dull, for Grover Cleveland and his running-mate, Adlai E. Stevenson, Democrats, had predictably defeated Republicans Benjamin Harrison and

Whitelaw Reid by a comfortable margin. The World's Columbian Exposition had opened in Chicago, but America was tiring of reading about it, as it was tired of reading about labor strife and conflict. Perhaps the most stirring news had been the stunning upset in New Orleans of the "Boston Strong Boy," John L. Sullivan, by "Gentleman Jim" Corbett for the world's heavyweight boxing championship. Ironically, what would turn out to be the most significant events of the months before the trial of Lizzie Borden had received little or no press notice: the Duryea brothers had built their first internal-combustion automobile, and shortly thereafter came the sequel destined to revolutionize the world's transportation— Henry Ford manufactured his first motorcar, which in a later model was, by an odd twist of fate, to be dubbed the "Tin Lizzie."

In this framework of relative tranquillity in the country it was natural that the nation's press would seize upon the sensational Borden trial as the story of the year. The public was hungry for the gruesome details of the double murders, and the press was prepared to satisfy that hunger with saturation coverage. On some days of the trial the Boston *Globe* devoted its entire front page and seven of the twelve inside pages of the same edition to the Borden case, and this concentration was not atypical of press focus. And as has been mentioned, the New York office of Reuter's, the British agency, was prepared to relay news to its transatlantic readers.

Into the journalistic swarm that had settled upon New Bedford the day before the trial strode Joseph Howard, probably the first syndicated news columnist in the nation. Controversial, flamboyant, the veteran Howard was the nineteenth-century version of today's romanticized notion of a celebrated reporter. He had first attracted national attention in the waning days of the Civil War when he invented a story of a universal compulsory military draft; this earned him a stay in jail and the censure of the government, but Howard merely termed his story. "a playful hoax." Later he had "scooped" other newsmen in the Crédit Mobilier scandal of 1873* which rocked Washington and the nation and brought the second Grant administration to its knees.

---

* The Crédit Mobilier was a construction company organized by a syndicate of wealthy entrepreneurs to build the Union Pacific Railroad. Congressional support for their project was achieved by allowing Congressmen and Senators to purchase stock in the construction company at par value, and often the dividends paid by the company were so large that the first dividend paid to a stockholding Congressman exceeded the price he had been charged for the par value stock. Fortunes were made; reputations were ruined. Occurring exactly one hundred

Howard's literary style was marked by an excessive use of adjectives to the point of being euphuistic, but his grandiloquence captured the American newspaper-reading public in 1893. He reported the trial for the Boston *Globe*, the New York *Recorder* and Pulitzer's New York *World*, signing his daily dispatches "Howard" in sprawling script.

Like all newsmen, Howard was attentive to and sensitive to the public pulse, and like all the correspondents covering the New Bedford trial, he was conscious of the solid, pre-trial demagogic support which Lizzie had received.

"The Bloomer Girls" and other articulate feminist organizations had rallied militantly around her. Shortly before the trial Mrs. Susan S. Fessenden, president of the powerful Woman's Christian Temperance Union, had thrilled the annual meeting of that national organization with her maudlin oratorical praise of Lizzie, "the poor helpless child."

"Is Lizzie Borden guilty?" Mrs. Fessenden screamed, rhetorically, at the W.C.T.U. Then with a line which was to become the lead lyric of a popular song, she answered herself, "No, no, a thousand times no!"

Lizzie's past, though somewhat spasmodic, endeavors for the Christian Endeavor Society and for the Fruit and Flower Mission of the Central Congregational Church were rewarded a thousandfold. These, coupled with the cloak of sanctimony lent to her by her two now well-publicized clerical escorts, the Reverend Jubb and the Reverend Buck, won for her the support of various well-meaning religious groups of all denominations and persuasions.

Before the trial began, scathing condemnations of the prosecution and the police by Lizzie's supporters were regular fare in the public press, and sickly sentimental descriptions of the early middle-aged spinster characterizing her as a "helpless little girl" were even the subject of some editorial

---

years before "Watergate," it was the most celebrated *widespread* political scandal until 1973. A number of Congressmen—led by Oakes Ames of Massachusetts and including (later President) James A. Garfield—were involved, as were several United States Senators. As political careers were tarnished, stained and ruined, the scandal reached the White House, smearing the reputation of Schuyler Colfax, Vice-President of the United States. Beginning in the first year of Grant's second administration, the shameful affair was investigated for years by several different commissions. The net result was that President Grant was pitifully powerless for the balance of his second term, the business of the nation suffered deplorably, and Grant's Presidency, already proven inept, was marked as one of the most corrupt in history.

comment. In short, the newspapers had printed so much of this pre-trial bombast and drivel that they began to believe it themselves. Slowly but perceptibly the sympathy of the press had swung in Lizzie's direction.

Reflecting upon this, one finds the concept of pre-trial prejudicial publicity in reverse operation. This was pre-trial *advantageous* publicity. On the eve of the trial the press had conditioned the minds of the public and probably the minds of prospective jurors *in favor* of the criminally accused defendant.

As the curtain rose on the trial of Lizzie Borden, it was the police and the prosecutors who wore the black hats. Lizzie's hat was white.

TRIAL I:

The Prosecution

ON 5 JUNE 1893 the attention of the nation was focused upon New Bedford and a two-story brick building with four white Doric columns and a white wooden portico. This was the Superior Court House, which translated the majesty of justice to the people of Bristol County and the Commonwealth of Massachusetts.

Despite the grace and dignity of the exterior of the building, its interior design is, and was in 1893, somewhat curious. The only courtroom in the structure is located on the second floor, and the public can reach it only by a flight of stairs from the ground-floor corridor, which ascends and empties into the comparatively small courtroom itself; thus the staircase opening yawns as a large cavity in the courtroom floor. Although there is no main door, there of course are secondary doors in the courtroom, one on either side of the judge's bench. The left door leads to the judge's chambers, or "judge's lobby," as it is called in Massachusetts; the right door is for the use of jurors and members of the bar. A third door near the center of the courtroom leads to a small detention room.

The judge's lobby was—and indeed so remained until 1972—a very small, cell-like room, barely suitable to accommodate one judge and certainly not large enough for three. The spectators' seats in the rear of the courtroom are spoke-backed, wooden benches which rise in tiers; in no event could they comfortably hold two hundred persons. Naturally the witness box and the jury box are to the left of the bench from the judge's position. For the Borden trial a series of long tables with four-legged wooden stools, arranged at either side of each table, had been placed along the courtroom wall, separated from the jury seats only by the court crier's box. Four large, brass, gas-burning chandeliers hung from the courtroom ceiling.

Picture this singular scene on this first Monday in June 1893, the clerk and the bailiffs standing so stiffly that they seemed part of the court fittings, the spectators' seats crowded to full capacity, the press tables so swarmed that some of the correspondents shared the tiny stools or stood. The unseasonably torrid weather was amplified by the body heat generated by the pressing crowd, which fluttered palm-leaf and folding fans to provide a semblance of coolness. At 11:25 A.M. the detention room door opened and Lizzie Borden was led to, and placed at, the bar for trial. At 11:28, with a resounding crash of the bailiff's staff, the Court entered and took its place upon the bench, Chief Justice Mason in the center, flanked by Justice Blodgett to his right, and Justice Dewey to the left. The court crier, from his box at the side of the courtroom, gave the cry:

> Hear ye, hear ye, hear ye! All those having anything to do before the Honorable, the Justices of the Superior Court gather round, give your attention, and you shall be heard. God Save the Commonwealth of Massachusetts! Be seated!

The format of a capital trial in 1893 in Massachusetts was much the same as it is today. After the selection of the jury, the prosecution would make an opening statement, disclosing what it intended to prove by the use of the witnesses who were to be heard. Following the last of its witnesses, the Commonwealth would rest its case "in chief," reserving the right to introduce rebuttal testimony after the defense had finished. The defense then would make an opening statement, introduce witnesses, and rest its case in the same manner as the prosecution had done. After hearing any rebuttal testimony, the defense counsel, and then the prosecutor, would make final arguments to the Court and jury. At that point in the proceedings—in 1893 until 1973—in Massachusetts the defendant could make an unsworn statement to the jury in which he could say virtually anything to clarify his position. Then the presiding judge, or one of them speaking for all three, would deliver instructions in the law, called "the charge," and the jury then would retire to deliberate upon its verdict.

After the Court presiding over Lizzie Borden's trial had been seated, the Reverend M. C. Julian of New Bedford offered a prayer for divine guidance to the tribunal and to the jury.

There had been one hundred forty-five prospective jurors, all of whom were polled and answered to their names. Chief Justice Mason briefly addressed the venire, which is the jury panel, and gave them some words of preliminary instruction.

District Attorney Hosea Knowlton then rose and addressed the Court, formally notifying the judges that "the Attorney General of the Commonwealth finds himself in such a condition of health that he fears to engage actively in the trial of this cause, and he has, therefore, assigned to the District Attorney of Bristol County, the District Attorney of Essex County, William H. Moody of Haverhill, as co-counsel for the prosecution at this trial."

Each of the prospective jurors was then individually interrogated by the Court. In all, fifty-four prospective jurors were excused by the Court after examination; thirty-one were excused because they said that they had already formulated an opinion as to Lizzie's innocence or guilt, sixteen because they held opinions against capital punishment; one was excused because he was related to Lizzie, and the balance because of advanced age. The attorneys for the defendant challenged fifteen prospective jurors; fourteen jurors who were examined were challenged by the Commonwealth.

After four hours of dreary examination and selection, twelve jurors at last were chosen. They were: George Potter of Westport, William F. Dean of Taunton, John Wilbur of Somerset, Frederic C. Wilbar of Raynham, Lemuel K. Wilber of Easton, William Westcot of Seekonk, Louis B. Hodges of Taunton, Augustus Swift of New Bedford, Frank G. Cole of Attleboro, John C. Finn of Taunton, Charles I. Richards of North Attleboro, and Allen H. Wordell of Dartmouth. Except for the coincidence that jurors No. 3, 4 and 5 were named Wilbur, Wilbar and Wilber,

The Borden Jury

FROM PORTER

respectively, the jury chosen was unremarkable. There was one black-smith, and the rest were farmers and country tradesmen; all but one came from the small farming communities of Bristol County.

The Court recessed at five o'clock to allow the twelve jurors selected to arrange their personal affairs, since the jury was to be locked up. At 5:30 P.M. the Court reconvened and appointed Charles I. Richards as foreman of the jury, and thereupon suspended for the day.

The second day of the trial began with the clerk's formal reading of the three indictments returned by the grand jury 2 December 1892—charging Lizzie Andrew Borden with the murder of Andrew Jackson Borden, the murder of Abby Durfee Borden, and the murders of Abby Durfee Borden and Andrew Jackson Borden. The reading then ended with this stylized, yet always stirring, language: ". . . to each of these indictments the defendant has pleaded not guilty and has placed herself upon the country, which country you are. Gentlemen of the jury, harken to the evidence."

The Chief Justice nodded to the prosecution table, and District Attorney William H. Moody rose, walked across the courtroom with a solemn, measured step, leaned upon the rail of the jury box, and began, "Mr. Foreman, Gentlemen of this jury . . ."

THE PROSECUTION OPENS

District Attorney Moody, at age thirty-nine, was the youngest of all the professional participants at the trial, and, in addition, he was about to try his first murder case; yet his manner was confident and possessed, his delivery flawless. From a professional point of view, Moody's opening statement of the prosecution's case was a masterpiece. To the professional in the law it is clear that he had mastered every detail of the factual situation; equally clearly he had carefully marshaled the facts. For more than two hours he addressed the jury, yet a careful study of his opening fails to reveal a single paragraph that did not have significance, a single sentence that did not have supportive importance. As he recited to the jury, in an almost conversational tone, all the facts the Commonwealth intended to prove, a clear pattern emerged. When he had finished his opening statement, the jury had, or should have had, stamped upon their minds a definitive outline of the case against Lizzie Borden.

As Moody indicated in his opening, the prosecution's approach to proof of guilt was trifurcated. Three basic propositions were advanced:

First: That Lizzie Borden was pre-disposed to and had pre-determined to murder Andrew J. Borden and Abby Durfee Borden.

Second: That Lizzie Borden did in fact murder Abby Durfee Borden and Andrew J. Borden, in that order, and with a substantial interval of time between the two killings.

Third: That by her statements and by her actions after the murders, and each of them, Lizzie Borden by word and act placed herself in a position which was entirely inconsistent with innocence. In fact, by her words and by her deeds after the murders, and each of them, Lizzie Borden had displayed a consciousness of guilt of the murders to the point that she revealed herself to be guilty beyond any reasonable doubt.

As Moody related the expected testimony from the prosecution's witnesses, he indicated how each of the witnesses would support one or more of the three basic premises of guilt.

With regard to Lizzie's pre-determination to kill, Moody offered to prove this by witnesses who would testify as to the hostility and dislike for Abby which Lizzie harbored and her general fear of loss of inheritance, all to show *motive* for the murders.

Certain other witnesses would appear in support of proof of Lizzie's pre-disposition to kill by testifying as to Lizzie's actions and words prior to the murders to indicate her *state of mind* at that time. This is what in the law is known as *mens rea*. To this end, witnesses were to testify, said Moody, as to the statements and the acts of Lizzie Borden, tending to show her intention to kill on 4 August 1892.

As to the second basic proposition—that Lizzie did, in fact, commit the murders—Moody spoke of witnesses who would indicate that Lizzie had *the strength and the means* available to her to commit the crimes. In addition, and perhaps most importantly, the evidence would show, explained Moody, that Lizzie Borden not only had the opportunity to commit the crimes, but she had *exclusive opportunity* to commit them.

Thirdly and finally, Moody discussed the witnesses who would provide evidence of Lizzie's statements and actions after the crimes: witnesses who would testify as to *her lies to prevent the detection of the first murder; her lies and inconsistent statements as to her own whereabouts; her lies and inconsistent statements as to her discovery of her father's corpse,* and as to the inevitability of her knowledge of the first murder; and, very significantly, witnesses would testify as to *unusual acts and statements in the several days following the murders and before her arrest.*

At twelve noon the temperature as recorded in the New Bedford newspaper for 6 June 1893 was ninety-three degrees; within the courtroom the temperature was much higher, yet the judges, the jury and the spectators sat enthralled as Moody unfurled his damning recital.

At one stage of his opening, Moody, holding a dress that was to be offered into evidence, tossed it carelessly upon the prosecution table. Lying on the table was a plain, opened handbag with tissue paper covering its contents. As the dress landed partially upon the bag the tissue was swept away, and there were exposed in plain view the hideous eyeless, fleshless skulls of the two victims.

Lizzie Borden at first covered her eyes with her fan, then her head fell against the police matron seated next to her, and she slid to the floor in a dead faint. Here is Joseph Howard's vivid description of this incident as it appeared in the Boston *Globe*:

> The sight of those skulls was pregnant with meaning and Mr. Moody's descriptions of their gashed and hacked mutilations must have intensified the vividness of the scene to the inner consciousness of the prisoner who then without sigh, or gasp, or convulsive movement, dropped her head and slid upon her official companion, her face blue red with congestive symptoms, an inert, consciousless mass of inanimate flesh.

In his long dispatch of the trial's second day Howard spoke in glowing terms of Moody's opening. This is most significant, since from before the first day of the trial until the acquittal and even after, Howard led all other correspondents in his lack of objective reporting. He was, or pretended to be, convinced of Lizzie's innocence long before the trial began, and he never missed an opportunity to let this be known—so much so that after the acquittal the grateful Lizzie held a reception in Howard's honor, and it was well deserved. However, Howard had written of Moody's opening:

> Mr. Moody has a good head, clear eye, a firm mouth, a pleasant voice and an engaging manner. But far and better away than that, he has the rare gift of common sense, and without attempts at vocal gymnastics tells a clean-cut, well-matured history of the crime, adroitly weaving therein his theory of the guilt of the prisoner and its whys and wherefores.
>
> Mr. Moody spoke about two hours in a purely conversational tone; conscientiously he has worked upon the case for nearly a year and is satiated with Bordenism and permeated with what seems to him incontrovertible proof of guilt.

Moody ended his opening with these words: "We shall ask you to say, if say you can, whether any other reasonable hypothesis except that of guilt of this prisoner can account for the sad occurrences which happened upon the morning of August 4th."

There was a short pause. Moody, his opening statement finished, turned, and, with a bow to the three judges, called his first witness to the stand.

Here, at the outset of the testimony which consumes most of the 1,930 pages of the official trial transcript prepared by Philip Burt, Court Stenographer for the Massachusetts Superior Court which heard the case in 1893, it is important that the reader know how the testimony material is presented in the following chapters.

First, all statements of fact adduced from the witnesses are taken from the transcript, and from the transcript only.

Second is the manner of presentation. Where significance or emphasis requires that the give-and-take of a formal question and a formal answer be preserved, the testimony is set down in the question-and-answer style in which it appears in the transcript.

To conserve space and for facility of reading, much of the transcript has been redacted by reframing the question-answer testimony to statement summary form, and the redactions are contained within quotation marks in boldface. Throughout, however, care has always been used to preserve in redaction the idiom and the flavor and manner of speech of each individual witness, and unslanted summary has always been attempted.

Descriptions of courtroom activities, and actions and demeanor of the witnesses *other than testimony* has been extracted from a variety of contemporary accounts.

Occasionally I express as a professional in the law my opinion of certain passages between witness and counsel, of certain statements by counsel, and certain rulings from the Bench: such comments are contained clearly between boldface brackets.

The prosecution's first witness was Thomas Kieran, a registered professional engineer, the engineer for the City of Fall River. Kieran testified that he had measured the distance from the Borden house on Second Street to the Fall River Central Police Station, and it was 1,300 feet; from the Borden house to the Fall River City Hall measured 900 feet. He had drawn a plan of the area showing Second Street, Main Street, Borden Street and Spring Street, showing the City Hall, the Post Office and other buildings. He had also drawn a plan of the Borden house and the neighborhood immediately surrounding it, and still another plan, drawn to the scale of four feet to one inch, depicting both the ground and the upstairs bedroom floors of the interior of the Borden house. All these plans were admitted into evidence and were marked as exhibits.

After Kieran had given his technical testimony, the Court ordered that the jury take a view of the Borden premises, the interior as well as the exterior of the house. This was done by agreement of counsel. In accordance with the law, the Court offered to the defendant the opportunity to accompany the jury on the view; Lizzie declined. Jennings, on behalf of the defendant, and District Attorney Moody, on behalf of the Commonwealth, went with the jury to Fall River. The Court then recessed until the following day.

On the third day of the trial Engineer Kieran was recalled to the witness stand by Knowlton. He testified that he had attempted an experiment in the closet of the front hall on the ground floor of the Borden house: he had placed a man in the closet, and he claimed that the door of the closet was easily shut with the man inside the closet, and with the door ajar the witness, Kieran, had failed to see the man inside while standing eight or ten feet from the closet and looking directly into it.

[This was an odd courtroom practice and seemed to set the standard for what was to follow in rulings throughout the trial. In the first place the witness was a witness for the prosecution, not for the defense. Secondly, what Kieran and another man did in their "hide and seek" experiments made at some time after the murders could not have the slightest material importance considering the issues which were then before the jury. Lastly, if the testimony, under any conceivable hypothesis, was admitted as supportive or collaborative of other evidence, there was, as yet, *no other* evidence to support or collaborate. Kieran was the first witness, and his provocative tale of "experiments" was the first and *only* evidence the jury had heard other than the introduction of the plans.

Parenthetically, there was a remarkable paucity of objections made to the Court in the Borden trial. By contrast, in a murder trial of this length today there would be scores, if not hundreds, of objections made by counsel.]

The second witness was James A. Walsh, a photographer doing business in Fall River. At the request of the Medical Examiner, Walsh had taken photographs of the Borden premises and of the corpses of both Mr. and Mrs. Borden as they had appeared on the day of the murders. These photographs were introduced into evidence and marked as exhibits.

A short, peppery man whose quick step to the witness stand belied his age was the first dramatic witness to take the stand, John Vinnicum Morse.

"My name is John Vinnicum Morse, age sixty-nine, present address South Dartmouth, Massachusetts. I have been living in the west for a number of years, but three years ago I returned east. I am the uncle of the defendant Lizzie Borden and her sister Emma because my sister Sarah Morse was the first wife of Andrew J. Borden and the mother of Emma and Lizzie.

"Andrew J. Borden married my sister Sarah in 1850, and there were three children, but one had died in infancy; the other two were Emma and Lizzie. My sister died in 1861, and Andrew J. Borden married Abby Durfee Gray in 1864. At the time of the murders Andrew Borden was sixty-nine, Abby Borden was sixty-three or sixty-four, Lizzie was thirty-two and Emma forty-two.

"On August 3rd I arrived at the Borden house at 1:30 P.M., and had the midday meal there finishing at about 3:00 P.M. That night, Wednesday, August 3rd, I slept in the guest chamber, the room where Mrs. Borden's body was discovered. I had brought no luggage with me of any kind. From time to time in the past I have come to Fall River on business and slept overnight in this guest chamber of the Borden home.

"On August 4th, the day of the murders, I arose at about 6 A.M., dressed and went down the front stairs to the first floor. At 7 A.M. I had taken breakfast with Mr. and Mrs. Borden. The breakfast consisted of bread, coffee, cakes. A bowl of fruit, including bananas, was on the table.

"After breakfast I left the house and went out the rear or side door. Andrew Borden showed me out and hooked the screen door as I left. At that time Mrs. Borden was dusting with a feather duster and wore nothing on her head. Just as I was leaving I saw Lizzie Borden in the kitchen, but I don't remember what she was doing at the time. I left the house at fifteen or twenty minutes before nine. First I went to the post office and then I walked to the home of my nephew and niece who live on Weybosset Street in Fall River, about a mile and a quarter from the Borden house.

"After my visit, I returned by taking a horse car along Main Street from Weybosset Street. I walked to the Borden premises from the nearest car stop. Before going into the house I stopped at a pear tree in the yard and picked up two or three pears and began to eat one of them. A man standing at the door told me that something had occurred inside the house, and I went inside immediately.

"I first saw Lizzie and then I passed into the sitting room and saw Mr. Borden's body; then I went partway up the stairs, far enough to see Mrs. Borden's body lying on the floor with blood on her face."

In cross-examination Morse said that he had seen Bridget in the morning before he left. The two or three times he saw her she was attending to her chores. In further response to Robinson's cross-examination the witness testified:

"I was in the yard eating pears only two or three minutes before Mr. Sawyer [the passer-by who had been ordered by Officer Allen to stand guard outside the Borden house] standing at the door, spoke to me about the occurrences inside. There was no one else in the yard except Sawyer and myself. Inside the house I saw Lizzie; she was sitting in the dining room on the lounge. Mrs. Churchill and Miss Russell were with her, but then they went into the living room where Mr. Borden's body was lying on the sofa. There were two or three police officers in the house and I saw blood spots on the door leading from the sitting room into the dining room and above Mr. Borden's head. I think that Emma washed these off on Sunday.
"I saw the police overhauling everything in a search, and they had full opportunity to look about the house; no one stopped them. They looked over the different rooms and found some hatchets, but I didn't examine them at all. When I saw them, Dr. Dolan, the medical examiner, had them in his hand."

In re-direct examination by the District Attorney, Morse admitted that he may have been a year or two off concerning the death of his sister, Andrew's first wife. He also testified that Second Street, where it passed the Borden house, was "macadamized," or hard-surfaced, and vehicles passing on the street made considerable noise all day. So ended the testimony of John Vinnicum Morse.

[Most importantly, this testimony established that Morse had played no rôle in the murders since, at all times material, he had been absent from the premises and at places which could be, and no doubt had been, thoroughly checked. Morse's testimony had contributed very little else of value, and this is somewhat perplexing. Certainly, tactiturn as he was, under the circumstances he must have had some words with Lizzie when he viewed the bodies. Yet neither Knowlton nor Robinson asked Morse if Lizzie had made any statements to him after the crimes had been committed.]

The purpose of the testimony of the prosecution's next five witnesses was to log the chronology of Andrew Borden's whereabouts from the time he left his home at shortly after 9 A.M. on 4 August until he returned home shortly after 10:30 A.M.

John T. Burrill, cashier of the National Union Bank, was with Andrew Borden from 9:15 to 9:45. Everett M. Cook, cashier of the First National Bank of Fall River, was with Borden from about 9:45 to 9:55 A.M. Jonathan Clegg, a hatter and a tenant of Borden's, had talked business with his landlord until 10:29 exactly. Borden had then headed in the direction of City Hall and Clegg had looked at the City Hall clock as Borden left. Joseph Shortsleeves, a carpenter who was working on a new store which Clegg, the hatter, had leased from Borden, was the next witness. The new store was a very short distance from Clegg's other store. Shortsleeves testified as follows:

"On the morning of the murder Andrew J. Borden, whom I have known for at least ten years, came into the store premises where I was working. From the floor he picked up a broken lock which was broken to pieces; he looked at it, put it back on the floor and went upstairs. He came down, picked up the broken lock again and walked out. He was at the store no more than two minutes when he left, headed in the direction of his home. The time was about 10:30 A.M."

It should be borne in mind that the banking institutions and the two stores owned by Borden and leased to Clegg were all located close together in the business district near City Hall, which, as the engineer witness Kieran had testified, was only 900 feet from No. 92 Second Street, which would be at the most an easy five-minute walk home.

Timorous, apprehensive, obviously nervous, with a high flush on her pretty face, Bridget Sullivan, having been called as the next witness, ascended the stand. In a soft, shy and hurried voice she testified:

"My name is Bridget Sullivan, age twenty-six. In the Borden household I was called Maggie by the Borden sisters, Miss Emma and Miss Lizzie, but all others call me by my given name Bridget. Seven years ago I came from Ireland, first stopping in Newport, Rhode Island, where I lived with relatives; then I went to Pennsylvania. Four years ago I came to Fall River, and I had worked for Mrs. Borden two years and seven months at the time of her death.

"My duties as housemaid did not include taking care of the bedrooms,

Bridget Sullivan
FROM PORTER

except my own. The Borden daughters took care of their own rooms and
Mrs. Borden took care of the guest room at the front part of the second
floor. In the summertime Miss Lizzie took care of the sweeping and
dusting of the parlor.

"On Wednesday evening, August 3rd, I had been visiting a friend who
lived on Third Street and when I returned I went directly to bed.

"On Thursday morning I arose at 6:15 A.M. feeling poorly, dressed and
went downstairs. I first went to the cellar, brought up some firewood and
lit a fire in the stove. At about 6:30 or 6:40—I can't tell the time

exactly—Mrs. Borden came downstairs. She was the first person to arrive and she came from her bedroom by way of the back staircase, since there are no communicating ways between the front and the back of the house on the second floor.

"About five minutes after Mrs. Borden came down, Mr. Borden did. He carried his slop pail. He first went outside and emptied the slop pail in the yard; then he unlocked the barn and went inside the barn door."

At this point in Bridget's testimony, Knowlton interrupted her and asked that she step down from the witness box in order to accommodate another witness, Mrs. Kelly, who had a pressing engagement. Mrs. Kelly, the Bordens' next door neighbor to the south, having been sworn, testified that she was Mrs. Caroline Kelly, wife of Dr. Kelly, and that on 4 August she had had a dentist's appointment. To keep her appointment she had hurried from her house, down Second Street past the Borden house. As she had passed, she had seen Andrew Borden headed from the back of his house to the front door; there he had stooped down.

"When I saw him at the front door," said Mrs. Kelly, "I was opposite his front gate, near enough to touch him, but his back was turned toward me; he was stooping down. This was at exactly twenty-eight minutes to eleven."

Bridget Sullivan was then recalled to the stand, after Mrs. Kelly finished her brief testimony.

[The practice of interrupting one witness to interpose another witness is not unheard of in trial procedure. This interruption, under all the circumstances, however, was difficult to understand. Bridget Sullivan was one of, if not the most important of, the prosecution's witnesses. On the other hand, Mrs. Kelly's testimony added little if anything to the prosecution's case. An interruption such as this distracts the jury, loses their attention, and, of course, breaks the continuity of the testimony of the important witness. Here also an interruption would tend to create in the jurors' minds the impression that Bridget's testimony was routine and not important; and this was certainly not the case.]

Bridget continued:

"I had done my ironing the day before. Mr. and Mrs. Borden had breakfast with Mr. Morse. Lizzie was not at the table. After breakfast the Bordens and Mr. Morse went into the sitting room and the bell rang for me to clear the dining room table. I sat down in the dining room and had my breakfast, then cleared the dishes and went into the kitchen. At this time Mr. Borden came into the kitchen, washed his teeth in the sink and took a bowl of wash water and went to his room.

"Five minutes later Miss Lizzie came into the kitchen. She said that she wanted no breakfast and that she would make herself a cup of coffee. At this time I felt sick to my stomach, so I went out into the yard and vomited. I stayed in the yard for about fifteen minutes and then went back into the kitchen. I never saw Mr. Borden again that morning until I let him in at the front door.

"At nine o'clock Mrs. Borden was dusting with a feather duster in the dining room and she told me to wash the windows on the first floor.

"I finished my work in the kitchen and shut all the first floor windows getting ready to wash them. I started for the barn to get the washing equipment when Miss Lizzie appeared and said to me, "Maggie, you're going to wash the windows?" I answered "Yes" and said, "You needn't lock the door. I'll be out around here; you can lock it if you want to." "

When asked if Lizzie had locked the screen door, Bridget answered that she had not, and continued with her testimony:

"I first washed the sitting-room windows; they are on the south side, the Kelly side, of the house. While washing them on the outside I met Dr. Kelly's servant girl and chatted with her. Next I did the parlor windows on the front of the house. There were three windows in the parlor: two on the front and one on the side of the house. I went to the barn six or seven times to get water during this procedure. I then rinsed all the windows on the outside, went into the house to wash the inside of the windows. I first went into the kitchen, then went into the sitting room to wash the inside of the sitting-room windows. When I came in, I hooked the screen door in the back; it was unhooked. I had seen nothing of anyone at this time since I had seen Lizzie at the screen door before I started.

"While washing the inside windows in the sitting room, I heard a person at the door, trying to unlock the door but could not. I went to the front door and unlocked it. There was no bell rung. I opened the door; Mr. Borden came in. There were three locks on the front door. As I unlocked the door I said, "Oh, pshaw!" and Miss Lizzie laughed upstairs. Her father was out there on the doorstep; she was upstairs. She was either in the entry or at the top of the stairs; I can't tell which.

"Mr. Borden came in, did not say a word. He was carrying a small package. After I let Mr. Borden in, I continued washing my window in the sitting room. I saw him sit down in the dining room, and Lizzie came downstairs in about five minutes. I heard her ask if she had any mail, and there was some conversation, but I did hear her say that Mrs. Borden had a note and had gone out.

"Mr. Borden came into the sitting room, took a key off the mantelpiece, and went upstairs to his room. The key was the key to his bedroom door. He came down to the sitting room, and sat in the sitting room, and I began to wash the dining-room windows. While I was washing the dining-room windows Lizzie came down. She came to me and said, "Maggie, are you going out this afternoon?"

"I said, "I don't know. I might and I might not. I don't feel very well."

"And she said, "Well, be sure and lock the door, for Mrs. Borden has gone out on a sick call and I might go out too."

"Said I, "Miss Lizzie, who is sick?"

"Said she, "I don't know. She had a note this morning. It must be in town."

"I finished washing the windows, and then I went into the kitchen where Lizzie was ironing handkerchiefs. Then Lizzie said, "There is a cheap sale of dress goods at Sargent's this afternoon at eight cents a yard."

"I replied, "I'm going to have one." "

Q. What did you do then?

A. I went upstairs to my room.

"After that time there was no sign or sound of anyone [Bridget Sullivan continued]. I went up to my room and laid in my bed. The next sound I heard was the City Hall bell ringing eleven o'clock. My clock was in the room, and I was lying in the bed at that time. At no time did I hear a sound of any kind. The next thing that occurred was that I heard Miss Lizzie holler, "Maggie, come down!"

"I said, "What's the matter?"

"She called, "Come down quick! Father's dead! Somebody came in and killed him!"

"This was ten or fifteen minutes after I heard the clock strike eleven.

"I ran downstairs. I had not at any time taken off my clothing or changed my clothing. Lizzie was wearing at that time a blue dress with a sprig in it. It was light blue. The sprig was a darker blue than the dress. It was a dress that Lizzie had procured last spring. It was made at the house by the regular dressmaker.

"When I came down the back stairs, Miss Lizzie was standing at the rear, or back, door, standing against the door. I started toward the sitting room, and she said, "Oh, Maggie, don't go in. I have got to have a doctor quick. Go over. I have to have the doctor."

"So I went over to Dr. Bowen's right away, and when I came back, I said to Miss Lizzie, "Miss Lizzie, where was you?" I says, "Didn't I leave the screen door locked?"

"She answers, "I was out in the back yard and heard a groan and came in, and the screen door was wide open."

"She asked me if I knew where Miss Russell lived. I said yes; she said to go and get her: "I don't want to be alone in the house."

"So I took from the entry my hat and shawl and went to Miss Russell. No outcry or alarm was given at this time to the neighbors. When I went to Dr. Bowen's, I had not found Dr. Bowen; his wife came to the door, and I told her that Mr. Borden was dead.

"I searched and found from someone where Miss Russell lived. She lived on Borden Street next to the baker's shop. I ran all the way. When I came from Miss Russell's, Mrs. Churchill was there and Dr. Bowen and Miss Lizzie and no one else.

"Dr. Bowen said, "He was murdered! He was murdered!"

"I said, "Miss Lizzie, if I knew where Mrs. Whitehead lived, I would go and see if Mrs. Borden was there and tell her Mr. Borden is very sick."

"Miss Lizzie replied, "Maggie, I am almost positive I heard her coming in. Won't you go upstairs to see?"

""I'm not going upstairs alone," I said.

"Before that Dr. Bowen said that he wanted a sheet, and I said I'd get the sheets from Mrs. Borden's room, and I had gone up and gotten one for him.

"So when I talked about Mrs. Whitehead to Miss Lizzie, she said, "I am positive I heard her coming in."

"I asked, "Are you sure?"

"She answered, "I am sure she is upstairs."

"Again I said, "I am not going upstairs."

"Mrs. Churchill said she would go upstairs with me. As we went upstairs, I saw the body under the bed. I ran to the room and stood at the foot of the bed. I saw the clothing of the body when I was part up the stairs.

"On Wednesday, the day before, I had not seen Miss Lizzie except at breakfast and at dinner."

[It was clear that the testimony of Bridget Sullivan supported all three of the basic propositions of proof of guilt as outlined by Moody in his opening. First, there was evidence of at least incompatibility between Lizzie and her stepmother for some time prior to the murders. Second, there was evidence which, if believed, showed that Lizzie had exclusive opportunity to commit the crimes. And third, there was evidence of consciousness of guilt in the testimony concerning the note from a sick friend which Mrs. Borden was supposed to have received.]

The direct examination finished, former Governor Robinson rose from the defense table and walked to the jury box to conduct his cross-examination of Bridget. This was a high point of the trial.

It was Robinson's first purpose to establish that a friendly, or at least reasonably friendly, relationship existed between the family members of the Borden household. More precisely, Robinson in fact sought from the witness testimony revealing a good relationship between Lizzie and her stepmother. He did not get far.

In response to his question Bridget replied, "Miss Lizzie answered her mother civilly. There was, as far as I know, no trouble that morning."

Pressing the point further, Robinson asked specifically about the mother-daughter relationship. Bridget's answer upset him: she responded, "I didn't see anything. I know when Mrs. Borden was sick one time, none of them went into the room while she was sick."

Then Robinson challenged her testimony by asking, "Didn't you testify at the inquest that they seemed to get along congenially?"

Bridget answered, "Yes."

In order to cast the witness in a poor light with the jury, Robinson then brought out the fact that Bridget, as a material witness, had as her two sureties Marshal Hilliard, City Marshal of Fall River, and State Police Officer Seaver, who was working on the Borden investigation. Further, he showed that Bridget since the inquest had been working as a domestic for a Mr. Hunt, the keeper of the jail. This was, of course, to show that Bridget had been influenced in her testimony by her association with police officials prior to the trial, and that since the murders she had not talked to either of the Borden sisters, nor to any of Lizzie's representatives.

Following this, Robinson launched into a full-scale cross-examination. Point by point, Bridget was asked questions almost identical to the questions she had been asked by the prosecutor. She again related that her duties did not take her to the front rooms of the second floor and that she seldom went to the front part of the house at all. She told, in response to Robinson's question, the complete menu for breakfast on 4 August: mutton broth, johnnycake, coffee, cookies and butter, bananas and other fruit. It was a very lengthy cross-examination, which produced nothing— except perhaps to provide fodder for wits in later years who declared that the Borden family's breakfast on this torrid day was cause in itself for murder.

[It is basic to the art of cross-examination in a criminal case that questions be avoided which allow the witness to repeat testimony that is damaging to the defendant. Robinson violated this basic completely. The jury was allowed to hear for a second time and reflect for a second time upon Bridget's damaging story: "I heard her tell her father that her mother had a note and had gone out." The jury also heard again that Lizzie had not been seen on Wednesday afternoon by Bridget and—a particular fact that was considered important to the prosecution, as will be seen in due course—that the whole family had been sick the day before the murders and that Mrs. Borden, thinking that she had been poisoned, had summoned Dr. Bowen to attend her. To allow a witness to repeat such harmful testimony unnecessarily in cross-examination is not the mark of an experienced trial lawyer.]

At the conclusion of Robinson's cross-examination the Court recessed until 9 A.M. Thursday, 8 June.

On the fourth day of the trial the early summer heat wave which had gripped New Bedford granted surcease to the sweltering city. A gentle rain fell outside the courtroom as the eleventh witness for the prosecution was called to the stand and testified:

"My name is Seabury W. Bowen. I am a licensed physician and surgeon, and I have practiced in Fall River for twenty-six years. My home is diagonally opposite the Borden house in Fall River, and I have lived there for twenty-seven years. During that time I have shared both a social and a professional relationship with the Bordens, as I have been their family physician.

"On the day of the murders, August 4th, I left my home early to make my professional calls and I returned from my last call in Tiverton, Rhode Island, sometime after 11 A.M. and before 11:30 A.M.

"When I approached my home, my wife, Mrs. Bowen, was waiting for me at the door, and as a result of my conversation with her I immediately crossed the street to the Borden house and went in the side door. When I entered, I saw Miss Lizzie Borden and Mrs. Churchill; they were in the back entry, close to the kitchen, at the time I came in. I immediately asked, "Lizzie, what is the matter?"

"She answered, "Father has been killed or stabbed."

"I can't recall whether she said, "Father has been killed," or "Father has been stabbed."

"I asked, "Where is your father?"

" "In the sitting room," she responded.

Seabury W. Bowen, M.D

"I went into the sitting room and saw the form of Mr. Borden lying on the sofa. His face was very badly cut with apparently a sharp instrument. There was blood all over his face; his face was covered with blood. I felt his pulse and satisfied myself that he was dead, and took a glance about the room and saw that nothing was disturbed at all. No furniture was disturbed, as I noticed it. The body was lying with its face toward the south or the right side, apparently at ease, as anyone would if they were lying asleep. I could hardly recognize the face. I then went into the kitchen. No, before I went into the kitchen, Miss Lizzie followed me part way through the dining room. As I entered the sitting room, when I found that he was dead, as I returned the same way, I asked Miss Lizzie questions. "

Question. Will you state them?

"The first question I asked was if she had seen anyone. Her reply was, "I have not." The second question was "Where have you been?" Her reply was, "In the barn, looking for some irons or iron.""

"She then said that she was afraid that her father had had trouble with the tenants, that she had overheard loud conversations several times recently. That was the extent of the conversation in the dining room.

"I then asked for a sheet to cover the body of Mr. Borden. As a consequence, Bridget Sullivan brought me the sheet. When the sheet was brought, Miss Lizzie asked me if I would telegraph to her sister Emma."

Q. And did you?

A. Yes.

"I telegraphed [Dr. Bowen continued], and when I returned from the telegraph station, up to that time there had been nothing said about Mrs. Borden. Before I went to the telegraph office, the question was asked, "Where is Mrs. Borden?" The inquiry was made, "Where is Mrs. Borden?" Miss Lizzie, I think, answered—I am not certain that she answered; the answer was that Mrs. Borden had received a note that morning to visit a sick friend and had gone out.

"When I returned from the telegraph office, having sent the message, I met Mrs. Churchill in the kitchen hallway. She said, "They have found Mrs. Borden upstairs in the front room."

"I went directly up the front stairs and stopped by the front chamber. At that point I looked over and saw the prostrate form of Mrs. Borden. When I first saw the body, I was directly in the door of the room. I went to the back of the bed—the foot of the bed—and between the form and the bed, and placed my hand on her head. It was a little dark in the room, somewhat dark, not very light. I found there were wounds in the head, felt of her pulse—that is, felt of her wrist—and found she was dead. I never made any statement that she had died of fright or [was] in faint.

"I went downstairs to the kitchen, said that Mrs. Borden was dead and that she was killed, I thought, by the same instrument. I said I thought it was fortunate for Lizzie that she was out of the way or else she would have been killed herself. I noticed that Lizzie had a different dress than when she went up to her room. I noticed the color of it; it was a pink wrapper morning dress. As to the dress that she had on before, as I testified at the inquest, I am indefinite as to the color, but it was a different dress; it was a drab color, very indefinite. Calico, I think. It was an ordinary, unattractive, common dress that I did not note especially."

Q. (*the District Attorney exhibiting a blue dress*) Does this appear to you, Doctor, to be a sort of a drab or colorless dress? Morning calico dress?

There was an objection. Chief Justice Mason excluded the question.

Q. Is this the dress she had on that morning?

A. I don't know, sir.

Cross-examination was conducted by Melvin O. Adams for the defendant. By contrast with Robinson, Adams was an effective cross-examiner. He adduced from the witness several minor facts which might have been helpful to the defense, and he carefully avoided allowing the witness to restate what Lizzie had said to him of her whereabouts at the time of her father's death: that she was "in the barn looking for some iron."

In cross-examination Dr. Bowen was questioned about not having seen Mrs. Borden's body until he got to the door of the guest room. He agreed to that, and he said that she was a big woman and that she occupied much of the space between the bureau and the bed. The shutters were partly closed and it was somewhat dark in the guest room.

Dr. Bowen was then asked at what time he sent the telegram. He responded:

"At 11:32, and I returned to the Borden house immediately, arriving there at 11:40. Ten or fifteen minutes later the medical examiner arrived.

"I accompanied Dr. Dolan, the medical examiner, and we inspected the bodies. Dr. Dolan, myself, and some assistant whom I do not remember. The autopsy was not held until three o'clock. I attended it at three o'clock that afternoon.

"I went downstairs after viewing the body. I went into the kitchen where Lizzie was with Mrs. Bowen [witness's wife, who had recently arrived], Mrs.Churchill, Miss Russell, and Bridget Sullivan. They were working over Lizzie, fanning her and rubbing her head. Then Lizzie went into the dining room and threw herself on the lounge at the end of the dining room. I told Lizzie then to go upstairs to her room. She went through the dining room and the corner of the sitting room. Mr. Borden's body was covered up with sheets in that room, and I subsequently saw Lizzie in her room upstairs at about one o'clock, between one and two o'clock the same day. At that time I gave her a preparation called Bromo Caffeine for quieting nervous excitement and headache, and I left a second dose to be taken within an hour. Later I prescribed Sulphate of Morphine, an eighth of a grain on Friday night, at bedtime the next day. On Saturday I doubled the dose of Sulphate of Morphine. She continued to take this tranquilizing drug up until the time of her arrest and the hearing, while she was at the stationhouse."

Thus Dr. Bowen's testimony ended, whereupon Bridget Sullivan was recalled to the witness stand by Robinson, and she testified:

"I went down in the cellar with three officers: Mr. Fleet, Mr. Medley, and Officer Doherty. In a box there were some hatchets, and they took them out of the box. The hatchets were in the cellar in the room where Mr. Borden kept the wood for the furnace. I saw them take three hatchets out of the box. I think there were three."

Q. While you were at the house, during the two years and nine months you lived there, was there some burglary there or robbery?

A. Yes.

Q. Was it twelve months before the murders or that time [the day of the killings]?

A. Yes, sir. I think it was. I'm not sure. In the daytime it occurred.

[At this point Chief Justice Mason interrupted to exclude this evidence *sua sponte* (i.e., on his own volition); there had been no objection, but the Chief Justice ruled, "Too long before the time to be material." The Chief Justice's ruling was of course entirely proper since the incident was too remote in time to be material to any issue posed here.

However, the robbery a year before the murders has significance as an indication of the intrafamilial relations in the Borden home. Actually, only Mrs. Borden's belongings were taken: some jewelry, a small amount of money and some streetcar tickets. Andrew Borden reported the matter to the police, and an investigation of short duration ensued, during which Lizzie produced a nail which she said she had found in the lock of a door in the house. This and other circumstances apparently convinced the police and Andrew Borden that Lizzie herself might have planned and set the robbery scene. The investigation of the robbery was dropped. Some authorities on the Borden case attribute to this incident Andrew Borden's odd practice of locking his and his wife's bedroom door and then leaving the key in clear view on the sitting-room mantel for Lizzie to see. An exercise in amateur psychology by Andrew?]

Bridget then testified that in the Fall after the burglary, there was a breaking-and-entering of the barn. Bridget said she could not remember exactly when; it might have been five or six months before. She could not fix the time. The breaking-and-entering of the barn was in the nighttime.

[Why this also was not excluded by the Chief Justice as being too remote in time is unexplained. Alice Russell was later to describe the incidents as pranks, merely boys seeking pigeons in the empty barn.]

Bridget then said that she never did say that Lizzie was crying at any time. Notwithstanding a plain inference by Robinson, the cross-examiner, that she had made that statement at the inquest, Bridget insisted that she had not.

Mrs. Adelaide Churchill

FROM PORTER

Adelaide B. Churchill was the next witness called to the stand. She was a widow, and had lived in the house north and next door to No. 92 for forty-three years, all her life; she had been born in the house. Her household consisted of her mother, her sister, her son, her niece, and a man employed by them. Her relationship with the Borden family was one of ordinary civil neighborliness.

She described Mr. Borden as a tall, thin man, Mrs. Borden as very fleshy and not very tall, "not as tall as I am," and continued:

"I went to the store at about eleven o'clock. The store was right in the next street. I was not there long. I bought groceries for dinner and returned to my home. I walked down Borden Street and up Second; I did not pass the Borden house. I saw Bridget Sullivan going across the street from Dr. Bowen's house to the Borden house. She looked very white; I thought someone was sick. She was running; she was moving very fast. I was about at the Burt house, which is just north of our house, at that time. I went to the north side of our house and entered the back door. I then looked out of the window, and I saw Lizzie on the inside of her screen door. She looked as though she were leaning against the casing of the door. She seemed excited, and I asked her what was the matter through the window, my kitchen window.

"I asked, "Lizzie, what is the matter?"

"She answered, "Oh, Mrs. Churchill, do come over! Someone has killed Father!"

"I shut down the window, passed through the kitchen and went to Mr. Borden's. I saw Lizzie and put my hand on her arm and said, "Oh, Lizzie. Where is your father?"

"Lizzie answered, "In the sitting room."

"I looked in the sitting room and saw the body. I then asked, "Where were you when it happened?"

"She replied, "I went to the barn to get a piece of iron."

"I asked, "Where is your mother?"

"She replied, "I don't know. She had got a note to go see someone who is sick, but I don't know but she is killed too. I thought I heard her come in."

"Lizzie also said, "Father must have an enemy, for we have all been sick, and we think the milk has been poisoned."

"Then Lizzie stated, "Dr. Bowen is not at home, and I must have a doctor."

"I asked, "Lizzie, shall I go and try to get someone to get a doctor?"

"And she answered, "Yes." And I went out.

"I crossed the street, looking for my hired man. I sent him to get a doctor and returned to the Borden house. Then Bridget came in, and Dr. Bowen came in. Dr. Bowen turned to me and said, "Addy, come in and see Mr. Borden."

"I responded, "Oh no, Doctor. I don't want to see him. I saw him this morning. I don't want to see him."

"Dr. Bowen asked for a sheet. Bridget and I went up the back stairs into Mrs. Borden's room with the key that Dr. Bowen had given her, and Bridget unlocked the door, and we got the sheet; we came down, handed the sheet to Dr. Bowen, and he covered Mr. Borden up.

"Soon after, Miss Russell arrived. About this time Lizzie said she wished someone would try to find Mrs. Borden, for she thought she had heard her come in. Bridget and I started to go to find her; we went through the dining room, out of the sitting room where Mr. Borden was sitting or lying, and up into the hall. Bridget was just ahead of me; she led the way. As I went upstairs, I turned my head to the left, and as I got up to where my eyes were on the level of the front hall [floor], I could see across the front hall into the guest room. At the far side, or the north side, of the room I saw something that looked like the form of a person, when my head was level with the floor of the second floor. The door of the guest room was open. I turned and went back. Miss Russell said, "Is there another?"

"I answered, "Yes, she is up there."

"That morning Lizzie also said that she would have to go to the cemetery, and I said, "Oh no, the undertaker will attend to everything for you."

"I never saw Lizzie in tears that morning at any time.

"When I left, Lizzie was in the dining room. She had been wearing a light blue-and-white dress with white groundwork; it seemed like calico. It had a light blue-and-white groundwork with a dark navy blue diamond printed on it."

At this point a dress was shown to her, and Mrs. Churchill said, "That is not the dress."

For some reason Robinson opened his cross-examination of Mrs. Churchill by questioning her about noise heard regularly on Second Street. The witness stated that Second Street was a very noisy street, so noisy, in fact, that when her windows were open, she could not hear normal sounds in her own house.

[This fact Robinson of course must have considered helpful to his case; but, upon reflection, it was a two-edged sword: it was equally helpful to the line of reasoning set out in Moody's opening for the prosecution, since it would account for Bridget Sullivan's hearing nothing when Mrs. Borden was killed and again when Mr. Borden was slaughtered.]

When Robinson inquired about the dress worn by Lizzie when Mrs. Churchill first saw her, the witness responded, "I only looked at the general effect; it looked like light blue-and-white groundwork to me, with a deep navy blue diamond printed on it. The diamond is the most distinct thing in my mind. It was a navy blue calico dress, cotton, either calico or cambric."

Next, very carefully, Robinson inquired about the ministrations to Lizzie, and the witness testified that, after Alice Russell had arrived, both she and Miss Russell bathed Lizzie's head with water and rubbed her hands. "I did not see any blood on her dress. When I left at twelve noon, I stood in front of her, rubbing both her hands and fanning her, and I did not see any blood on her hands or on her face, nor any disarrangement of her hair."

[This was very effective testimony from Robinson's point of view, and he handled the questioning well. However, he then turned to the matter of Lizzie's trip to the barn, and here again, as he had done with other witnesses, Robinson, by his questions in cross-examination, allowed the jury to hear for a second time Mrs. Churchill's testimony, which was damaging to his client: she repeated verbatim the conversation she had had with Lizzie relative to Lizzie's trip to the barn while her father was being murdered—"*Q.* Where were you when it happened? *A.* I went to the barn to get a piece of iron."]

Then Robinson asked a question: "Did Bridget tell you about Mrs. Borden having a note?"

Mrs. Churchill answered, "She said Mrs. Borden had a note to go to see someone who was sick, and she was dusting the sitting room and she hurried off, and [she, i.e., Lizzie] says, 'She didn't tell me where she was going. She generally does.' "

Robinson wisely chose to end his cross-examination on that note. He emphasized the statement by restating it and then asked:

Q. Bridget said that?

A. Yes, sir.

Q. That was not what Lizzie said?

A. No, sir.

This confusion did not escape District Attorney Moody, however. He signaled Mrs. Churchill to remain on the witness stand for two clarifying questions in re-direct examination:

Question by Moody. Lest there be any mistake, Mrs. Churchill, you don't speak of this talk with Bridget with reference to the note as in substitution, but in addition to what Miss Lizzie Borden told you?

A. It was after Lizzie had told me.

Q. Then Bridget told you what you have told us.

A. Yes, after that.

[Although Moody may have thought at the time that he had made it perfectly clear who had first told the story of the note, in actuality he had not. In his argument to the jury at the conclusion of the trial Robinson shrewdly dwelt upon this question at length. He argued that both Lizzie and Bridget had spoken of Mrs. Borden having received a note and that each spoke of it separately and independently of the other, and that therefore it was true that a note had been received. This of course was a distortion of Mrs. Churchill's testimony recorded above, but it could, and apparently did, confuse the jury, and the importance of the nebulous note to the prosecution's case was greatly diminished, if not completely erased.]

Despite Lizzie's social aspirations she appears to have had few, if any, intimate friends in her lifetime except for the next witness. A spinster, much older than Lizzie, somewhat dowdy in appearance—and perhaps feeling a sense of disloyalty, but with a determination, almost a compulsion, to tell the truth as she knew it—Miss Alice Russell took the witness stand.

"My name is Alice M. Russell. I am unmarried, and I have lived in Fall River a great many years. I formerly lived in the house now occupied by Dr. Kelly, next door to the Bordens, and I know the Borden family very well. I now live on Borden Street between Third and Fourth streets next to the bakery shop and only a very short distance from the Borden house."

On Wednesday night, 3 August, or the night before the murders took place, Lizzie Borden made a visit to Miss Russell at her house. She arrived about seven o'clock. She stayed until about nine or five minutes past nine. Miss Russell continued:

"Lizzie said at that time, "I have taken your advice, and I have written to [friends in] Marion that I will come."

"I replied, "I am glad that you are going to Marion."

"Lizzie said, "Well, I don't know. I feel depressed. I feel as if something was hanging over me that I cannot throw off, and it comes over me at times, no matter where I am." And then she said, "When I was at the table the other day, when I was at Marion, the girls were laughing and talking and having a good time, and this feeling came over me, and one of them spoke and said, 'Lizzie, why don't you talk?' I don't know what was said after that."

"Then Lizzie said, "I don't know. Father has so much trouble."

"She also told me that Mr. and Mrs. Borden were awfully sick last night (Tuesday), and I said, "Why? What is the matter? Something they have eaten?"

"She answered, "We were all sick, all but Maggie."

"Then I asked, "Something you think you have eaten?"

"She said, "We don't know. We had some baker's bread and all ate of it but Maggie, and Maggie wasn't sick."

"To this I responded, "Well, it couldn't have been the bread. If it had been baker's bread, I should suppose other people would be sick, and I haven't heard of anybody."

"And she said, "That is so.""

"Then Lizzie stated to me, "Sometimes I think our milk might be poisoned.""

"And I said, "Well, how do you get your milk? How could it be poisoned?""

"She answered, "We have the milk come in a can and set on the steps over night, and the next morning when they bring the milk they take the empty can.""

"I said, "Well, if they put anything in the can, the farmer would see it.""

"Then I asked her what time the milk came, and she replied, "I think about four o'clock.""

"I said, "Well, it is light at four o'clock. I shouldn't think anyone would dare to come then and tamper with the cans for fear somebody would see them.""

"She agreed and said, "I shouldn't think so.""

"Then Lizzie continued, "They were awfully sick, and I wasn't sick. I didn't vomit, but I heard them vomiting and stepped to the door and asked if I could do anything, and they said no." She told me that they were better in the morning and that Mrs. Borden, though, thought that she had been poisoned, and she called Dr. Bowen to treat her.

"Lizzie said, "I don't know. I feel afraid sometimes that Father has got an enemy, for he has so much trouble with his men that come to see him." And she told me of a man that came to see him. She didn't see him, but she heard her father say, "I don't care to let my property for such business." And she said the man answered sternly, "I shouldn't think you would care what you let your property for."

"Then she told me, "Father was mad and ordered him out of the house." She also told me of seeing a man run around the house one night when she went home. I have forgotten where she had been. In addition she stated, "And you know the barn has been broken into twice."

"And I said, "Oh well, you know well that that was somebody after pigeons. There is nothing in there for them to go after but pigeons."

" "Well," she said, "they have broken into the house in broad daylight with Emma and Maggie and me there.""

"I said, "I never heard of that before.""

"She answered, "Father forbade our telling it.""

"So I asked her about it and she said it was in Mrs. Borden's room, what she called her dressing room. She said her things were ransacked,

Courtroom Sketch of Miss Alice Russell

FROM PORTER

and they took a watch and chain and money and car tickets and something else that I can't remember, and there was a nail left in the keyhole, and she didn't know why that was left, whether they got in with it or what.

"I asked her if her father did anything about it, and she said, "He gave it to the police, but they didn't find out anything." She said, "Father expected they would catch the thief by the tickets." She remarked, "Just as if anybody would use those tickets."

"Lizzie said, "I feel as if I wanted to sleep with my eyes half open—with one eye open half the time—for fear they will burn the house down over us."

"She told me about her fears of someone breaking in before she told me about breaking into the barn. Then Lizzie stated to me, "I am afraid somebody will do something. I don't know but what somebody will do something." She said, speaking of her father, "Somebody will do something because he is so discourteous." And then she said, "Dr. Bowen came over after Mrs. Borden went over for him, and Father didn't like it because she was going and she told him where she was going, and he said, 'Well, my money shan't pay for it.' She went over to Dr. Bowen's and she told him she was afraid they were poisoned, and Dr. Bowen laughed and said, 'No, there wasn't any poison,' and she came back, and Dr. Bowen came over." And Lizzie said, "I was so ashamed the way Father treated Dr. Bowen. I was so mortified." "

The next day, the day of the murders, Miss Russell was summoned by Bridget to the Borden house. She entered and saw Lizzie. In the course of Miss Russell's initial inquiry about the tragedy, Lizzie said that she had been in the barn. Miss Russell said, "I asked her why she went to the barn, and Lizzie said, 'I went to get a piece of tin or iron to fix my screen.' And I recall that she asked for someone to find Mrs. Borden."

Q. Had she told you anything about where Mrs. Borden was?

A. I don't remember.

Q. Anything about a note?

A. I heard the note talked over. I don't know who told it.

Miss Russell described later going upstairs in Lizzie's room when Lizzie asked for an undertaker; she said she wanted Winwood. Then Miss Russell saw Lizzie coming out of her room wearing a pink-and-white-striped wrapper. She testified that no one had suggested to Lizzie at that time that she change her dress.

Miss Russell said Thursday night she slept in Mr. and Mrs. Borden's room, and she did not see Lizzie again that night after they had gone to the cellar. (Miss Russell stayed at the Borden house Thursday night, Friday night, Saturday night and Sunday night, occupying Mr. and Mrs. Borden's room or Emma's room; she went home Monday.) Thursday night at the Bordens' she went to the cellar with Lizzie; she carried a lantern and Lizzie had a slop pail. Asked if there was clothing in the cellar when she went there, Miss Russell said, "Yes, the clothing taken from the bodies, and that clothing was in the washroom in the cellar."

She testified that on Sunday morning she prepared the breakfast, and after the dishes had been cleared away and before noon, she went into the kitchen and saw Lizzie at the other end of the stove and Miss Emma at the sink. Lizzie was at the stove with the remains of a dress in her hand, and her sister turned and said, "What are you going to do?" Lizzie answered, "I'm going to burn this old thing up. It is covered with paint."

"Then I left the room [Miss Russell continued]. I returned to the room again, and the cupboard door was open, and Lizzie appeared to be either ripping something down or tearing part of a garment. I don't know what part.

"I said to her, "I wouldn't let anybody see me do that, Lizzie." She didn't make any answer. I left the room.

"Later I saw Mr. Hanscom, and then I said to Lizzie, "I'm afraid, Lizzie, that the worst thing you could have done was to burn that dress. I have been asked about your dresses."

"Lizzie answered, "Oh, what made you let me do it? Why didn't you tell me?"

"On the day of the murder there was a search for a note by Dr. Bowen. He said, "Lizzie, do you know anything about the note your mother had?"

"She hesitated and said well, no, she didn't.

"And he said, "Well, I have looked in the wastebasket."

"And I think I said—no, he said, "Have you looked in her pocket?"

"And I think I said, "Well, then she must have put it in the fire."

"And Lizzie said, "Yes, she must have put it in the fire," meaning, of course, Mrs. Borden, the deceased.**"**

Moody closed his direct examination by returning to the dress-burning episode as follows:

Q. Miss Russell, will you tell us what kind of a dress—give us a description of the dress that she burned, that you have testified about on Sunday morning?

A. It was a cheap cotton Bedford cord with a small dark blue figure on a light blue ground.

In cross-examination Robinson drew from the witness that at the time of the dress-burning incident there was a police officer outside the Borden house, and that Miss Russell had seen no blood upon the dress when Lizzie held it prior to burning it.

He also questioned Miss Russell about blood on Lizzie's person or clothing late Thursday morning, the day of the murders, when Miss Russell and Mrs. Churchill had attempted to comfort Lizzie. The witness responded that she had seen no blood.

Thus ended Miss Russell's testimony.

[It was clear that the importance of Alice Russell's testimony to the prosecution rested in part upon the stories that Lizzie had related to Miss Russell on the evening before the murders—stories of robberies, threats and fear. Harking back to Moody's opening for the prosecution, here was evidence of pre-determination to kill, evidence of attempts to divert suspicion before the crimes had been committed. But most important of all was Miss Russell's incriminating recital of the dress-burning incident of the Sunday morning after the murders, as evidence of consciousness of guilt.]

The next witness was John Cunningham. He was sworn and testified that he was a newsdealer in Fall River.

Cunningham had seen Mrs. Churchill running, had learned from her handyman that there was something the matter at the Borden house, and had gone to a telephone and called the City Marshal. Marshal Hilliard had answered the telephone at the Central Police Station, the time later established as 11:15 A.M.

Cunningham further told of having seen Bridget and later Miss Russell going toward the Borden house, and meeting Officer Allen and going to the Borden premises himself. There were two newspaper reporters—one from the Fall River *Globe* and one from the Fall River *News*—entering the premises at the same time. They went around to the south side of the house between the Borden house and the Kelly house, noticed no footprints in the grass; they went around to the back yard and also saw nothing there. They tried the cellar door, but it was locked. They did not go into the house. At the time they went onto the Borden premises, the passer-by named George Sawyer, who had been set as an impromptu guard at the door, was standing in front of the house.

The next witness was George W. Allen, a police officer in Fall River for five years. He testified that at 11:15 Marshal Hilliard received a telephone call, and as a result Allen went directly to the Borden house. It took him four minutes to walk—or run—to No. 92. He continued:

"When I arrived, the front door was locked and bolted. I entered by the side rear door, saw Miss Lizzie, viewed the body of Andrew Borden, and left immediately. I told Mr. Sawyer [the workman passing by whom Allen impressed into service] to stay there until I came back, and left the premises. I went back to the station and spoke to the Marshal. When I returned with another officer, Mullaly, I went up the stairs and saw Mrs. Borden's body from the stairs, just as I made the turn of the stairs. The cellar door was bolted. There was a table with some books on it near the body, and there was no blood on it."

In cross-examination by Robinson it was brought out that the message was received by Marshal Hilliard at 11:15 exactly.

Next to testify was Francis X. Wixon, a Deputy Sheriff of Bristol County. He was with the Marshal at the time of receiving the telephone call, and he placed the time at about 11:15 A.M.

Wixon went to the Borden house and saw Mr. Borden's body. The wounds on Mr. Borden's face appeared to be fresh wounds—

". . . quite fresh wounds; the blood was a bright color, the same as I had seen in army wounds. I did not see any coagulation of the blood.

"I then went upstairs and viewed Mrs. Borden's body. The blood on her body was very dark and coagulated. She lay upon the floor, face down. The blood was very dark; I should think it looked to me as though it was dark maroon color. It had thickened up."

John Fleet, Deputy City Marshal of Fall River, was next called to the witness stand. Fleet testified that he was informed of the Borden murder at his home, that he took a buggy to the Borden house where he arrived at about 11:45. He went inside; he first met John Vinnicum Morse, Bridget Sullivan, and Mrs. Churchill when he went into the kitchen. He then went into the sitting room and saw Dr. Dolan standing over the body of Mr. Borden. Going upstairs, he viewed the body of Mrs. Borden. Then he went into the room where Miss Lizzie Borden was with the Reverend Mr. Buck and Miss Russell; it was Lizzie's bedroom upstairs at the head of the stairs, and he had a talk with her. Asked to state what the talk was about, Fleet answered:

"I went in there and told her who I was—made known who I was (I was in citizen's clothes then as I am now)—and I asked her if she knew

Deputy Marshal John Fleet

anything about the murders. She said that she did not. All she knew was that Mr. Borden—her father, as she put it—came home after 10:30 or 10:45, went into the sitting room, sat down in the large chair, took out some papers and looked at them. She was ironing in the dining room some handkerchiefs, as she stated. She saw that her father was feeble; she went to him and advised and assisted him to lay upon the sofa. She then went into the dining room to her ironing, but left after her father was laid down and went out in the yard and up in the barn. I asked her how long she remained in the barn; she said she remained up in the barn about a half hour. I then asked her what she meant by "up" in the barn. She said, "I mean up in the barn, upstairs, sir." She said after she had been up there half an hour, she came down again, went into the house, and found her father on the lounge in the position in which she had left him but killed or dead.

"I then asked her what she did, finding him in that condition, and she said that she went to the back stairs and called Maggie. I asked her who Maggie was; she answered that Maggie was the servant girl, and she said that she told Maggie to go for Dr. Bowen, and she went, but Dr. Bowen was not in the house. He lives opposite Mr. Borden. She then told the girl to go for Miss Russell, and Miss Russell came, and so did Dr. Bowen soon after.

"I asked Miss Lizzie Borden, "Who was in the house this morning or last night?"

"She said that there was no one but her father, Mrs. Borden, Bridget, Mr. Morse and herself. I asked her who was this Mr. Morse.

"She replied, "He is my uncle, and he came here yesterday and slept in the room where Mrs. Borden was found dead."

"Do you think that Mr. Morse had anything to do with the killing of your parents?"

"She said no; she didn't think that he had because Mr. Morse left the house this morning before nine o'clock and did not return until after the murders.

"I asked her if she thought that Bridget could have done this, and she said that she didn't think that she could or did, that Bridget—I would say here that I did not use the word Bridget at that time because she had given me the name as Maggie; I should say Maggie. I asked her if she thought Maggie had anything to do with the killing of Mr. and Mrs. Borden. She said no, that Maggie had gone upstairs previous to her father's lying down on the lounge, and when she came from the barn, she called Maggie downstairs.

"I asked her, "Anything else?""

"I then asked her if she had any idea who could have killed her father and mother.

"Then she said, "She's not my mother, sir. She is my stepmother. My mother died when I was a child.""

"I then asked her if there had been anyone around this morning whom she would suspect of having done the killings, and she said that she had not seen anyone, but about nine o'clock that morning a man came to the door and was talking with her father. I asked her what they were talking about, and she said she thought they were talking about a store, and he spoke like an Englishman.

"I think that's about all the conversation I had with her at that time. Oh no, Miss Russell was in the room, and she said to Lizzie, "Tell him all; tell him what you was telling me.""

"She looked at Miss Russell, and then she says, "About two weeks ago a man came to the house, to the front door, and had some talk with Father and talked as though he was angry.""

"And I asked her what he was talking about.

"And she said, "He was talking about a store, and Father said to him, 'I cannot let you have the store for that purpose.' The man seemed to be angry. I then came downstairs." ""

Q. Was anything said about a note at that time?

A. Oh yes. That was on the occasion of the second interview.

"I then went downstairs into the sitting room and looked around the building [Fleet resumed], then again upstairs, where I found Mr. Borden's room locked. I went down to the kitchen entry, then upstairs and found Bridget's room locked and also the room next to it with a bed in it. I found the other rooms in the attic locked. I then went downstairs in the cellar and found Officers Mullaly and Devine there. They had two axes and two hatchets from the cellar floor."

Q. What was done with the hatchets and the two axes?

A. The two hatchets and axes were left there that day. The larger hatchet with a rust stain on it and a red spot about the handle that had apparently been washed or wiped was placed behind some boxes in the cellar.

Q. (*showing two axes to the witness*) Are these two axes the ones to which you refer?

A. They seem to be.

"I then told Officer Medley to go to Providence on the 12:30 train [Fleet continued]. I then went upstairs to make a search of Lizzie's room. I used the front stairs. Mr. Minahan, who is now dead, and Mr. Wilson, both police officers, went with me. I went to Lizzie's door, rapped on the door; Dr. Bowen came to it, holding the door, opening the door, I should say, about six inches and asked what was wanted. I told him we had come there as police officers to search this room and search the building. He then turned around to Miss Borden and told me to wait a moment. He then opened the door again and said that Lizzie wanted to know if it was absolutely necessary for us to search that room. I told him as officers, murders having been committed, it was our duty so to do, and we wanted to get in there. He closed the door again and said something to Miss Borden and finally opened the door and admitted us. We proceeded to search, looking through some drawers and the closet and bedroom.

"While the search was still going on, I said to Lizzie, "You said this morning that you was up in the barn for half an hour. Do you say that now?"

"She says, "I didn't say half an hour. I say twenty minutes to half an hour."

" "Well, we will call it twenty minutes then."

"She says, "I say from twenty minutes to half an hour, sir."

"I then asked her which was the last time that she saw her stepmother, when and where. She said that the last time she saw her stepmother was about nine o'clock, and Mrs. Borden was then in the room where she was found dead, making the bed—that is to say, she was making the bed in the room where she was found dead at nine o'clock. Lizzie then said that someone brought a letter or note to Mrs. Borden, and she thought her stepmother had gone out and Lizzie had not known of her return.

"We searched her room and as we came to the head of her bed, I found a door there and went to open it. She said that that door was locked and bolted from the other side and we could not go through there, and I found that it was locked on her side. The door was hooked with a common hook and staple. Lizzie said she hoped we would get through with this quick, that she was getting tired, or words to that effect; it was making her tired, and we told her we should get through as soon as we possibly could. It was an unpleasant duty, that is, considering her father and stepmother were dead, that is all.

"We searched that room and then we went to the room where Mrs. Borden was found dead. Lizzie said there was no use in searching that room, that nobody could get into her room or throw anything in, that she always locked her door, even if she went downstairs, when she left the room or went downstairs."

*Question by Moody.*You said that you went into the guest chamber. Describe what you saw there.

"I saw Mrs. Borden laid down between the bed and the dressing case [Fleet answered], face downward with her head all broke in or cut and she was dead. I saw a door which would lead into Lizzie's room, and on Lizzie's side was a bookcase and, I think, desk combined. That door was locked. In the room and near the body I noticed blood spots. The body was laying in a pool of blood, and there was blood upon the pillow cases and also upon the dressing case.

"After this I got the keys and asked Lizzie what was in this room, and she said that was a clothes press. It was locked; Lizzie got the keys and opened, or unlocked, the door. We just looked over the clothing in the room, looked around the floor and up on the shelf. We did not search very closely.

"Then we got the keys from Maggie and went to Mr. Borden's room. When I found Mr. and Mrs. Borden's room, the door was locked.

"Then we went up in the attic and searched Bridget's room very closely, and the closet together with the adjoining other rooms at the west end of the attic.

"Then we went down to the cellar, and the other officers and Dr. Dolan were still in the cellar. I asked Officer Mullaly where he got the axes and the hatchet. As I asked him, I found in a box in the middle of the cellar on a shelf near an old-fashioned chimney the head of a hatchet. The box was about a foot long—it might have been a little longer—and four or five inches deep."

Q. (producing the hatchet) Is this the hatchet?
A. Yes, it looks like the hatchet that I found there. Pretty sure that's the one.

"This piece of wood that was in the head of the hatchet was broken off close, very close to the hatchet. The hatchet was covered with white ashes; not on one side but on both were ashes on the head of the hatchet. The other articles had dust on them, but this was ashes. There was a difference. The handle appeared as though it had been newly broken; the break in the wood was new."

Returning to the discovery of the bodies, Moody inquired of Fleet concerning the type of blood found on each body. Fleet said that on Mr. Borden's body he found that the blood was light and thin and red, and that the blood on Mrs. Borden's body was of a darker color and was congealed and black.

In response to another question by Moody, Fleet continued that the following Saturday, after the funeral party had left, Fleet had taken part in a search along with Marshal Hilliard, Detective Seaver, the State Police Officer, Attorney Jennings, and Officer Desmond. The search lasted well into the afternoon. The dresses in the house were examined very closely, and they found no dress with paint on it—nor with blood, for that matter.

Fleet had gone into the barn and found it extremely hot there; the day was very hot. There was hay in the barn, and the hay was in volume about half a stack, well-ordered and undisturbed. There also was a bench upstairs in the loft.

Cross-examination by Robinson was extremely lengthy and, from the point of view of the defendant, established nothing; it was most inconclusive. It developed that there were a great many police officers on the premises on the day of the murders; all were searching the house. Robinson became somewhat facetious at this point and asked how many police officers there were on the force. He was told one hundred and twenty-five. Robinson asked if they were all there. Fleet answered No.

The witness testified that although they had examined the various rooms, they had not looked closely at the dresses on this occasion. They were looking for a man in the closet rather than for dresses, although he did glance at the dresses to a limited extent. Fleet repeated that since they were looking for a man on 4 August, they were not looking particularly closely at the dresses hanging in the closet. He did take some dresses from Lizzie's closet that day and put them on the bed. He saw no blood on them, nor did he see any paint.

At the beginning of the fifth day of the trial, Friday, 9 June, Deputy Marshal Fleet once more was recalled to the stand. The cross-examination which Robinson had begun the day before was resumed. Again it was a very lengthy cross-examination, establishing very little, except that the witness repeated what he had testified to on direct examination at great length. Fleet's basic story remained unshaken.

He discussed the hatchets. He had left the hatchets on the first day where they were found in the cellar. There was a substantial amount of ashes, about six bushels of ashes in a pile in the cellar near where the hatchets were found. These were coal ashes or ashes derived from the burning of coal, since there was a central-heating system in the house.

In cross-examination Robinson passed over that part of Fleet's testimony which concerned itself with his conversation with Lizzie in her bedroom when Dr. Bowen was present, and concentrated upon the search of the clothes closet and the failure of the police to find blood-stained clothing.

That hatchet which was newly broken had ashes upon it rather than dust. It was found "some few feet from the ash pile." Fleet testified that the broken end of the hatchet did not look the same as it did when he found it; it was newly broken when he found it; it did not look so newly broken at the time of the trial. "Some time has lapsed. It was clearly a new break," said Fleet as Robinson completed his repetitious cross-examination.

[An analysis of Marshal Fleet's lengthy testimony reveals that he was perhaps the strongest of the prosecution's witnesses so far. His testimony gave support to each of the propositions of guilt which Moody had advanced in his opening.

As to pre-disposition to murder, Fleet added another dimension to the picture of hostility between Lizzie and her stepmother, which Moody was carefully painting. Not only did Fleet support Miss Russell's testimony by telling of Lizzie repeating her story of the "angry" man seeking to rent the store, but when Fleet spoke of Mrs. Borden as Lizzie's mother, Lizzie had, he testified, interrupted him by saying, "She is *not* my mother, sir. She is my stepmother. My mother died when I was a child."

Turning to the issue of means to commit the crimes, the handleless hatchet, newly broken and rubbed in coal ashes, was important evidence. In addition, Fleet's testimony of the extreme heat in the barn loft was significant as bearing upon the falsity of Lizzie's story to him of having remained there for about one-half hour on the day of the murders.

Finally, on the issue of consciousness of guilt, Fleet's testimony regarding Lizzie's story of the mercurial note to Mrs. Borden was supportive of the testimony of the other witnesses.

Parenthetically, Fleet had committed his lengthy story in a full handwritten report, an early photostatic copy of which has come into the possession of this writer.]

At the conclusion of the cross-examination of the witness Fleet, Philip Harrington was sworn. A Captain of the police force of Fall River, he had been promoted from the rank of Sergeant since the Borden murders had taken place.

He said he had arrived at the Borden house at about 12:20 P.M. on the day of the murders. He went into the house, saw other officers and several ladies whom he did not know. He looked at Mr. Borden's body. When he examined it, Mr. Borden was wearing black pants and a pair of lace shoes. He raised the sheet and looked at the face. Small drops of blood were still trickling down the side of the face.

Harrington went upstairs and looked at Mrs. Borden's body. The blood on the head of the body was quite dark and coagulated.

"I went into Lizzie Borden's room, stood at the foot of the bed, and asked her if she would tell me all she knew about this matter [Harrington testified].

"She said, "I can tell you nothing about it."

"I asked her when she last saw her father, and she replied, "When he returned from the post office with a small package in his hand and some mail. I asked him if he had any for me, and he said no. He then sat down to read the paper, and I went out to the barn. I remained there twenty minutes. I returned and found him dead."

"I then asked, "When going to or coming from the yard, did you see anybody in or around the yard or anybody going up or down the street?"

"She said, "No, sir."

" "While in the barn," I asked, "did you hear any noise in or about the yard or anybody walking there?"

"She responded, "No, sir."

"I said, "Not even the opening or closing of the screen door? Why not? You were but a short distance and you would have heard the noise if any was made." "

Q. What did she say?
A. She said, "I was up in the loft."

"I then [Harrington resumed] said to Lizzie, "What motive?"

"And she replied, "I don't know."

" "Was it robbery?"

" "I think not, for everything appears all right, even to the watch in his pocket and the ring on his finger."

"I asked her about the rest of the house, and she said everything appeared all right. She also said, "A few weeks ago Father had angry words with a man about something."

"I asked, "What was it?"

"She answered, "I don't know, but they were very angry at the time, and the stranger went away."

" "Did you see him at all?"

" "No, sir [Lizzie answered Harrington]. "They were in another room, but from the tone of their voices I knew everything wasn't pleasant between them."

" "Did you hear your father say anything about him?"

" "No, sir. About two weeks ago he came again. They had a very animated conversation, during which they got angry again, and I heard Father say, 'No, sir, I will not let my store for any such business.' But before they separated, I heard Father say, 'When you are in town, come again, and I will let you know about it.' "

"I said to her [Miss Lizzie], "Owing to the atrociousness of this crime, perhaps you are not in a mental condition to give us a clear statement of the facts, as you will be on tomorrow. By that time you may recollect more about the man who wished to hire the store. You may remember having heard his name or having seen him, and thereby be enabled to give a description of him. You may recollect having heard your father say something."

"Then she made a stiff curtsey and said, "No, I can tell you all I know now just as well as at any other time."

"She was not in tears at any part of the interview. Her voice was at all times steady.

"I asked her to fix the time accurately with regard to how long she'd been out of the house. She said, "No, sir. I was there only twenty minutes."

"At that time Lizzie was wearing a striped house wrap with pink and light stripe alternating; pink is the most prominent color, a loose house wrapper.

"Then I went to the kitchen, and while I was in the kitchen, just as I went to pass by Dr. Bowen, between him and the stove, I saw some scraps of notepaper in his hand. I asked him what they were."

Q. You say you saw Dr. Bowen with some scraps of notepaper in his hand?

A. Yes, sir.

Q. Where was he standing?

A. He was standing a little west of the door that led into the rear hall or stairway.

"I asked him what they were [Harrington continued], referring to the pieces of paper, and he said, "Oh, I guess it is nothing."

"I saw the word "Emma" in a lefthand corner. I asked Dr. Bowen what about the paper, what it contained, and he said, "Oh, I think it is nothing. It is something, I think, about my daughter going through somewhere."

Then he turned slightly to his left, took the lid from the stove, and threw the paper in—or the pieces in. I looked in the fire, and I saw, as he threw the scraps in, that there had been paper burned there before. It was rolled up and still held a cylindrical form. The roll of paper was about twelve inches long, I should say, and not over two inches wide.

"Then the Medical Examiner, Dr. Dolan, came in. He had two or three cans in his hand and one or two hatchets, I think three hatchets. He gave me instructions, and I stood guard over the cans and the hatchets. Then we went to the barn, and I received orders there, and I threw the hay from one side or end of the barn to the other and examined it thoroughly, as I thought. At that time the temperature in degrees I cannot say, but it was extremely hot. It was very dusty there, very uninviting; the floor, bench, and hay and old-fashioned fireplace which stood in the west-end corner and some windows were covered with dust. The windows were all closed, and were covered with cobwebs. It was very disagreeable breathing there because of the dust. It was suffocating hot."

Cross-examination by Robinson produced the fact that the interview which Harrington had had with Lizzie was about one o'clock on the day of the murders, and the witness was dressed in uniform at the time.

The nineteenth witness to take the stand was Patrick H. Doherty, a member of the police force of Fall River, who testified:

"When I arrived at the Borden house, I saw Dr. Bowen. He and I looked at Mr. Borden's body. The blood was fresh in my estimation. I went upstairs, saw the body of Mrs. Borden, observed the blood; it seemed hard, as if it had been there for some time. I saw blood spots on the pillow shams and a bunch of hair on the bed, black hair. It was a piece of hair which had been severed, I think. It was about half as large as my fist. I left it there.

"I went to the kitchen and saw Miss Borden—Miss Lizzie Borden—and Mrs. Churchill. I said, "Miss Borden, where were you when this was done?"

"She said, "It must have been done while I was in the barn."

"I said, "Was there a Portuguese working for your father over the river?"

"She said, "No, sir. Mr. Johnson and Mr. Eddy worked for my father."

"I asked, "Were they here this morning?"

"She replied, "No, sir. Mr. Eddy is sick. They would not hurt my father anyhow."

"I asked her if she had heard any noise or outcries. She said, "No, sir. I heard a peculiar noise.""

" "What kind of noise, Miss Borden?"

" "I think it was something like a scraping noise." This ended my conversation with Lizzie which took place in the kitchen.

"Later I saw her in her room. I went to the door, went to open it; I opened it two or three inches, and she said, "One minute," and shut the door on me, and it was a minute, I should think, before she opened the door for me, fully a minute. I went in the room and just glanced around, that's all.

"When I saw her downstairs, I thought she had a light blue dress with a bosom in the waist, or something like a bosom. I have a faint recollection; that is all I can say about it. I thought she had a light blue dress. I thought there was a small figure on the dress, a little spot, like."

Q. (*showing Officer Doherty a dress*) Was this the dress?

A. No, I don't think so. I searched the barn later. In the loft it was very warm. The breathing was very bad. It was stifling hot there.

In cross-examination he revealed that he did not look at any of the dresses in the house. The remainder of the cross-examination by Robinson of this witness was very inconclusive: Doherty simply repeated the same testimony that he had given in direct examination.

The next witness was Michael Mullaly, who was also a police officer of Fall River.

Mullaly arrived at the house at 11:37 A.M. He went into the side door. He first saw Mrs. Churchill and Bridget Sullivan, Dr. Bowen, Miss Russell, and Miss Lizzie Borden.

"I had a talk with Miss Lizzie Borden [Mullaly testified]. Lizzie Borden told me that she was out in the yard, and when she came in, she found him dead on the sofa. I then inquired of her if she knew what kind of property her father had on his person, and she told me that her father had a silver watch and chain, a pocketbook with money in it, and a gold ring on his little finger. I then asked her whether there was a hatchet or an axe on the premises, and she told me there was. I then learned the property which she had described was on his person.

"I then went and viewed Mrs. Borden's body. The blood looked thick and clotted.

"I went with Bridget down into the cellar, looking for the hatchets and axes. Bridget led the way. Went to the cellar and she took from a box two hatchets. I saw the hatchet which Mr. Fleet took—or the part of the hatchet; [*the witness is shown the hatchet*] it looked very much like it, only the

The Handleless Hatchet

CHARLES CAROLL PHOTOGRAPH,
AND COURTESY OF THE FALL RIVER HISTORICAL SOCIETY

break was cleaner. It looked at the time as though it was just broken; it looked like a fresh break. It was covered with dust and ashes or something like that. The handle was broken fresh. Both sides of it were covered with ashes, both sides of the blade, that is.

"I had some conversation with Lizzie Borden. I inquired of her whether she saw anyone around the premises, and she told me she did. She said she saw a man around there sometime before with dark clothes on."

In cross-examination Robinson again took Mullaly over the same territory as had been covered in direct examination: the witness described seeing a pile of ashes in the cellar; he testified that there was another piece of the handle of the hatchet which was broken, which he saw, but he did not know where it was now—it was a piece that corresponded with the rest of the handle, and it had a fresh break in it, and the other piece did too.

Q. Was it the handle to a hatchet?

A. It was what I call a hatchet handle. It was somewhat shorter than the handles of the other hatchets.

At this point Robinson asked District Attorney Knowlton to produce the rest of the handle of the hatchet, and Knowlton said that he never had had it.

Robinson said, "The Government does not know where it is?"

Knowlton replied, "I do not know where it is. This is the first time I ever heard of it."

Q. (*Robinson to the witness Mullaly*) Did you ever tell anyone of this before?

A. No, sir, I never did.

In re-direct examination Moody questioned the officer about this handle:

Q. Do you say it fitted into these breaks?

A. I did not try to fit it in.

Q. Did you notice anything in reference to the handle of the hatchet?

A. They were fresh broken.

Q. Did you notice anything with respect to the ashes on the handle?

A. Ashes were on both sides of it.

Q. On the handle of the hatchet?

A. Oh, the handle. I did not notice no ashes on the handle.

This apparently came as a surprise to both counsel, and Robinson requested that the witness remain in the courtroom while he recalled John Fleet, the Deputy Marshal. Robinson put Fleet on the stand, showed him the hatchet and said:

Q. (*by Robinson*) Was this what you found?

A. (*by Fleet*) Yes, sir.

Q. Did you find anything else except old tools?

A. No, sir.

Q. Sure about that?

A. Yes, sir.

Q. Now this is all you found in the box except some old tools, is that right?

A. That is all we found in connection with that hatchet.

Q. You did not find the handle—the broken piece—not at all?

A. No, sir.

Q. You did not see it, did you?

A. No, sir.

Q. Did Mullaly take it out of the box?

A. Not that I know of.

Q. It was not there?

A. Not that I know of.

Q. But you could have seen it if it was there?

A. Yes, sir.

Q. You have no doubt about that at all?

A. What?

Q. That you'd have found the other piece of handle had it been in there.

A. No, sir.

Re-direct by Moody to Fleet:

Q. Did you see anything other than the metallic substance except this piece of wood that was driven into the eye of the hatchet in that box?

A. I don't recollect that I did.

Q. (*by Robinson*) There was no hatchet handle belonging to that picked up right there?

A. No, sir.

Q. Or anywhere around there?

A. No, sir.

Q. Or any piece of wood besides that that had any fresh break in it?

A. Not that came from that hatchet.

Q. Or in the box in any way?

A. No, sir, not in the box.

Q. Or around there?

A. No, sir, not that I'm aware of. I didn't see it.

Officer Charles H. Wilson of the Fall River police force next took the stand.

When he had arrived at the Borden house, Wilson testified, he had overheard Deputy Marshal Fleet talking to Miss Borden. Miss Borden said that she saw her mother at about nine o'clock in the guest chamber making the bed, but that she had received a note and she thought she had gone out. She said that she was out in the barn from twenty minutes to a half an hour.

"Anything further?" the District Attorney asked; and Officer Wilson responded:

"When we went in the room, she said it was not necessary to search one room because it was locked, and no one could go in and throw anything in there, as if she ever went out, even downstairs, she always locked the door after her. She asked if it was absolutely necessary to search the room. No, the doctor asked that. Mr. Fleet said it was, and we went in. He said to be as quick as we could about it, that she was sick."

Re LIZZIE'S INQUEST TESTIMONY

Miss Annie M. White, the stenographer at the inquest of August 1892, was called to the stand. The appearance of the stenographer with her notes signaled the opening of the first of the two great evidentiary disputes which were to plague the Court at the trial. This was the question of the admissibility of Lizzie Borden's statements made to Judge Blaisdell during her testimony at the inquest held 9, 10 and 11 August 1892, a few days after the murders.

All counsel agreed that the evidentiary problem posed by Lizzie's statements was complex and that they desired to argue to the Court outside the jury's presence.

Because it was Friday the Court postponed facing the problem until Monday, 12 June, thus allowing counsel to file statements and have time over the weekend to prepare arguments.

[A full discussion of this evidentiary matter will be given in a later chapter, "Behind the Verdict." It is sufficient here to note that after hearing, the Court resolved the issue in favor of the defendant Lizzie Borden, and Annie White, the stenographer, did not testify, and her notes, particularly Lizzie's unbelievably inconsistent and incredibly damaging testimony, was not read to the jury because it was considered an involuntary statement of the defendant.

This was a major victory for the defense, and the ruling of the Court seems biased and was sharply criticized by eminent professionals in the law in 1893, as will be discussed in connection with events following the trial.]

The next witness to be called during what was left of the fifth day was George A. Pettee. He had known Andrew Borden for many, many years; in fact, he had lived in the Borden house twenty-two years before, being one of the preceding owners of No. 92.

He passed the house at ten o'clock on the morning of the murders, and he saw Bridget washing windows. He heard about the murders after eleven o'clock when he was in Vernon Wade's store. He testified further:

"I went over to the house and into it, and Dr. Bowen showed me Mr. Borden's body by taking the sheet away. It seemed to me the blood was quite fresh. I could detect movement of the blood. Dr. Bowen invited me to go upstairs and view Mrs. Borden's body, and I did so. It was quite dark in there and I couldn't see well. I put my hand on her head in order that I might see and feel the condition the head was in. The hair was dry and it was matted, no fresh blood. When I went up to the house it was twelve o'clock."

The sixth trial day, a relatively short session on Saturday, 10 August, opened with filing of counsel's statements concerning admissibility of Lizzie's inquest testimony, then Lieutenant Francis L. Edson of the Fall River police was sworn as a witness.

He said he went to the Borden house on the night of the murders—that is to say, Thursday night—and on Friday morning he found in the cellar two wood axes, a hand axe and a small shingle hatchet. He took them from the house and turned them over to Marshal Hilliard. He had nothing to do with the possession of the handleless hatchet.

On Monday, 8 August, he was present at a further search of the premises with Captain Desmond, Connors, Inspector Medley, Officer Quigley, Attorney Jennings, and O. M. Hanscom, a superintendent of the Pinkerton Detective Agency who was associated with Jennings. As far as he could observe, Edson testified, the search was a thorough one. He saw Officer Medley take from the house a hatchet head; Medley had it in his pocket, and showed it to the witness only partly since it was wrapped in paper. "The hatchet had no handle, and there was no handle in Medley's possession that he showed to me. I saw no loose handle around there, and I don't know where Medley got the handleless hatchet," the Lieutenant said.

He then testified that a man he referred to only as McHenry was also present at the search. The witness did not know who the man was beyond the fact that he was not a police officer; Edson had never seen him around police headquarters before, and assumed him to be a friend of State Police Officer Seaver's. "He is not a resident of Fall River," said the witness. "At that time he hailed from Providence."

Q. Is he still traveling?

A. He might be. He was looking around to find something. He hasn't been in police headquarters since that day.

Q. Was McHenry around police headquarters often?

A. I saw him a great many times, and I can't remember whether he was or he wasn't. I'm not positive.

Q. Was he paid by the police?

A. I never saw his name on the police rolls.

[The man was Edwin D. McHenry, a private detective whose activities, though tangential, were to play a rôle in a significant aspect of the Borden case, as we shall see.]

Police Inspector William H. Medley was then called, and testified that he had arrived at the Borden house at 11:40 on 4 August 1892. He had a brief conversation with Lizzie Borden in which she said that she had been "upstairs in the barn." He went immediately to the barn. Here follows the questioning of Inspector Medley:

Q. After you went into the barn, what did you do? Describe in detail.

A. I went upstairs until I reached about three or four steps from the top, and while there, part of my body was above the floor, above the level of the floor, and I looked around the barn to see if there was any evidence of anything having been disturbed, and I didn't notice that anything had or seemed to have been disturbed, and I stooped down low to see if I could discern any marks on the floor of the barn having been made there. I did that by stooping down and looking across the bottom of the barn floor. I didn't see any, and I reached out my hand

Inspector William H. Medley

FROM PORTER

to see if I could make an impression on the floor of the barn, and I did by putting my hand down so fashion, and found that I made an impression on the barn floor.

Q. Describe what there was on or about the floor by which you made an impression.

A. Seemed to be accumulated hay dust and other dust.

Q. How distinctly could you see the marks which you made with your hand?

A. I could see them quite distinctly when I looked for them.

Q. Go on and describe anything else which you did.

A. Then I stepped up on the top and took four or five steps on the outer edge of the barn floor, the edge nearest the stairs, then came up to see if I could discern those, and I did.

Q. How did you look to see if you could discern those footsteps which you had made?

A. I did it in the first place by stooping down and casting my eye on a level with the barn floor, and could see them plainly.

Q. Did you see any other footsteps in that dust than those which you made yourself?

A. No, sir.

Q. After you had made that examination, what did you do?

A. I came downstairs and searched around the pile of lumber and other stuff there was in the yard, looking for anything that we could find, and after a while I met Mr. Fleet.

Q. Wait a moment now. Did you notice what the temperature was in the loft of the barn as you went up there?

A. Well, I know it was hot, that is all, very hot. You know it was a hot day.

[Inspector Medley's testimony had been brief, but it had also been extremely important to the prosecution's case. If he were believed—and he had no discernible reason to tell an untruth—the jury could be expected to decide that Lizzie Borden had not been in the hayloft at all: her explanation of her whereabouts when her father was killed was a tissue of lies.]

The morning of Monday, 12 June, the seventh day of the trial, was consumed by arguments by counsel on the evidentiary problem of Lizzie's inquest statements, and shortly after noon the Court announced its ruling that her testimony was inadmissible.

Then Dr. William A. Dolan, Medical Examiner for Bristol County, ascended the stand. He testified:

"Quite by chance I arrived at the Borden house about 11:45 A.M., 4 August. I stayed a short time talking with Dr. Bowen, who had already been there. With Dr. Bowen I examined the body of Mr. Borden first. I found his hand was warm, and the blood was still oozing from his wounds and was bright red in color.

"I then went upstairs and examined the body of Mrs. Borden, noted that her blood was coagulated and of a dark color. I felt her hand and her head, and they were cold. The blood on her head was dry.

"I left the Borden house and returned at three o'clock that afternoon when I conducted autopsies on both of the bodies on the dining room table. I removed the stomachs from both bodies, tying each at both ends and putting them into separate, clean jars which I sealed.

"On August 11th a more thorough autopsy was performed. With me at that time was Dr. Francis W. Draper of Boston. Dr. Draper made casts of both skulls at this time. We also examined the intestines of both bodies. We measured and closely inspected each of the wounds on each skull. They varied from one half inch to approximately five inches long.

"I decapitated both bodies and prepared the skulls by carefully removing flesh and cartilage without interfering with the integrity of the bone."

When asked by District Attorney Moody with regard to the priority of the deaths, Dr. Dolan responded that it was his opinion, given with reasonable medical probability, that Mrs. Borden died first: "I should say from one and a half to two hours or from one hour to one and a half hours before Mr. Borden." He said that he had based his opinion not only upon his observations of the condition of the blood of both bodies, the warmth of Mr. Borden's body and the coolness of Mrs. Borden's body, but also upon the observations in examining the intestines of both at the autopsy with regard to the digestive processes, assuming Mr. and Mrs. Borden had breakfasted together.

In response to questions by Adams in cross-examination, Dr. Dolan said: "The autopsy, which took place at the Oak Grove Cemetery, took place on the eleventh of August, the day of the funeral, and the bodies were interred after the heads had been removed. The family, the daughters Emma and Lizzie, were not notified that the interment had been performed when the bodies had no heads."

The Court adjourned at 5 P.M. till Tuesday morning, 13 June, at nine o'clock.

Medical Examiner William A. Dolan

The eighth trial day opened with lengthy questioning by Adams which developed only a repetition of Dr. Dolan's detailed testimony with regard to the length of the wounds and their location, and whether or not they penetrated into the brain cavity.

The witness was shown the handleless hatchet, and he said that he had first seen it only a short time earlier in the Marshal's office.

Q. Have you examined the handleless hatchet?

A. I have.

Q. Do you consider it as a good edge, a sharp cutting edge?

A. I do. It is sharp. From the appearance of things I would place the assailant of Mr. Borden at the head of the lounge, between the parlor door and the head of the lounge, and the blows were swung from left to right.

Q. If the assailant, using the instrument you have described, or a similar one, had cut the artery which you have described, would it not have been natural that the assailant would have been covered with blood? Or would have been splattered or sprinkled with blood?

A. Not necessarily.

Q. How do you explain that they would not have been?

A. Because the blood would not spurt in that direction. It would not necessarily spurt in the direction of the assailant.

Adams, now using a cast of Andrew Borden's skull in his questioning, continued:

Q. No more than the ordinary strength of a person was required to administer these blows?

A. Moderate force was used; no more than moderate force to give these blows was used.

[The long cross-examination by Adams with regard to the location of the blood spots failed to change the fact that Dr. Dolan had made an important point: the butchery of Lizzie Borden's father could have been committed without necessarily covering the assailant with blood.]

Q. Now taking the position of Mrs. Borden, the pillow shams, the bedspreads, the spots on the pillow shams, mirrors and baseboard, where in your opinion did the assailant stand when inflicting these injuries?

A. Astride the body.

Q. And over it.

A. Yes, sir.

Q. How did the assailant face?

A. Faced the east wall.

At this point Juror Hodges became faint, affected by the grisly dialogue. Ironically, Juror Hodges was a blacksmith. The jury was allowed to retire to their rooms. After a short time the jury returned, and Dr. Dolan continued, testifying concerning blood spots.

"When I got the dress, I did say it looked like blood, and I also sent for shoes and stockings of Miss Borden on Saturday. I sent the Marshal for them. He brought me shoes and stockings, only one pair, low shoes, laced."

Q. Did you examine them for blood?

A. I did.

Q. Did you find any?

A. Yes, sir.

Q. Whereabouts?

A. On the sole. I think it was blood, yes, sir.

Q. And the white skirt. Did you receive that?

A. Yes.

Q. And you found upon it a pinhead spot on the front of it that looked like blood, did you?

A. Yes.

Q. Did you claim that it was human blood?

A. I don't know whether or not it was human blood, but it is blood. I didn't test it further.

The remainder of the eighth day of the trial continued to be given over to medical testimony, presented by District Attorney Moody for the prosecution. The three expert witnesses who testified for the Commonwealth were all eminently qualified.

[In general, a so-called expert witness is a person who testifies about a subject matter beyond the sophistication of the ordinary witness. Whereas the ordinary witness may normally testify only as to things and matters which he himself knows of his own knowledge, or has observed, or in some cases heard, he may not opine; he may not give opinion evidence. On the other hand, if a person is, in the opinion of the trial Justices, specially qualified in a field of human endeavor beyond the ken of the ordinary person, and if this witness, by reason of background, education, training and experience in a specialized field, satisfies the Court of his qualifications, he may opine; he may give an opinion within the boundaries of his specialty. Such a specialty is medicine, and medical doctors who appear to the Court to be qualified may give opinion evidence in matters relating to the field of medicine. The qualifications and credentials of the next three following witnesses, when recited, were obviously unimpeachable. Accordingly, each of the three was declared qualified by the Court to opine, and did.

In offering this testimony, Moody was supporting his second major proposition of proof of guilt—that Lizzie Borden did, in fact, murder her stepmother and her father in that order. The purpose of the evidence was threefold: 1) to establish priority of the deaths of the victims; 2) to demonstrate that Lizzie Borden had available to her an appropriate weapon to accomplish the murders, and 3) that she was physically capable of inflicting the death wounds. In short, Moody was offering to prove that Lizzie had the means to commit the crimes.]

The first of the three medical experts took the witness stand and testified as follows:

"My name is Edward S. Wood. I am a physician and a chemist. For twenty-two years I have been a Professor of Chemistry at the Harvard Medical School. I received my medical training at the Harvard Medical School and at the Massachusetts General Hospital. My specialty in medicine lies in the medical-legal field, and I have testified in several hundred criminal cases, including a very large number of capital cases.

"On August 5th, 1892, I received at the Harvard Medical School a sealed box from the Railroad Express. The box contained four jars: one labeled "milk of August 3, 1892," the second labeled "milk of August 4, 1892," the third jar labeled "stomach of Andrew J. Borden," and the fourth "stomach of Mrs. Andrew J. Borden."

"I first examined the stomach of Mrs. Andrew J. Borden. It was a normal stomach, and its contents were, upon my examination, found to be of solid consistency: four-fifths solid food and one-fifth liquid. In the stomach contents I found partially digested starch: wheat found normally in bread or cake, slightly digested muscular fibre, meat, and an undigested skin of an apple. The process of digestion indicated to me that death had taken place within two to three hours of the ingestion of this food.

"I next examined the stomach of Andrew J. Borden and found it to be a normal organ. The contents, however, differed from those found in the stomach of Mrs. Borden; first, there was much more of contents; second, they consisted of nine-tenths liquid and one-tenth solid matter, only a few starch granules, a few muscle fibres from meat, and some vegetable tissue, the residue of a digested apple or pear. The contents of Mr. Borden's stomach indicated that normal digestive process had taken place; nearly all the solid food had been expelled from the stomach into the intestines, and the stomach digestive process was almost complete. It was my opinion that the digestive process had been operative for approximately four hours before death."

Q. Does digestion stop with death?
A. Yes.

Next Moody posed an hypothetical question to Dr. Wood. He asked him to assume that both parties had partaken of substantially the same breakfast at substantially the same time: what then was the opinion of the Doctor as to the difference in time of death? Dr. Wood answered that Mrs. Borden had predeceased her husband by approximately one and one-half hours.

The witness then stated that he had heard the testimony by various witnesses at the trial with regard to the condition of the blood observed upon and around the bodies. He said that the difference in the condition of blood as described corroborated the results of the tests which he himself had made upon the stomachs and the intestines of Mr. and Mrs. Borden. He then categorically repeated that in his opinion within reasonable medical certainty, Andrew J. Borden died in the neighborhood of one and one-half hours after Abby Durfee Borden had expired.

Dr. Wood continued:

"I received by Railroad Express on the 10th of August two axes, two hatchets, a blue dress, skirt and waist, a white skirt, a piece of the sitting-room carpet, a piece of the bedroom carpet, a piece of false hair, a braid or switch, a hair from Mrs. Borden's head, a hair from Mr. Borden's head, and a hair taken from the head of a hatchet. The two hatchets and the two axes I tested, and they were shown to be free of blood. The hair found on the hatchet appeared to be animal hair, probably the hair from a cow, but it definitely was not human hair. The blue skirt I observed had a brownish stain upon it, but I found that that was not blood, nor was there any suggestion of blood upon the shirtwaist.

"The white skirt which I had received did have upon it a small spot, six inches from the bottom of the skirt. This spot was one-sixteenth of an inch in diameter, about the size of the head of a pin. It was more extensive and plainer on the outside than on the inside of the skirt. I subjected this spot to examination and I found it to be blood. I further found that the microscopic measurement of the blood corpuscles averaged one-3,243rd of an inch. This measurement is within the limits of human blood, and the blood spot on the white skirt therefore is consistent with its being a human blood stain. The fact that it was plainer and more extensive on the outside of the skirt, that it was larger in diameter on the outside of the skirt, indicates that it came onto the skirt from the outside and not from the inside."

[This last statement of the witness Dr. Wood is significant because Robinson in his argument to the jury was to say that Lizzie Borden was in a menstrual period on or about 4 August and thus this small blood-stain was accounted for. Professor Wood's testimony here seems absolutely to refute this explanation of Robinson's for the presence of the blood. It is to be noted that the matter was not pressed by the prosecution, perhaps because the subject seemed indelicate.]

"I next examined the pieces of carpet which had been received [Dr. Wood continued], and I found upon testing that both pieces absorbed and dried human blood with equal rapidity.

"On August 30th I received the hatchet head or the handleless hatchet, and it has been in my possession ever since. My examination revealed that both sides of the hatchet head were uniformly rusted, that there were several reddish spots upon the head, although I could not determine that these were blood stains. I soaked the hatchet for several days in a solution which accounts for the darkening of the fractured part of the wood handle. When I received it, there was white dirt, like ashes, clearly visible with a magnifying glass, which covered both sides of the hatchet head. This substance resembles ashes, and was, and continues to be at this time, strongly adherent to both sides of the blade. It resisted rubbing. The hatchet, in my opinion, had been wet when placed in, or in contact with, the white material, and this white material had permeated the many crevices of the blade's surface and had stuck very tightly."

Dr. Wood then testified, in response to an hypothetical question posed to him by District Attorney Moody, that the handleless hatchet could have been used to inflict the wounds found on the victims and cleaned by ashes to eliminate the detection of blood if the handle was broken after the weapon was used. His reasoning was that some blood would have appeared at the break in the wood if it had been used as the weapon when it was broken. However, if it were used as the weapon and later broken, it could have been the death weapon.

In closing, Moody shifted the subject of direct examination and inquired of the witness as follows:

Q. What is the nature of prussic acid?

A. It is a poison acid, gaseous. It is one of the most deadly poisons we know; any solution which contains one grain of prussic acid is a fatal dose.

[This seemingly casual departure from the line of questioning was in preparation for pivotal evidence which the District Attorney expected to adduce at a later time—as shall be seen.]

Cross-examination of Dr. Wood was conducted for the defense by Adams, and he first inquired concerning the small blood spot found on the white skirt six inches from the bottom. The witness testified that the skirt was seven feet one inch in circumference and that the spot which was the subject of the question would be found on the back of the skirt six inches from the bottom. Adams pursued this subject further:

Q. Are you able to say that that spot was not a spot of blood which might have gotten on the skirt from the menstrual flow of the woman?

A. No, sir, I am not. It may have been menstrual blood or it may not, so
far as I can determine.

Then switching to the subject of the handleless hatchet, Adams was at
first unable to shake Professor Wood's testimony. In asking an hypothetical question, Adams inquired if the Professor would not have reached the
same conclusion if the hatchet had fallen into ashes or into a pile of ashes.
To this question Dr. Wood responded that it was his opinion that the
hatchet head had been forcibly rubbed with ashes, for the crevices in the
head, or blade, were tightly packed with the white substance.

Adams did, however, after a lengthy questioning, succeed in adducing
from the witness the fact that Dr. Wood could not determine from any
examination which he had made how freshly broken the hatchet handle
was.

In re-direct examination Moody asked the witness as to blood spattering
and was answered: "Blood might spatter under these circumstances in any
direction and might not spatter in every direction. There is no way to
determine whether any given surface near the wound would receive
spattering of blood; it would vary according to accidental circumstances."

In re-cross-examination Adams pressed the issue of blood spattering,
and Dr. Wood stated that the assailant standing behind Andrew Borden
would almost certainly receive spatters of blood on the upper part of his
body; if the assailant stood astride Mrs. Borden, he would receive spatters
on the lower part of his body. The Doctor, however, could in no way form
any opinion as to the number of spatters of blood, if any, which the
assailant would receive.

A Boston physician, Frank W. Draper, M.D., was next to take the
witness stand for the prosecution. Dr. Draper had practiced medicine in
Boston for twenty-four years. He was a graduate of the Harvard Medical
School, and he had been Medical Examiner for Suffolk County, which
includes Boston, since 1877, when he had been appointed the first Medical
Examiner in the Commonwealth, pursuant to the Act of 1877. He was a
professor at the Harvard Medical School; his title was Professor of
Medical Jurisprudence.

On 10 August Dr. Draper had come to Fall River and had been taken
to the Oak Grove Cemetery to examine the bodies of Mr. and Mrs.
Borden. He said that his examination revealed that the bodies were
somewhat decomposed and that he had received a plaster cast of the skulls
of both Mr. and Mrs. Borden, and, while at the cemetery, he had drawn
pencil marks upon the skulls, indicating the exact location and length of
each of the many wounds on each skull. Although, as he said, he of course

could not testify as to the sequence of the many blows which appeared on the skulls, he had numbered them for his convenience in explanation.

Taking first the plaster cast of the skull of Andrew Borden, Dr. Draper explained the wounds as follows: The first had penetrated the nose and upper lips to the tip of the chin; it measured four inches in length; it had severed the cheek and the nose. The second was above the left eyebrow and had broken through the skull and entered the brain. The third had cut through the eye deeply and exactly and had crushed the cheekbone; it measured four and one-half inches and had been delivered from left to right. The fourth was a double wound of the skull, as was the fifth; both blows had been delivered from the front backward, as Dr. Draper put it, "from before backwards." Then he detailed a whole group of wounds around the left ear, "all of them crushing into the brain itself." One wound at the top of the skull gave with "approximate accuracy the length of the blade which would enter there: three and one-half inches." Four of the wounds had penetrated the bone of the skull and had sunk into the brain.

Then taking the plaster cast of Mrs. Borden's skull, Dr. Draper indicated the first wound, which was a flap wound over the left ear. This, he said, had been delivered from the front backward and was a long cut. There were two wounds on the top of the head back of the crown; both of them had penetrated the skull and entered into the brain. The next wound he described had entered the ear and was deep enough to penetrate the skull. He then showed pencil marks indicating a group of deep wounds at

Hair Found Near Mrs. Borden's Body

the back of the head. Two of these three wounds went into the skull through to the brain. Finally, he showed a group of twelve wounds above the right ear "distributed in a fan shape"; varying in depth, these wounds were altogether a complete smashing of the skull. Finally, Dr. Draper told of finding a wound on the body at the neck, near the middle of the neck line, where the neck joins the shoulders. This blow, he said, had been delivered from right to left as the assailant stood over the body.

"During the autopsy which I performed at the Oak Grove Cemetery [Dr. Draper testified], the stomachs of both bodies were missing, but the intestines were not, and I examined the contents of the intestines. From my examination I concluded that the priority of death was that Mr. Borden had died at least one hour after Mrs. Borden."

At this time in the direct examination of Dr. Draper there was a pause. The prosecutor turned, stepped to the prosecution table, took a large package from the floor and placed it upon the table. There was then a shuffling of papers, and then occurred one of the most sensational moments of the trial. As the prosecutor walked again toward the witness stand, he held in his hand the actual fleshless, crushed skull of Andrew J. Borden. This gruesome relic shocked spectators, Court, and jury alike. Passing the ghastly object to the witness, Dr. Draper accepted it and then produced from his pocket a piece of tin plate which he said measured exactly 3½ inches in length. Using the piece of tin plate, the witness then inserted it into each of the many wounds on the crushed skull, showing how each blow had been administered. The 3½-inch tin plate fit exactly into each wound.

This demonstration finished, the prosecutor handed Dr. Draper the handleless hatchet, and the Doctor, using the handleless hatchet, repeated his demonstration by fitting the cutting edge of the hatchet into each of the many wounds of the skull. The blade of the handleless hatchet measured precisely 3½ inches.

Q. Are you able to say whether or not this weapon could be capable of making these wounds?

A. I believe it is.

Then Dr. Draper continued his demonstration of fitting the handleless hatchet into the wounds. He demonstrated that only a 3½-inch blade would fit into each of the wounds; using a tin plate with a 4-inch cutting edge, he showed that it was too long for a number of the skull wounds, although he was able to place the 4-inch cutting edge into some of them.

Q. In your opinion, Dr. Draper, could the results you found have been produced by the use of an ordinary hatchet in the hands of a woman of ordinary strength?

A. They could, yes, sir.

"I believe that the assailant of Mrs. Borden stood astride her prostrate body as she was lying face downward on the floor [Dr. Draper continued]. One wound on the left side of the head was given while Mrs. Borden was standing facing her assailant.

"I also believe that Mr. Borden had his face turned well to the right while he was lying on the sofa when he was first struck, and all other blows which were received on his head were inflicted when the head was in much the same position."

The prosecutor inquired of the witness as to the spattering of blood, or lack of it. The response of Dr. Draper was that testimony in this regard would be mere guesswork: there was no way to determine the direction of spattering or the radius of the spattering of blood. "I have no opinion as to whether the person inflicting the blows would be spattered or not," he said. "There is no rule for direction or amount of spattering of blood in these circumstances. It would be sheer guesswork on my part."

Cross-examination of the witness Draper was conducted by Adams. After a long review of the hideous wounds, the defense attorney drew from the witness the fact that ten blows delivered to Andrew J. Borden's head from a close distance would create a strong likelihood that the assailant would receive blood spattering on the upper part of his body.

Then occurred an incident which backfired upon the cross-examiner. First Adams asked this question, waving the handleless hatchet:

Q. This handleless hatchet is not an uncommon type of hatchet, is it?

A. No.

Thereupon Adams produced a new hatchet, completely unrelated to the case, and passed it to Dr. Draper, asking him to fit the blade of the hatchet which Adams produced into the various wounds on the skull. With the jury giving full attention to the movement of Dr. Draper's hand in attempting to fit into the wounds the blade of the hatchet just produced, it became obvious that the hatchet blade would not fit all the wounds. Dr. Draper remarked that the blade simply was not ground enough, and this fact was obvious to the jury. The hatchet was $3\frac{3}{8}$ inches long at the blade edge.

This demonstrative evidence adduced the following significant testimony from the witness Draper: "It must be a hatchet with an edge that will accurately apply itself to these wounds of the bone; it is both the length of the hatchet and the thinness of the edge of the blade at certain places in this individual handleless hatchet that led me to the opinion that this handleless hatchet could inflict these wounds which I have observed."

Then Adams engaged in another attempt at demonstrative evidence. First he detailed with the witness the gruesome story of the removal of flesh and eyes and cartilage from the two skulls at the Oak Grove Cemetery, and then he detailed each of the nineteen cutting wounds found on Mrs. Borden's head. After that, he turned his back to the witness and asked Dr. Draper to draw on his (Adams's) coat a chalk mark indicating the exact location of the wound which Dr. Draper had found at the base of the neck, where the neck met the shoulders of Mrs. Borden's body. The witness accommodated him and drew the chalk mark, whereupon Adams, playing to the jury, said facetiously, "I trust that I shall not be numbered and marked as an exhibit."

This remark—in context in questionable taste—served a purpose: it convulsed the spectators and the jury with laughter, for, after nearly an entire day of sickening medical testimony, it came as comic relief.

Finally, moving to the question as to whether or not the presence of an abundance of hair, both false and natural, upon the head of Mrs. Borden would have cushioned the blows and have caused a greater exertion of force to create the crushing of the skull which had been testified to, Adams asked Dr. Draper:

Q. Does the degree in which the hair would serve as an obstacle to the passage of the weapon into the head alter your opinion that the inflicting of the wounds was within the ability of an average woman to inflict the blows?

A. It does not alter my opinion that the inflicting of these blows was within the physical capability of an average woman of average strength.

Distinguished, elderly, David W. Cheever, a Boston physician for many years, was the next expert witness called by the Commonwealth. Dr. Cheever was the Professor of Surgery and Anatomy at the Harvard Medical School and had served as a Professor of Anatomy since 1850, a period of forty-three years.

"On May 31st I for the first time viewed the skulls of Andrew J. Borden and Mrs. Borden. I have heard the medical testimony which was given here in this courtroom at the trial. Based upon my understanding of the testimony with regard to the coolness of Mrs. Borden's body, with regard to the blood coagulated on Mrs. Borden's head, and the liquid and dripping blood found on Mr. Borden's head at the time of the discovery of the bodies on August 4th, based further on the description of the digestive system after an examination of the organs of Andrew J. Borden as well as the description of the digestive system as testified to after examination of the organs of Mrs. Borden's body, it is my considered opinion that Mrs. Borden died first and by a considerable time interval, a minimum of one hour and a maximum of two hours.

"I made an examination of the wounds appearing on the two skulls, and I concluded that the cutting edge to cause these wounds was three and one-half inches long and no longer. I reached this conclusion after examining all the wounds and applying to these wounds the so-called handleless hatchet. I have tried the handleless hatchet on each of the wounds on both of the skulls and I find that its blade fits accurately."

Thereupon Dr. Cheever took the handleless hatchet and the skull of Andrew Borden and demonstrated how in each wound the handleless hatchet fitted exactly. He then testified:

"I have concluded that the scalp wound which appeared on Mrs. Borden's head was inflicted when the assailant was face-to-face with Mrs. Borden and that the other wounds were delivered by the assailant while he was standing up astride Mrs. Borden's prone body.

"Judging from my examination, from the nature of the wounds, and from the circumstances as I understand them to be, all of these wounds could have been inflicted by a hatchet wielded by a woman of ordinary strength. With regard to spattering of blood I can say with certainty that no one can tell the direction of blood spattering or its radius."

In cross-examination Dr. Cheever explained that the spattering of blood depended in large measure upon which of the many blows cut the artery and killed the victim: if the person was already dead, there would be little spattering from subsequent blows, for the circulation within the dead body would be feeble, if existing at all, and therefore a small amount of blood would spurt since a small amount of blood would be passing from the heart. The testimony of Dr. Cheever ended with a lengthy cross-examination during which the witness repeated his opinion that blood spattering and blood spotting upon the assailant would be guesswork. He did concede, however, that Mrs. Borden's assailant would in all likelihood have blood on his shoes.

The medical testimony on the eighth day of the trial was now complete. The prosecution had succeeded in adducing forceful testimony from eminent authorities that Mrs. Borden had predeceased her husband by approximately one and one-half hours; that blood spattering and the presence or absence of blood spots was sheer speculation; that the attacks upon the victims had been hideous, bestial, and atrocious; that the so-called handleless hatchet was a likely weapon to have been used; and that an ordinary woman of ordinary strength wielding such a hatchet could have inflicted the terrible wounds. As Moody had forecast in his opening, here was the evidence of physical strength and available means.

The cross-examination of Dr. Cheever was completed at 5 P.M., and the Court adjourned until the ninth day of the trial, the next day, Wednesday, 14 June 1893.

The ninth day was hot and humid, and the early morning sun baked the small New Bedford courthouse. Within, Rufus B. Hilliard was called to the witness stand to testify. He had been for fourteen years the City Marshal of Fall River. He stated that he had received the telephone call from Cunningham and had dispatched Police Officer Allen immediately to the Borden house as a result of the call. It was not, however, until three o'clock in the afternoon that Hilliard first went to the Borden house on 4 August 1892. Although he did not have a conversation with Lizzie Borden that day, he did to some extent participate in the search of the premises. This led him to the barn, and he had found there that the barn door was closed and, upon entering and ascending to the loft, he found that the loft was suffocatingly hot.

On Saturday afternoon while the funeral was in progress, Hilliard, with others, had more thoroughly searched the Borden house, and although he himself had made no personal examination of the various dresses, Hilliard had asked Attorney Jennings for the dress which Lizzie had worn on the morning of 4 August. Jennings left Hilliard and returned carrying a dress, which he had procured from Lizzie, together with a petticoat. These Jennings turned over to Hilliard, who in turn gave them to the Medical Examiner.

That evening, 6 August, at 7:45 P.M. Marshal Hilliard, together with Mayor Coughlin, had gone to the Borden house. They had observed a very large crowd of people gathered in front of the house. Here follows the Marshal's testimony:

Marshal Rufus B. Hilliard

FROM PORTER

"I sent for officers to clear the street, and then the Mayor and I saw Lizzie and Emma and Mr. Morse in the parlor. Mayor Coughlin asked that the members of the family remain in the house for a few days, and he offered to them police protection and suggested that they send persons for the mail rather than go to the post office for it.

"Lizzie then said, "What! Is there anybody suspected in this house?"

"The Mayor said, "Well, perhaps Mr. Morse can answer that question [presumably a reference to Morse's being harassed by a mob the day after the murders]."

"Then Lizzie said, "I want to know the truth," and she repeated that twice.

"Mayor Coughlin then said, "Well, I regret very much to say, Miss Borden, but you are suspected."

"With that Miss Emma spoke up and said, "We have tried to keep it from her as long as we could."

"Mayor Coughlin then asked Lizzie where she was when her father was killed, and Lizzie replied that she was in the barn. When the Mayor asked for what purpose she was in the barn, Lizzie said that she went out to get some lead to make sinkers with. The Mayor asked how long she was there, and Lizzie replied that she was there twenty minutes.

"Then Lizzie said, "Well, I am ready to go at any time." ""

Robinson cross-examined Marshal Hilliard, stressing the thoroughness

of the search which was conducted on Saturday, 6 August, by the police
officials. The cross-examination was extremely lengthy. It was adduced
that, when Mayor Coughlin and Marshal Hilliard went to the Borden
house on Saturday night, no warrants for Lizzie's arrest had been issued:
the first warrant for her arrest was issued on Monday noon.

There was an offer of proof made by Moody on behalf of the
Commonwealth to show that Mayor Coughlin's visit to the Borden house
was made in good faith, merely to offer police protection because John
Vinnicum Morse, while walking to the post office the night before, had
been threatened by crowds. Chief Justice Mason excluded this evidence.

The next witness was John W. Coughlin, physician, surgeon, and
Mayor of Fall River. He told of his visit, accompanied by Marshal
Hilliard, to the Borden home on Saturday, and his testimony with regard
to the conversation that took place between the Mayor and the Marshal
and the members of the Borden household was exactly as Marshal Hilliard
had related it.

There was a short cross-examination, after which Moody rose and
addressed the Court as follows: "Your Honors did not announce the exact
grounds of the decision. This witness has spoken a little more about the
previous night." This was of course a reference to the exclusion by the
Court of Lizzie Borden's inquest statements. Chief Justice Mason,
responding for the Court, answered, "It does not change the situation."

Mrs. Hannah H. Gifford, a dressmaker of Fall River, next testified that
she had been making clothing for Lizzie Borden for a period of seven or
eight years, that all of her business transactions with Lizzie had taken
place in her place of business and that she herself had never been in the
Borden home.

Questioned about a conversation that Mrs. Gifford had had with Lizzie
about Mrs. Borden in the Spring of 1892, the dressmaker testified:

"I was speaking to Lizzie of a garment I had made for Mrs. Borden,
and instead of saying "Mrs. Borden," I said "Mother," and Lizzie says,
"Don't say that to me, for she is a mean good-for-nothing."

"I said, "Oh, Lizzie, you don't mean that."

"And she said, "Yes, I don't have much to do with her; I stay in my
room most of the time."

"I said, "You come down to your meals, don't you?"

"And she said, "Yes, but we don't eat with them if we can help it." "

The next witness to take the stand was Miss Anna H. Borden. Not a relative of Lizzie's—or at least a close relative—she had been Lizzie's traveling companion and had shared a cabin with Lizzie on the steamship which carried them both to Europe in the Summer of 1890.

Moody, in offering this witness, addressed the Court, and told Chief Justice Mason and his associates that Anna Borden would testify that en route home from Europe Lizzie Borden had several times complained to Anna Borden and had expressed her great reluctance to return to her "unhappy home" and had made other, more compelling, expressions of her extreme resentment toward Mrs. Borden.

To this evidence Robinson objected and, after a brief argument, the Court excluded all testimony from this witness. The exclusion of the evidence was on the sound grounds that the statements were too ambiguous in character and too remote in point of view of time.

Lucy Collet was then sworn and testified that on the morning of the murders she had gone to Dr. Chagnon's house behind No. 92, and had sat on the steps—there being no one at home at the Chagnons'—from ten minutes to eleven until sometime after eleven, and had seen no one coming from the direction of the Borden house. The effect of her testimony was somewhat diminished by the fact that she seemed slightly confused as to the exact time when she sat on the porch of the Chagnon house.

Thomas Bold, a resident handyman of Mrs. Churchill's, next took the witness stand and stated that on the morning of the murders he had been washing carriages near the Churchill house in such a position that he could have seen anyone leaving the Borden yard. He stated that he had washed the carriage for some time before Mrs. Churchill came to summon him for aid. The substance and the purpose of his testimony was expressed in the following exchange:

Q. Now during the time that you were washing carriages there, did you see anyone go in or come out of the Borden yard or go through the yard in which you were?

A. No, sir, I did not.

In cross-examination Robinson was able to show that the witness was in a position where he could see only part of the Borden yard during the period of time which was material.

The next witness was Patrick McGowan, a mason's laborer. This witness had been working in the Crowe yard, which is behind the Borden house, on the morning of 4 August. He thus was in a position to see a portion of the back of the Borden house from 10:08 for about twenty minutes, and he saw no one leaving the Borden yard, or premises.

An elderly woman, Mrs. Aruba P. Kirby, next testified that she lived across Third Street behind the Borden premises and that on the morning of 4 August—for the entire morning—she had been in her kitchen. From her kitchen window she had a clear view of the rear Borden fence, and from time to time on 4 August she had looked out the window.

Q. Now during any time that you could see—during the time you could see—did you see anyone pass in and out?

A. No, sir.

[Mrs. Kirby's daughter in 1973 still resided in the same house on Third Street. She was a lady of such advanced age that it was not possible to converse with her. The kitchen window is at the front of the house, looking across the street toward the Bordens', and therefore it would have been possible to see a portion of the passageway leading to the rear fence of the Borden premises.]

Joseph Derosier, a twenty-three-year-old workman, was the next witness. He testified that he had been sawing wood in the Crowe yard behind the Borden house all day on 4 August 1892—from 7 A.M. to 5 P.M. He was asked if on the morning of the murders he had seen anyone go through the Crowe yard over the fence into the Borden yard or come from the Borden yard over the fence into the Crowe yard. His answer was "No, sir." The witness was French, spoke English with great difficulty, and therefore his testimony was given through a court interpreter.

John Denny, another stonemason who had been working in Crowe's yard, next testified. He said that he had been at work on the Crowe premises from quarter of seven on 4 August to twelve o'clock.

Q. Had you seen any stranger or anyone come from the direction of Mr. Borden's premises and go out onto Third Street?

A. No, sir.

Q. Had you seen anyone at any time during the morning of August 4th take the contrary course, coming from Third Street and going into the Borden premises?

A. No, sir.

[Obviously Moody's purpose in introducing the witnesses Collet, Bold, McGowan, Kirby, and Derosier and Denny was to support one of the prosecution's propositions of proof of guilt: exclusive opportunity. The testimony of Moody's next witness was equally obviously designed to support another prong of the prosecution's case against Lizzie: consciousness of guilt.]

Hannah Reagan was one of the two policewomen of Fall River, and her principal duty was to act as matron for female prisoners at the Fall River jail, which was housed in the Central Police Station. Some ten months earlier, Lizzie Borden had been in her custody and had been lodged during the preliminary, or probable-cause, hearing before Judge Blaisdell, in the matron's quarters—that is, in Mrs. Reagan's own room.

On the morning of 24 August 1892, while Lizzie was awaiting the opening of the hearing, Emma Borden had come to the jail to visit her sister Lizzie. Here is how Mrs. Reagan related the occurrence:

"Miss Emma Borden came to my room about twenty minutes to nine o'clock on the twenty-fourth day of August, and I let her in, and she spoke to her sister Lizzie. I left the two women talking together, and I went into a toilet room about four feet from where Lizzie Borden was lying on a couch, and I heard very loud talk, and I came to my door, and it was Miss Lizzie Borden; she was lying on her left side, and her sister Emma was talking to her, and Lizzie says, "Emma, you have gave me away, haven't you?"

"She says, "No, Lizzie, I have not."

" "You have," Lizzie says, "and I will let you see. I won't give in one inch." And Lizzie sat right up and put up her finger, and I stood in the doorway, looking at both of them."

Q. Was Lizzie Borden's tone loud or low?

A. I could not hear what Miss Emma said, only "I did not, Lizzie. I did not give you away, Lizzie." Lizzie says, "You have." Lizzie spoke in a loud voice.

Q. What occurred then?

A. Lizzie laid down on the couch and faced out the window and closed her eyes. Emma got a chair and sat down beside her sister and stayed until sometime after eleven o'clock in the morning.

Q. During the time that the two sisters sat that way, did Miss Lizzie speak to her sister at all?

A. No, sir.

Q. When Emma left, was anything said, any goodbye or anything?

A. No, sir. She never spoke to her sister any more that morning.

Q. Did they see you at the time while this conversation was going on?

A. Both of them see me. They turned right. Lizzie lay this way [*illustrating*], and her sister was standing right beside her.

Andrew Jennings conducted the cross-examination for the defense, and apparently he considered it important to undo this testimony. Mrs. Reagan testified that Jennings himself, the cross-examiner, had come to the jail to visit Lizzie after Emma left and that Mr. Buck, the minister, had also visited in the late afternoon of that day. In fact, Mr. Buck visited almost every day at the Central Police Station. Mrs. Reagan testified that she did not recall whether a Mrs. Holmes or a Mrs. Brigham had visited Lizzie that afternoon, whereupon Jennings refreshed the witness's memory by recalling a trick which was performed in the afternoon in the presence of Mrs. Brigham; the trick concerned the breaking of an egg in a certain manner with her hand. Mrs. Reagan testified that she had bet a quarter with Lizzie that she (Lizzie) could not break the egg in the required manner, and, when she could not, Lizzie said, "That is the first thing that I undertook to do that I never could."

Q. Didn't you have a pleasant time that afternoon, all of you?
A. Yes, sir. We laughed about the breaking of the egg.

Miss Emma had been in the room at the time of the egg-breaking trick which was in the afternoon, following the incident of the conversation which Mrs. Reagan had testified to. "But," said Mrs. Reagan, "although Emma was in the room on her second visit of the day, she did not participate in the egg-breaking trick."

Mrs. Reagan had informed members of the press of the statements made by Lizzie in the morning, and they had been published subsequently in the newspaper.

Q. Did you tell any reporter that it was all a lie?
A. No, sir, I did not.
Q. Did the Reverend Mr. Buck speak to you about it?
A. No, sir, he did not.
Q. Didn't you tell me that it wasn't true?
A. No, sir, I did not.
Q. Subsequent to that, was a paper drawn for you to sign?
A. Yes, sir.

Then Jennings produced and read the following paper:

This is to certify that my attention has been called to a report said to have been made by me in regard to a quarrel between Lizzie and her

Police Matron Hannah Reagan

FROM PORTER

sister Emma in which Lizzie said to Emma, "You have given me away," and that I expressly and positively deny that any such conversation took place, and I further deny that I ever heard anything that could be construed as a quarrel between the two sisters.

This was a document drawn by Jennings immediately after the newspapers had carried Mrs. Reagan's statements with regard to the sisters' quarrel. It had not been signed by Mrs. Reagan. It was Attorney Jennings's contention that he had drafted the document for Mrs. Reagan's signature, but that Marshal Hilliard had induced Mrs. Reagan not to sign the denial. This resulted in a shouting altercation between Jennings, Hilliard and a newspaperman named Porter (which is underscored in the testimony of Charles J. Holmes later for the defense).

Q. Didn't you say that you were willing to sign that paper, but the Marshal wouldn't let you?
A. No, sir, I did not.
Q. Did you at any time have a conversation with Mrs. Holmes about that paper?
A. No, sir.
Q. Or about the quarrel?
A. No, sir.

In re-direct examination Mrs. Reagan testified that she had told the story to a reporter of the Fall River *Globe*, Edwin H. Porter.

[Porter was to be the author of the *Fall River Tragedy*, a history of the Borden murders published privately shortly after the trial in 1893. In his book Porter naturally devotes considerable space to Mrs. Reagan's testimony, since he himself played a major rôle in its earlier dissemination to the press. Apropos Porter's book, it is said that, when published after the trial, virtually all copies were purchased and destroyed by Lizzie Borden. So far as I have been able to determine, only three copies now exist: one of these three being in my temporary custody at this writing.]

In his re-cross-examination of Mrs. Reagan, Jennings involved himself personally in the incident. He attempted to show that he, acting as Lizzie Borden's attorney, had drawn the document and that Mrs. Reagan was willing to sign it and admit the truth of its contents, but that her superior, Marshal Hilliard, had prevented her from doing so. The witness denied that she had any knowledge or memory of this.

THE MATTER OF POISON

The appearance on the stand of the next witness, Eli Bence, was to mark the end of the prosecution's case and also to precipitate the most controversial evidentiary question to arise in the course of the trial of Lizzie Borden.

In capsuled form, the prosecution was prepared to present substantial testimony from various witnesses to prove that on the afternoon of 3 August, the day before the murders, Lizzie Borden had attempted to purchase prussic acid, perhaps the deadliest of poisons, from two different drugstores. Since this highly volatile substance was sold by druggists only by prescription, she failed.

[The prosecution was of course offering this evidence—foreshadowed at the end of Dr. Wood's testimony—as being supportive of the fact that Lizzie Borden had had a pre-disposition to kill on the afternoon before the murders: in short, pre-determination. Ultimately the Court excluded all the evidence with regard to her prussic acid purchase. This was another great evidentiary victory for the defense, and another telling blow to the prosecution's case. This evidentiary ruling by the Court will be more fully discussed in a later chapter; in addition, I have prepared a brief on the question, as Appendix III.]

A *voir dire* was conducted. Translated loosely from the French, this means "to see what is to be said"—and that is exactly a definition of the legal practice the Court adopted here. Normally when conducting a voir dire, the Court hears arguments of counsel and the proposed testimony of the witnesses, all outside the presence of the jury; and, with the jury withdrawn, the Court makes a determination as to whether or not the evidence should be heard by the jury.

Eli Bence testified that he was by occupation a drug clerk, employed at D. R. Smith's drugstore in Fall River and that he had been in that business for thirteen or fourteen years.

At this stage of Bence's testimony, Robinson interrupted and asked the Court to have the jury withdrawn for the voir dire. Chief Justice Mason ordered that the jury retire.

Moody stated to the Court in the absence of the jury that he expected Bence to testify that on the third day of August Lizzie Borden came to the shop in which Bence and another man were employed and asked for ten cents worth of prussic acid, stating that she wished it for the purpose of cleaning a sealskin cape, but that she failed to procure the poison: Bence had informed her that he did not sell prussic acid unless by a physician's prescription. Lizzie then said that she had bought it several times, to which Bence replied, "Well, my good lady, it is something we don't sell unless by a prescription from a doctor, as it is a very dangerous thing to handle." Bence understood her to say that she wanted the acid to clean a sealskin cape.

As we shall see in due course, Robinson argued successfully against the admissibility of this testimony. It is enough to note at this time that the evidence was excluded, the jury was returned to the courtroom—and, surprisingly and summarily, District Attorney Knowlton rose and stated, "The Commonwealth rests its case, in chief."

TRIAL II:

The Defense

LIZZIE BORDEN did not take the witness stand in her own defense, nor did Robinson, Jennings and Adams, her battery of attorneys, offer anything which might be characterized fairly as an *affirmative* defense. Instead they relied upon two basic propositions: first, testimony to establish that Lizzie's background had been reputable and unimpeachable, that she had been engaged in religious and charitable enterprises in the past, and therefore was incapable of committing the crimes; and second, witnesses to contradict, if not the credibility, at least the accuracy of the prosecution's many witnesses.

Attorney Andrew Jennings made the short opening argument for the defense. Normally the purpose of the opening by defense counsel is to inform the jury what they could expect to hear specifically from defense witnesses in proof of innocence or in contradiction of guilt. Broad, sweeping statements to generate sympathy for the defendant, summaries of testimony, and statements of the law are reserved for closing arguments.

Jennings's opening remarks, however, departed from the norm.

He began with a personalized plea for the defendant, relating how he himself had known the family of Andrew Borden for many years, and telling of his high regard for them all, including Lizzie. He next spoke in maudlin fashion about Lizzie's relationship to her father; he dwelt at considerable length upon Lizzie's church and charitable activities, and on her domesticity.

Jennings then said, "The proof that the law requires is that Lizzie Andrew Borden did it, *and [that] there is absolutely no opportunity for anyone else to have done it.*"

[There is something distasteful—even unprofessional—about an attorney interjecting his own personal views of the character of the defendant in an address to the jury, since it casts him in a testifying rôle without the burden of a witness's oath and without being subjected to cross-examination.

More objectionable, however, is Jennings's assertion concerning required proof of sole opportunity. This was a blatant misstatement of the law of Massachusetts as it is and as it was in 1893, nor is it or was it the law in any of the United States; and so far as I know, it was never the law anywhere in the entire English-speaking world. Since Jennings was an able and experienced lawyer, it is difficult to attribute his statement to ignorance of the law.]

Concluding with vague allusions to strange persons seen in the neighborhood of the Borden house at various times—persons whom Jennings said "had not been located or identified," and whom he appeared to cite solely for the purpose of confusing the issue—he finished his twenty-eight minute opening and returned to the table where his associates sat. Robinson then rose and called his first witness.

TESTIMONY FOR THE DEFENSE

Miss Martha Chagnon testified that she was the daughter of Dr. Chagnon and lived with her parents on Third Street behind the Borden house.

At 11 P.M. on 3 August, the night before the murders, she had heard a noise which had disturbed her, and she had notified her mother: it was a pounding sound, "as though someone was pounding on wood." Although the noise had continued for four or five minutes, she had done nothing to investigate. The windows of her house were closed at the time.

When District Attorney Knowlton cross-examined the witness, the following colloquy took place:

Q. How could you tell the direction from which the sound came?

(*No answer*)

Q. Was it only that you thought the sound came from that way, the direction of the Borden house?

A. Yes, sir.

Q. And that was all there was to it?

A. Yes.

Knowlton further developed that Miss Chagnon previously had testified that the sound she heard came from an icehouse and sounded like the

Courtroom Drawing of Lizzie on Trial

FROM *LESLIE'S WEEKLY*

dumping of ice; the icehouse was in a different direction from the Borden premises. Also, she testified that her family had a large Newfoundland dog which was on the wooden piazza of the Chagnon house that night.

Mrs. Marienne Chagnon, mother of the previous witness, then testified that she also had heard the sound on the night before the murders. She was very much confused as to the direction from which the sound came, and she admitted that dogs in the neighborhood sometimes went into her wooden rubbish barrels, located at the rear of her house toward the Bordens'.

[How any of this lengthy testimony was in any way material to the issues before the jury is a mystery. In the first place, if the sounds were in fact heard, they were heard on the night of 3 August, and there was no question but all members at that time of the Borden household, if not happy and well, were alive on the following morning. Secondly, the direction from which the sounds came and the producing cause of the sounds were both subjects of complete speculation.

Unrelated as this testimony was to the fact of the murders, it did forecast the pattern which the defense attorneys were to adopt. The witnesses who followed were allowed to, and did, testify as to the appearances of vague and unidentified persons and to events that could not reasonably be in any way associated with the fact of the crimes. This appears to have been a "smokescreen" technique, designed by the defense only to confuse the issues and the jury.]

Mary A. Durfee testified that she had seen a man talking angrily to Andrew Borden on the steps of his house "before the previous Thanksgiving." The witness gave no indication as to who the man was, what the conversation was about; she stated only that Borden, standing on his steps, was seen talking to another person.

The following colloquy attempted to fix the time of the perfectly innocuous incident, which, it was alleged, took place nearly a full year before the murders.

Q. Won't you fix the time more perfectly?

A. Well, no, I cannot. It was before Thanksgiving, I know.

Q. Before the previous Thanksgiving?

A. Yes, I lost my sister, and I know it happened before my sister died, and she died the 27th of October, I believe. The 27th of October she died, and what I heard, I heard before then because I went home and told it.

Charles N. Gifford of Fall River next testified that on the day before the murders he had seen a man unknown to him sitting on the front steps of a house on Third Street outside the gate of the house—that is, on the street side of the fence. He was followed on the stand by Uriah Kirby, owner of the house, which was on the opposite side of Third Street from the Chagnons'. Kirby merely corroborated Gifford's story that a man unknown to him had been sitting on his steps outside his gate on the day before the murders. The unknown man and Kirby had had no conversation. Kirby said that the person appeared to be sleeping and, when he was shaken, his hat fell off to the ground, and Kirby entered his home, leaving the man sitting on the step.

Not less remote in materiality than this incident—which took place some distance from the Borden house on the day before the murders, on a different city street—was the substance of the testimony of the next witness, Mark P. Chase, who stated that he had seen a man seated in a buggy on Second Street on the day of the murders. The man was a stranger to Chase. The buggy was parked on Second Street north of the Borden house and considerably farther up the hill.

Understandably, Chief Justice Mason ruled that this evidence was incompetent. Nonetheless the jury had heard it.

Benjamin J. Handy, the next witness, testified that he had seen a pale, well-dressed young man walking slowly down Second Street on the morning of the murders between 10:20 and 10:40. Handy said that the young man's "eyes were on the sidewalk" as he walked. In cross-examination it was developed that this witness was a close friend of Lizzie Borden's, the owner of the summer cottage in Marion whose household Lizzie had announced an intention to visit.

Finally, Mrs. Delia S. Manley testified that she had seen a young man at 9:45 A.M. on 4 August standing on Second Street near the Borden house. She said that she merely noticed him but could not identify him, although he had stood in her clear view.

[Obviously the preceding testimony of this cluster of witnesses was designed to establish in some remote way the presence of vague, unidentified persons in the area. Equally obviously these vague, unidentified persons, some of whom were seen at times not at all material, could be seen on a busy city street, at any time, on any day. Clearly this accumulation of lengthy and pointless testimony could be considered useful to the defense only because it might distract the jury from more substantial evidence advanced against the defendant by the prosecution.]

Jerome C. Borden, a relative of Lizzie's, was the next defense witness. He lived on Fourth Street, a short distance from No. 92 Second Street. On the day after the murders he had visited the Borden house and had entered the front door without anyone opening it for him. There was, however, a police officer on duty at the time, standing at the door.

Recognizing the terribly damaging nature of the testimony of Officers Medley and Harrington that the barn-loft floor, when they had viewed it less than one-half hour before and after noon, respectively, on the day of the murders, was covered with completely undisturbed dust, and that therefore Lizzie's story of her visit to the loft was of necessity false, the defense attempted with the next two witnesses to contradict it.

A newspaper reporter for the Fall River *Daily News*, Walter P. Stevens, testified that he had gone to the Borden house with Officer Mullaly on the morning of 4 August soon after the murders were discovered, and had examined the premises, including the yard and the barn. He had found the cellar door at the rear of the house locked, and then he had gone to the barn, where, he said, he found the door open. He did not know if his visit to the barn was before or after Medley had gone to the loft.

Robinson tried to show that this witness had heard others upstairs in the barn at a time before Officer Medley had testified that he had gone into the loft. Stevens said that it was twelve o'clock when he was on the premises, but he had not seen Medley.

Then Alfred Clarkson, a steam engineer, took the stand and said that he had gone onto the Borden premises on the morning of the murders and had gone into the barn and up to the loft. He further said that there were other persons in the barn and that it was about 11:38 A.M. He had not seen Officer Medley.

In cross-examination by District Attorney Moody, Clarkson admitted that Officer Medley could have been there, but he had not seen him. Being pressed as to exact time, Clarkson admitted that he had previously testified that he arrived at the Borden premises at 11:40 A.M. and that the time of his visit to the barn was only his best estimate; he had not "looked at his watch."

The next witness spoke English with a foreign accent. He was Hyman Lubinsky, an ice-cream peddler who sold his wares from a horse-drawn cart. Lubinsky stabled his horses on upper Second Street at Gardner's livery, which was at the far end of Second Street from the Borden house.

Q. (*by Robinson*) Did you go by the Borden house the morning of August 4th in your team?

A. Yes, sir. I left Gardner's stable a few minutes after eleven and drove
   down Second Street toward the Borden house.

Q. When you got to the Borden house, did you see anybody?

A. I saw a lady come out the way from the barn right to the stairs at the
   back of the house. She wore a dark dress, had nothing on her head,
   and she was walking slowly. I have seen the servant girl there before,
   and this woman was not the servant.

In cross-examination Lubinsky stated that he had fed his horses at 11:30
that day and had peddled ice cream for two and one-half hours before
feeding. When he saw the woman he spoke of, his horses were trotting
downhill past the Borden house. The woman was only two or three feet
from the steps leading to the side, or kitchen, entrance, as he observed her
while passing on Second Street. Lubinsky testified that he had sought out
Officer Mullaly and told him the story two days after the murders.

Although District Attorney Knowlton pressed the witness hard on the
issue of the exact time of his observation of the woman in the barn,
Lubinsky insisted it was shortly after 11:00 A.M. Later the witness said that
he had told his story to Arthur S. Philipps, the assistant who had
conducted early investigations for Attorney Jennings, but that he had not
been called upon to testify at any of the preliminary hearings.

Charles E. Gardner, who operated the stable on Second Street where
Lubinsky's horses were kept, was next called to the stand. Gardner stated
that on 4 August Lubinsky left his stable between five and ten minutes
past eleven o'clock. He fixed the time because on that day Lubinsky had to
wait for his horses since they were being fed.

Knowlton conducted a very effective cross-examination of this witness.
He adduced that Gardner himself had passed the Borden house in his own
team fifteen minutes after Lubinsky had left his stable. When Gardner
passed No. 92 Second Street, he said he observed no activity. Thus if
Gardner's testimony as to times was accurate, he himself passed the
Borden house after 11:30, when there was a great deal of activity there.
Clearly this witness's corroboration of Lubinsky's testimony as to time was
badly shaken by Knowlton's cross-examination.

Charles Newhall of Worcester, a "drummer," or traveling salesman,
who had accompanied Gardner on his trip down Second Street in the late
morning of 4 August after Lubinsky had left Gardner's stable, did not help
much in fixing the exact times. When asked what time he and Gardner
had left the Second Street stable, Newhall replied that he did not know
exactly. District Attorney Knowlton did not cross-examine the witness
Newhall.

[It seems clear that the defense thought that Lubinsky's testimony, if believed, was very helpful: it placed a woman coming from the barn to the Borden house at just about the time when Lizzie said she had. Nonetheless, District Attorney Knowlton demonstrated a great display of confidence by not cross-examining Newhall. It is well to emphasize here that Lubinsky had stated that he had, two days after the murders, recorded his full story with Officer Mullaly of the Fall River police, and, as we shall see in the discussion of rebuttal testimony, he had also related it to Philipps, Jennings's assistant.]

The next two witnesses called by the defense were young men. The purpose in presenting them to the jury was to show that they had been in the barn loft before Officers Medley and Harrington had had an opportunity to view what was described as the dust-covered floor, and thus to detract from the effectiveness of the police officers' testimony.

Everett Brown of Third Street, Fall River, said that he, with a friend named Thomas Barlow, arrived at the Borden house when a man, Charles Sawyer, was on guard at the door. The boys went into the barn and dared one another to go up into the loft, where Brown said they remained for five minutes. They descended and then were put out of the yard by police officers. When Brown was asked about the time of his visit to the barn, he responded that he knew nothing about the time at all; he simply could not say what time it was. He also said, "I might have seen Officer Medley, or I might not. I wasn't taking notice of who I saw there."

Thomas Barlow, Brown's friend, was a Fall River youth who worked in a poolroom stacking up pool balls. He said, "Me and Brownie went in the side gate, went to the barn and up to the hayloft. It was cooler in the barn than outside. People were there trying to look in the windows. The police officers put us out of the yard."

Barlow was very confused as to the time of the visit to the barn loft, and in cross-examination he changed his story with regard to the temperature in the barn. Among other things, he testified that he and his friend "had been fooling around" or playing in the streets, pushing one another off of the sidewalk, so that it required fifteen minutes for them to travel three short blocks. When he and Brown had reached the barn, Barlow said that he had unpinned the lock and entered "to see if anyone was in there."

Q. Did you think the man you were seeking had fastened himself in the barn from outside?

A. Well, no.

[Neither boy could fix the time of their loft visit, if indeed there had been a visit, with any degree of accuracy; from the tenor of their testimony they could hardly be characterized as reliable witnesses.

The testimony which followed theirs presented a problem of relevance and materiality which on its face appears to be quite simple, but certainly the Court did not treat it so.]

The next witness, Joseph Lemay, required an interpreter because he spoke only French. Former Governor Robinson proposed to prove, through Lemay, that on the 16th day of August—twelve days after the murders—the witness Lemay saw on his farm, located four miles from the city of Fall River, a strange-appearing person. This stranger had a hatchet in his hand and spoke to Lemay. Lemay understood him to have said, "Poor Mr. Borden." Then the man leaped over a stone wall on Lemay's farm and ran away.

District Attorney Moody argued to the Court that the event which Lemay related occurred nearly two weeks after the murders and about four miles from Fall River at a time when every crank in the Fall River area was brooding and talking about the crimes. Moody argued: "To admit this wild and imaginative story could accomplish nothing but confusion to the jury. This and other stories had all been investigated and found to be the result of disordered minds and imagination—to admit this evidence would be to obstruct justice, for it has no bearing whatsoever upon the case of Lizzie Andrew Borden."

The session adjourned early to allow for discussion and deliberation concerning the admissibility of this evidence, with Chief Justice Mason indicating that the Court would render its decision the following day.

On the eleventh day of the trial the Court began by announcing that the testimony of Joseph Lemay would be excluded.

Immediately thereafter Governor Robinson called to the stand Sarah B. Hart of Tiverton, Rhode Island, who testified that she was with her sister, Mrs. Manley—who had already testified for the defense—when they saw a young man leaning on the fence between the Borden and Churchill houses on Second Street on 4 August, sometime before 10:00 A.M.

Charles S. Sawyer was the next defense witness. He was a house painter, and a reading of the transcript of his testimony compels the conclusion that he was a dull-witted house painter. He had been immediately across Second Street when Officer Allen ran from the Borden house to return to the station immediately after verifying the murders. Allen had called upon Sawyer to stand guard at the door of the Borden house until he returned. Because he was never relieved, Sawyer remained at his post until after 6:00 P.M. that night.

Although he had been in an extremely advantageous position to make observations, his testimony certainly did not reflect this. He had seen Lizzie Borden once, shortly after he took his position guarding the door, and he remembered that Miss Russell and Mrs. Churchill were fanning her; he said that he noticed nothing unusual about Miss Borden and could not remember anything about the clothing which she was wearing at this time. He also was unsure of the order in which the various police officers arrived at the scene. When asked about the boys, Brown and Barlow, being in the yard, he responded that there were "lots of boys in the yard" and many people around. He did remember seeing the witness Arthur Clarkson in and about the premises, but he did not recall at what time he saw him.

[The only conceivable purpose for placing Sawyer upon the witness stand was to support Clarkson's testimony that he had been on the Borden premises soon after the murders; otherwise Sawyer's testimony was of no value—either to the defense or to the prosecution.

However, testimony from the next series of witnesses patently was expected to counteract part of the prosecution's claim of consciousness of guilt displayed by Lizzie after the murders, and was mainly concerned with accounts of the quarrel between Lizzie and Emma Borden—testified to by police matron Hannah Reagan near the close of the prosecution's case, in chief—which allegedly occurred on 24 August 1892 while the defendant was being held for her preliminary hearing.]

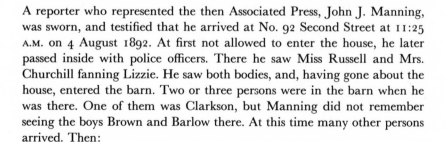

A reporter who represented the then Associated Press, John J. Manning, was sworn, and testified that he arrived at No. 92 Second Street at 11:25 A.M. on 4 August 1892. At first not allowed to enter the house, he later passed inside with police officers. There he saw Miss Russell and Mrs. Churchill fanning Lizzie. He saw both bodies, and, having gone about the house, entered the barn. Two or three persons were in the barn when he was there. One of them was Clarkson, but Manning did not remember seeing the boys Brown and Barlow there. At this time many other persons arrived. Then:

Q. Do you recall the publication of a story told by Mrs. Reagan about a quarrel between Lizzie Borden and her sister Emma?

A. Yes, it was published in the Boston *Globe*. That night, however, I talked to Mrs. Reagan, and she said, "There was nothing in it." I asked her if the story was true, and she said again, "There was nothing in it."

In cross-examination by District Attorney Knowlton the witness Manning admitted that Mrs. Reagan might have said, "What I have to say about the quarrel, I will say on the witness stand."

Thomas F. Hickey, a reporter for the Boston *Herald*, next testified that he had been sent by his editor to interview Mrs. Reagan in her room.

Q. What did you do?

A. I remember going into Mrs. Reagan's room and making a remark something like this: "I see you are getting yourself into the paper, Mrs. Reagan." She laughed and said, "Yes, but they have got to take that all back." After some other questions which I have forgotten now, I asked her again about the alleged quarrel between Lizzie and Emma Borden. Mrs. Reagan said to me, "There is no truth at all in the story that was printed."

District Attorney Knowlton conducted an interesting cross-examination.

Q. (*by Knowlton*) You represented the Boston *Herald?*

A. Yes, sir.

Q. And whatever was published was [also] published in the Boston *Globe?*

A. Yes, sir.

Q. And the Boston *Globe* and the Boston *Herald* are papers of considerable prominence in the city of Boston?

A. Yes, sir.

Q. And in one sense they are sort of rivals, is not that so, Mr. Hickey?

A. Yes, sir.

Q. The Boston *Globe* and Boston *Herald* are pretty active competitors, aren't they?

A. Yes, sir.

Q. And when one gets an item of news that the other doesn't, that is considered what they call a "scoop" in journalism, isn't it?

A. Yes, sir.

Q. And in this particular instance the Boston *Globe* got what they call a scoop on your men?

A. Yes, sir.

Q. And of course your object was to show that the scoop was good for nothing, wasn't it?

James E. Winwood, Fall River undertaker, then was sworn, and was asked by Jennings if in preparing Andrew Borden's body for burial he had observed a ring upon Borden's finger; the undertaker stated that he did not remember.

[This inconclusive testimony had been intended to show—as Emma Borden would recount on the stand later—that her father always wore a ring that Lizzie had given him a number of years before his death. Although this ring had no bearing whatsoever on the issue, it would be invoked by Robinson in his closing argument.]

Mrs. Marianna Holmes next took the witness stand, testifying:

"I have known Lizzie Borden since her childhood. She went to school with my daughters. She attends the Central Congregational Church and is active in the various church enterprises. She is a member of the Christian Endeavor Society. And she is a member of the Board at the Hospital of the Good Samaritan. I also knew her stepmother, and I have seen Miss Lizzie and her stepmother at church together.

"I arrived at the Borden house on August 4th at one o'clock and went to Miss Lizzie's room. I was in the room when the officers knocked upon the door, and Miss Lizzie said, "Open the door." When the officers asked questions, Lizzie said, "Please be brief, for I am very weary." She told the officers that she had been in the barn for something to fasten the screens. I cannot tell you whether she said "a piece of iron," or "a piece of tin," or "something." I heard her say all those things to different people.

"When the officers asked to search her room, Lizzie said, "Search," and made no objection whatever."

Q. Mrs. Holmes, do you remember the publication of a story about a quarrel between Lizzie and her sister, Emma Borden?

A. I do.

Q. Did you later speak to Mrs. Reagan?

A. Yes. Mrs. Reagan said, "No, Mrs. Holmes, it isn't so, for that was the afternoon that we were talking about the egg."

Q. Do you remember a time when there was talk about Mrs. Reagan signing a paper?

A. Yes, but the conversation was not to me.

Charles J. Holmes, husband of the previous witness, next testified that he knew something about the paper which was prepared for Mrs. Reagan to sign. He knew the substance of the document, which was, in effect, that the statement attributed to Mrs. Reagan in the press was not true, and that the argument alleged to have taken place between Lizzie and her sister Emma in the matron's room did not happen at all. Holmes testified that the Reverend Mr. Buck read this written statement to Mrs. Reagan and asked her to sign the statement. Mrs. Reagan took the statement downstairs to Marshal Hilliard's office, and Holmes said that he had heard parts of an altercation after the refusal of Marshal Hilliard to have the paper signed by Mrs. Reagan. Holmes stated that Mrs. Reagan had said nothing on this occasion. Holmes further testified that a shouting altercation involved a news reporter whose name was Edwin H. Porter. He described Porter as a man with only one eye (Porter, as noted earlier, was a reporter for the Fall River *Globe*, and used his articles as the basis for a book about the murders, published after the trial).

Holmes said that after the Reverend Mr. Buck had read the affidavit to Mrs. Reagan, she said that the contents of the affidavit were true.

Q. The affidavit was trying to get a denial of something that was published in a newspaper?

A. It was to prove no such statement had been made by Mrs. Reagan.

Q. Did Mrs. Reagan sign the affidavit?

A. She did not.

Q. And never has signed it, as far as you know?

A. No, not as far as I know.

John R. Caldwell, a reporter, then testified that he had seen Mrs. Reagan take the affidavit, which the Reverend Mr. Buck had given her and go down into Marshal Hilliard's office. Marshal Hilliard said to Mrs. Reagan, "If you sign that paper, it will be against my express orders." Then Marshal Hilliard ordered Caldwell out of his office.

In cross-examination Caldwell was asked if he heard Marshal Hilliard tell Mrs. Reagan that whatever she would say about the quarrel, she would say in court. The witness said he did not recall that.

Mary E. Brigham, a lifelong acquaintance of Lizzie Borden, was the next witness. Miss Brigham testified that she saw the Reverend Mr. Buck give Mrs. Reagan the affidavit, and Mrs. Reagan left for the Marshal's office. Later Mrs. Reagan returned to the matron's room where Miss Brigham was seated, and Miss Brigham testified:

"She acted mad. She sat down in the rocking chair near me and said to me, "It is all a lie from beginning to end. I was willing to sign that paper, but the Marshal wouldn't let me do it. He told me to go to my room and obey orders." "

EMMA BORDEN'S TESTIMONY

In the afternoon session of its eleventh day the trial of Lizzie Borden took a dramatic turn, for it was then that the defense attorneys called to the stand their most effective witness, whom they had contrived to save for the end. Whether or not she had been carefully coached, rehearsed or otherwise prepared, we shall never know, but the most telling blow the defense struck was the direct examination of the shy, diffident Emma Borden, Lizzie's sister, who became a veritable lion on the witness stand.

By an even stranger stroke of fate District Attorney Knowlton, who before the trial had been a reluctant prosecutor and who up to this point was allowing his associate, District Attorney Moody, to handle much of the trial itself, now, in his examination of Emma, became a tenacious, almost vicious, cross-examiner. He was persistent; his questions were incisive. Time and again he elicited from Emma Borden answers which flew in the face of the weight of the evidence.

Following is Emma's testimony:

"My name is Emma L. Borden, sister of Lizzie A. Borden. We have lived for twenty-one years at 92 Second Street with my father and stepmother."

Here counsel interrupted to indicate that there was an agreement as to Lizzie Borden's financial worth: a checking account of $2,190, a savings account of $641, and shares of stock in the Fall River National Bank and in the Merchant's Manufacturing Company. Emma then continued:

"My father, for ten or fifteen years, wore a ring upon his finger, given to him by my sister Lizzie. He wore it when he died and when he was buried.

"I have an inventory of the dresses belonging to Lizzie and myself as of August 4th, 1892; there were eighteen in all: ten of them were blue dresses; eight blue dresses belonged to Lizzie.

"I was told that the Saturday, August 6th, search of our home had been extremely thorough, and every box and bag had been examined. At times my sister and myself rendered assistance to the officers making the search that day, and we never made the slightest objection to the proceedings.

"My sister had a Bedford cord dress, light blue with a darker figure in it, which was made by Mrs. Raymond the dressmaker in the first week of May. It was a very inexpensive dress with a ruffle around the bottom, and it was very long so that it sometimes trailed the floor.

"At the time the dress was made, the painters were painting the house, and as a result, Lizzie, when wearing it shortly after it was made, stained it with paint. There were paint marks along the front, and on one side toward the bottom, and on the wrong side of the skirt.

"On Saturday, the day of the search, I saw it hanging in the clothes press near the front entry. I went in to hang a dress; there was no vacant nail, and I noticed this dress of Lizzie's. Later I said to my sister, "Lizzie, you have not destroyed that old dress yet. Why don't you?"

"When I said that to Lizzie, the dress was very dirty, very much soiled and faded. I don't remember seeing her wear it for several weeks before I went away [on the visit to Fairhaven during which the murders occurred]. The dress could not possibly be used for anything else; it was not only soiled but badly faded. It was a shade that in washing would be completely ruined—the effect of it. It was so long it dragged on the floor and quickly soiled because it was very light. It was an inch and a half longer than Lizzie's pink wrapper. The sleeves were so full that she couldn't get anything on over it. She couldn't have had it on under the pink wrapper when she was lying on her couch on August 4th.

"I next saw the Bedford cord dress Sunday morning, August 7th, after breakfast at about nine o'clock. I was washing dishes, and I heard Lizzie's voice. I turned around and saw she was standing at the kitchen stove; the dress was hanging on her arm, and she said, "I think I shall burn this old dress up."

"I said to her, "Why don't you?" or "You had better" or something like that. I can't tell the exact words, but it meant, "Do it," and then I turned back to washing dishes and didn't pay any more attention to her at that time."

Q. Were the officers all about at that time?
A. They were all about the yard.
Q. Was Miss Russell there?
A. Yes.

"After the burning of the dress [Emma continued], Miss Russell said nothing about it on Sunday morning.

"On Monday, however, Miss Russell came to us and said Mr. Hanscom, the detective, had asked her if all the dresses were there that were there on the day of the tragedy, and she told him "Yes"—"And of course," she said, "it is a falsehood." No, I am ahead of my story! She came and said she told Mr. Hanscom a falsehood, and I asked her what there was to tell a falsehood about, and she said Mr. Hanscom had asked if all the dresses were there that were there the day of the tragedy, and she told him "Yes." The carriage was waiting for her to go on some errand, and when she came back, we had some conversation and it was decided to have her go and tell Mr. Hanscom that she had told him a falsehood, and tell him we told her to do so. She went into the parlor, and in a few minutes she came back and said she had told him. That is all I can recall."

Q. Now at the time when Miss Russell said, "It was the worst thing that could be done . . ."

A. (*interrupting*) Oh, yes, sir, that Monday morning, when she came into the dining room, we asked why she told a falsehood, and she said, "The burning of the dress was the worst thing that Lizzie could have done," and my sister said to her, "Why didn't you tell me? Why did you let me do it!"

If Emma had been coached before narrating her long exposition concerning the dress-burning, she almost forgot to tell the last part of the story, but Jennings had come to her rescue with his reminding question.

Then, turning to the sisters' quarrel at the matron's room in the jail, Jennings led Emma through all the details of Mrs. Reagan's story. The witness denied everything. She stated that no quarrel or harsh words had ever passed between the sisters and that Mrs. Reagan's story was a complete and utter lie, manufactured from whole cloth.

With this, District Attorney Knowlton began his cross-examination. He first pointed out that Emma had been at Fairhaven for two weeks visiting the Brownells at a house owned by one Delano and that Lizzie had visited there one day after being in New Bedford.

Q. Did your stepmother have relatives in Fall River?

A. Yes, sir, a half-sister, Mrs. Whitehead, on Fourth Street [the mother of Mrs. Potter, with whom the writer visited Fall River in 1972].

Q. Did she own the whole house she lived in?

A. No.

Q. Who owned the rest of it?

A. My stepmother. My father bought it and gave it to her five or six years ago. He paid $1,500.

Q. Did that make trouble within the family?

A. Yes.

Q. Between whom?

A. Between my father and Mrs. Borden and my sister and I.

Q. Did it make trouble between your sister Lizzie and your stepmother?

A. Yes, Lizzie found fault with it.

Q. Did your father after the fault-finding give you both some money?

A. Yes, Grandfather's house on Ferry Street.

Q. Were the relationships between your sister and stepmother the same thereafter?

A. I think so.

Q. Have you ever said differently?

A. I think not.

Q. Wasn't it at this time that Lizzie ceased calling Mrs. Borden "Mother"?

A. I don't remember.

Q. Did you say that the relationship between Lizzie and your stepmother was not cordial thereafter?

A. I don't think I have.

Q. You testified at the inquest, didn't you?

A. Yes.

Q. Do you remember when I asked you then if the relations between your sister and Mrs. Borden were cordial?

A. I do not remember.

Q. Didn't you answer at the inquest, "I don't know how to answer that; we always spoke"? Do you remember that answer?

A. I do now.

Q. I said, "That might be or might not be cordial," and you answered, "Well, perhaps I should say no, then."

A. I don't remember.

Q. Do you remember your answer to my question, "Do you mean the relationship between your sister and Mrs. Borden was cordial," and your answer was "No"?

A. I don't remember.

Q. Did you say, "We felt that she was not interested in us, and at one time father gave her some property; that was the cause of lack of cordiality"? Do you remember saying that?

A. No.

Q. Do you remember me asking you if the giving of the property to you healed the breach, and you answered, "No"?

A. I don't remember.

Q. Do you know of anyone who was on terms of ill will with your stepmother?

A. No.

Q. Any enemies she had?

A. No.

Knowlton then adduced the fact that Lizzie had taken from Emma the large second-floor bedroom, and Emma occupied the smaller room, and that this had occurred several years before.

Next he pursued the issue of the missing and mysterious note:

Q. Have you ever caused a search for the note Mrs. Borden was supposed to have received?

A. I only looked in a little bag she carried sometimes, and we put an advertisement in the newspaper for several days asking for information from the sender or the messenger, with no response.

[This was a tactical blunder by Emma, for other testimony indicated that Lizzie had early announced the note was burned: if Lizzie was telling the truth, why insert an advertisement in the newspapers for several days?]

Knowlton also drew from Emma that she and Lizzie had, immediately after the murders, hired Oscar W. Hanscom, the Pinkerton detective. The folly of doing this was soon apparent to either the Borden sisters or their attorneys, for Hanscom disappeared from the scene a short time after he was employed. Emma, in her testimony in cross-examination, minimized Detective Hanscom's rôle.

The story told by Mrs. Reagan of the argument was vehemently denied again in cross-examination, but Knowlton persisted:

Q. There was nothing then that sounds like anything you said that Mrs. Reagan told?

A. Nothing whatever!

Q. There was no sitting silent for any length of time that morning?

A. I can't remember; I don't know. I was there; that is all.

Now turning to the dress-burning incident, Knowlton carefully first drew from Emma indications of present hostility toward Miss Russell.

Q. Miss Russell was an intimate friend of Lizzie's, was she not?

A. No, sir.

Q. Did she see her often?

A. Yes.

Q. On excellent terms?

A. On good terms.

Q. Associated in church work together?

A. No.

Q. Miss Russell stayed at your house Thursday, Friday and Saturday nights?

A. Yes.

Q. Sunday night?

A. I don't know; I think she did, but I am not sure.

Q. When Lizzie was to burn the dress [on Sunday morning] did you hear Miss Russell testify that she first said, "Lizzie, what are you going to do?"

A. I think she did so state, but I don't remember it so.

Q. Did you say, as Miss Russell said you did, "What are you going to do with that dress, Lizzie?"

A. I don't remember saying it.

Q. Is the reason you didn't say so because you had spoken to Lizzie about it the previous night?

A. The reason I didn't say so is because I didn't say so!

Q. You swear you didn't say so?

A. I swear I didn't say it.

Q. Didn't you just tell me you didn't remember saying it?

A. Yes.

Q. Did Lizzie wear the dress after the paint was on it?

A. Yes, until it got soiled and faded.

Q. Did you hear Miss Russell say, "Lizzie, I wouldn't let anyone see me do that?"

A. I did not.

Q. You mean it was not said?

A. I don't say it was not said; I say I didn't hear it.

Emma stepped down from the witness stand.

[District Attorney Knowlton's incisive questioning had cast a new and different light on Emma's direct testimony. He had shown it to be replete with improbabilities, one of the most notable being that the dress—made in May, according to Emma, and stained by paint a few days after it was made, so that it was worn only in the mornings—had become faded by early August. At the conclusion of her testimony it is clear to the professional in the law that she had been too carefully coached.]

Mrs. Mary A. Raymond was then called by Robinson. She stated that in May she had made the Bedford cord dress in question. The house was being painted at the time. The dress was light blue with a dark figure, long, and trimmed with a ruffle. The dressmaker testified that while she was at the Borden house Lizzie did get some paint on the dress at the bottom ruffle.

Mrs. Phoebe B. M. Bowen, wife of Dr. Bowen, next testified that on 4 August she had gone to the Borden house and observed Miss Russell and Mrs. Churchill ministering to Lizzie. Mrs. Bowen stated that at the time Lizzie wore a dress of dark material with a white design in it. She had seen Lizzie's hands and they were white and clean; there was no blood on them.

In cross-examination Knowlton asked if Lizzie's hands were clean. The witness answered Yes and was then asked if they gave the appearance of Lizzie's having handled objects in a dusty barn loft; they did not.

There was some confusion as to Mrs. Bowen's description of the dress Lizzie wore: it emerged that in previous testimony Mrs. Bowen had given a different description of Lizzie's dress as being of blue material with a light sprig in it.

The defense then rested its case. Moody addressed the Court, saying that the end of the defense had come unexpectedly to him, and he wished to arrange for a few rebuttal witnesses. The Court recessed for one hour to accommodate him.

In rebuttal the prosecution first recalled Marshal Rufus Hilliard to state what occurred when Mrs. Reagan came to him with the affidavit given her by the Reverend Mr. Buck. Buck had asked Mrs. Reagan to sign the affidavit condemning as a lie the publication of her statements about the Borden sisters' quarrel.

Marshal Hilliard testified:

"Reverend Buck and Mrs. Reagan came into my office. Mr. Buck handed me a paper and said Mrs. Reagan would sign it if I said so. I read the paper and said, "Mrs. Reagan, if you sign that paper, you do it in direct violation of my orders. If you have anything to say about this, you will say it on the witness stand in court." I told her to go to her room and attend to her duty.**"**

With its next rebuttal witness the prosecution sought to destroy the weight of the testimony by Hyman Lubinsky, by pointing out its inaccuracy as to time. Officer Mullaly was called to testify that he knew Hyman Lubinsky and that on 8 August Lubinsky had come to him and told him he had been coming down Second Street on 4 August, the day of the murders, and, passing the Borden house, he had seen a woman near the barn and the house. Mullaly wrote Lubinsky's story down as Lubinsky told it on 8 August. Lubinsky said at that time that when he saw the woman it was exactly 10:30 A.M., and Mullaly had so written the fact down and reported it to his superiors on 8 August.

[Mullaly's short rebuttal testimony seemed to nullify the proposition advanced by the defense through Lubinsky: that Lizzie was in the barn after 11:00 A.M. when she said she was. In this connection it should be noted that Andrew Borden had not returned home until about 10:40 A.M.]

Annie M. White, the stenographer at the preliminary inquest, was called to read one statement made at the inquest by Alfred Clarkson, who had testified for the defense concerning his early arrival at the Borden house, and seeing persons in the barn shortly after his arrival and thus before Officer Medley's inspection of the barn and loft.

The contradictory testimony which Clarkson had been given at the inquest was read:

Q. (*to Clarkson*) At what time did you arrive at the Borden house the morning of the murders?

A. 11:40 A.M.

[This in all likelihood would place Clarkson at the barn after Officer Medley had come, viewed the dust-covered floor of the loft and gone. Annie White's evidence, from her inquest notes, was admissible as a prior contradictory statement made by the witness previous to the trial and inconsistent with his trial testimony.]

Both sides now rested; the evidence was complete. Chief Justice Mason cautioned the jury to keep their minds open until after the arguments and the charge had been heard and until they had reached the jury room for their deliberations.

He then re-swore the court officers to take charge of the jury and adjourned the court until Monday, 19 June, for arguments of counsel.

Arguments, Charge and Verdict

W HATEVER George D. Robinson lacked in professional artistry as a trial lawyer, it was more than compensated for by his showmanship. His final argument to the jury was lengthy, perhaps necessarily disjointed, imaginative, illogical, laced with histrionics with a dash of deception. Nonetheless it was a dramatic performance. He cast himself in the rôle of the country lawyer confiding in twelve true-blue, country-bred Americans, confiding in them with regard to the noble causes of patriotism, God, motherhood, the protection of womanhood—especially from the hangman's noose—the sanctity of the home, and, incidentally, the acquittal of Lizzie Borden: all causes to be cherished and admired, all causes which sophisticated city folks did not, simply could not, understand. In effect, he established a close rapport with the jury by using the tools of rhetoric, poetry, bombast, threats, pleas, and a gross distortion of such damaging evidence as that concerning the elusive note from a sick friend. The facts proven were handled by Robinson loosely, but his grip on the country jury was tight.

He began by saluting the jury as men: "men of Bristol County, with hearts, with souls, men with rights who came from homes, firesides, wives and daughters, men who recognize the bonds that unite"; men of patriotism, "some of you have worn the blue, faced the cannon shot, heard the thunder of war, seen blood flow in streams"; good, wholesome country men, like himself, who, when they fished, used sinkers as Lizzie suggested she did, and as Robinson himself did—"that's the way we bob around for fish up in the country"; men of God, religious men who would understand that "just as the little sparrow does not fall unnoticed to the ground, so Lizzie Borden is shielded by His Providence from above."

To such men as these jurors, said Robinson, "it would be morally and physically impossible" for Lizzie Borden to have committed these crimes, and it was inconceivable that they could think otherwise, for this was a jury of true men whom Robinson did not have to remind—but he would anyway—that:

> . . . *to thine own self be true*
> *And it must follow, as the night the day,*
> *Thou canst not then be false to any man.*

It is important to note here that throughout his long address Robinson stressed the choice open to the jury: *sentence Lizzie Borden to death—a sentence beyond recall—or set her free.*

Then Robinson denounced the entire Fall River police force for what he characterized as discourteous conduct in questioning Lizzie on the day of the murder, his particular target being Deputy Marshal Fleet for "plying the grieving woman with questions shortly after her great bereavement."

[This typifies the subtle absurdities which marked Robinson's argument. What other course could the police pursue after the discovery of a double murder but to question immediately the only person who appeared to have any knowledge of the crimes—who had, in fact, discovered one of them, and prompted discovery of the second?]

He naturally stressed the absence of blood from Lizzie's person and clothing immediately after the murders were discovered, but he carefully avoided mentioning the testimony of the three distinguished medical experts—whose testimony had not been challenged at the time by defense counsel—that the amount and direction of spattering were sheer conjecture. He explained away the single blood spot on the petticoat with a hearty, knowing, man-to-man allusion to the delicate subject which he called "monthly illness."

Lizzie's statement to Marshal Fleet that "she is *not* my mother, she is my stepmother," provoked a discourse from Robinson concerning the glories of motherhood, ending with, "There never goes out of the heart the feeling for the dead mother who is gone."

He stressed the importance of Lubinsky's testimony, declaring, "Lizzie's life was possibly saved by a passer-by, a humble ice cream peddler, Hyman Lubinsky."

[Here it should be remarked that it appears that at one time the defense had apparently discounted Lubinsky's value as a witness: Lubinsky had told his story to Philipps, Jennings's assistant, well before the probable-cause hearing was held by Judge Blaisdell, and Lubinsky did not testify for the defense at that preliminary proceeding.]

As to Lizzie's visit to the barn when her father was murdered, Robinson added something new, something never heard at the trial from any witness—or, for that matter, even suggested. Instead of spending the five or ten minutes she was supposed to have spent in the excrutiatingly hot barn loft munching a few pears, Lizzie, said Robinson, might have spent them in the shade of a pear tree in the yard; "she was entitled to a moment of leisure," added Robinson.

[This not only was a distortion of the evidence before the jury: it was sheer invention of evidence not presented before the jury at all.]

As to Emma's testimony with regard to the dress-burning incident— which was so badly shaken in cross-examination and which was so obviously rehearsed—Robinson airily dismissed it with, "I will not apologize for Emma. It is creditable that she stands by her sister."

On and on Robinson spoke, not arguing the facts by meeting them head-on, but by alluding to them and throwing dust in the jurors' eyes. For example, he referred thus to the handleless hatchet, which the medical experts had stated fitted accurately into all the wounds on the skulls of both Mr. and Mrs. Borden: "This is an Underhill hatchet," said Robinson, "made by the Underhill Manufacturing Company; thousands of these were made and sold—you and I remember them as boys."

But it was the issue of the existence of the note that Mrs. Borden was supposed to have received from a sick friend, which Robinson distorted purposefully and wholly. This was an extremely important issue, for the case against Lizzie Borden could stand or fall on this point. Said Robinson: "Bridget told Mrs. Churchill, 'Mrs. Borden had a note to go and see someone who was sick as she was dusting the sitting room, and she hurried off'; and Bridget said, 'she didn't tell me where she was going; she generally does.'" Now this, said Robinson, is what Bridget told Mrs. Churchill. Therefore he argued that both Lizzie *and* Bridget had learned from Mrs. Borden that she had a note. "Mrs. Borden had told Lizzie. Mrs. Borden had told Bridget. Mrs. Borden had given Bridget the work to do washing windows; she said to Bridget, 'I have got a note to go out and see someone who is sick.' That was when she [Mrs. Borden] was dusting in the sitting room.

"You *must* find [italics here and hereafter supplied]," said Robinson, "that Mrs. Borden had a note and told both Lizzie and Bridget about it.

"Where is the note?" Robinson asked; "we would be glad to see it."
Explaining the lack of response to the concentrated search for the note, or
for its sender, or for its carrier, and including the newspaper advertise-
ments, Robinson said, "Why, you will find men in this county who don't
know this trial is going on." Then he added that sometimes people do not
want to become involved, "especially women—they have a dread of such
things. The note may have been part of the assassin's scheme, we don't
know. But that a note arrived there, *you can not question!*"

[Even a casual reading of the testimony indicates that the story of the note
was first told to Mr. Borden by Lizzie, then told to Bridget by Lizzie, and
later parroted by Bridget to Mrs. Churchill. Mrs. Churchill had made this
clear in her re-direct examination by Moody. From the testimony, there
could be no doubt that the note was an invention of Lizzie Borden's and
hers alone.]

Robinson, after reminding the jury that

> *The eyes that can not weep*
> *are the saddest eyes of all*

and that Andrew Borden had gone to his grave wearing on his hand the
symbol of "the pledge of faith and love, the ring which belonged to his
little girl [Lizzie]," he pointed at the jury and pointed to the defendant,
then shouted: "To find her guilty, you must believe her to be a fiend! Does
she look it?"

Robinson sank into his seat exhausted; for hours he had played his rôle,
for which his years of political speeches had served him well—he had
played upon the minds of the jurors as he would upon twelve delicate
instruments. He was sentimental, maudlin, confident, suitably clumsy in
speech, even humorous at times when he compared "city hotel fare" with
"good old country cooking"; he was a country lawyer that day, someone
whom the jury could trust and believe. And they did. Perhaps Charles
Macklin, that contentious actor, was right: theatricals and the trial of law
cases, he said, were kindred arts.

ARGUMENT FOR THE PROSECUTION

By contrast to the effective, shrewd, sleight-of-hand argument delivered by
Robinson, the closing arguments for the Commonwealth, delivered by
District Attorney Hosea Knowlton, were short, at times apologetic, and,
taken altogether, completely failed to sum up effectively the strong case
which Moody had outlined in his opening, and which the prosecution had

proven against Lizzie Andrew Borden.

He began with a lengthy tribute to the defendant as "a Christian woman, with the rank of lady, the equal of your wife and mine, a woman we believed incapable of such a crime. I do not underestimate," said Knowlton, "the strength of good Christian character. . . . The prisoner is a woman, one of a sex all high-minded men revere, all generous men love."

[The reader of the beginning of Knowlton's argument would be hard put to determine which side he represented. Such statements as these quoted above from Knowlton's argument go far beyond being fair to the defendant. Coming as they did from the prosecutor, they were unfair to the people of the Commonwealth.]

This is not to say that the tenor of Knowlton's closing argument was consistently defense-oriented. It was not; but it was half-hearted at best, at times manifesting futility. For example, there appears this surprising statement by the prosecutor: "It is scarcely worth while to recapitulate the evidence. I will not do it." One need have no experience whatever in the trial of criminal cases to recognize that it is the whole, sole purpose of closing arguments to recapitulate the evidence.

Nevertheless, Knowlton did score some telling points. His discussion of the gross atrocity of the crimes, followed by a mention of the hostility between Lizzie and her stepmother, a woman, as Knowlton said, "without an enemy in the world," led him to the logical conclusion: "The butchery shows no thief or burglar did this—only great hatred would inspire this." He went on to point out that Lizzie was in the house alone with her stepmother when the latter was slaughtered; that Mrs. Borden weighed two hundred pounds and therefore she could not have fallen, felled by a hatchet blow, without Lizzie's having heard the sound.

Knowlton then committed an unnecessarily risky act. Speaking of the mercurial note to Mrs. Borden, he said, "I stake the entire case on your belief of the truth or falsity of that proposition [that there was no note, none had ever been delivered, and that it was merely an invention of Lizzie's]."

One asks why? The note *was* important to the prosecution's case, the evidence that no note ever existed was forceful and compelling; but the entire case against Lizzie Borden did not or should not have stood or fallen depending on proof of its existence. With that odd gesture by Knowlton the Court interrupted his argument and suspended for the day.

The interruption was unfortunate, but the blame for it can hardly be placed at the doorstep of the District Attorney. It was—and is—the custom of Courts in all trials, but especially in capital trials, to time the proceedings so that closing arguments of either counsel will not be interrupted. The reason is obvious: otherwise continuity of argument is lost and the jury is distracted.

The thirteenth day of the trial was an uncomfortably hot one and, as District Attorney Knowlton resumed his closing argument, he mentioned to the jury his appreciation of their discomfort caused by the heat. He then picked up his argument where he had left it the day before by saying, "I shall press the bitter and unwelcome facts," and related that there was evidence of malice existent in the Borden household for many months. Here he pointed out a legalistic principle that certainly in this case needed to be stressed: motive is not an essential element of the crime of murder, and although evidence of motive is surely competent—that is, germane— in the proof of the prosecution's case, *the prosecutor need not prove motive to establish guilt.*

Then came this incredible statement from the prosecutor: "I should be slow to believe Lizzie Andrew Borden killed her father. I hope she did not."

Then, discussing the absence of blood from Lizzie's clothes and person after the discovery of Andrew Borden's body, he said, "I cannot answer how she concealed evidence of the murder of Andrew Borden"; she had, said Knowlton, plenty of time to conceal bloodstains produced by the murder of Abby Durfee Borden. He further argued that the dress given to the police was not the dress seen on Lizzie by Mrs. Churchill on the morning of the murders, and that the burning of the Bedford cord dress by Lizzie on Sunday morning was a "singular act." You must believe Alice Russell or Emma about the dress-burning, said Knowlton: one is lying; destruction of evidence is incriminating evidence in itself, it reveals consciousness of guilt.

In speaking about the handleless hatchet, Knowlton called to the jury's attention that the handle was broken not by accident, but by design, and he stressed again for emphasis that the $3\frac{1}{2}$-inch blade accurately fitted each wound.

By far the most effective part of Knowlton's argument, if not the only effective part, was delivered at its closing. Pointing out the complete *absurdity* of the hypothesis that the Bordens were the victims of an intruder (and thus by his contention actually in support of the strongest premise of guilt of Lizzie Borden—exclusive opportunity!) Knowlton described the actions of the imaginary intruder in these words:

". . . He came into the house where there was no chance to get in, he hid in closets where no blood was found, he went from room to room where no traces of blood were found in passageways or stairs, he came out when there was no opportunity to come out without being seen by all the world, that unknown assassin who knew all the ins and outs of the family, who knew Bridget Sullivan was going upstairs to sleep when she didn't know it herself, who knew when Lizzie was going to the barn when she didn't know it herself, who knew that Mrs. Borden would be up there dusting the guest room when no person could have foreseen it, who knew that he could get through and escape the eye of Lizzie and would find that screen door open at the exact time when it was possible to run in; that unknown assassin never would have carried the weapon away, carried the bloody weapon with him into the streets. It would have been left beside his victims. The fact that no hatchet was found there is in itself evidence. . . .

"Would the unknown assassin," continued Knowlton, "have written the note? To have his victim leave the house? That note was never sent. The note was never written."

Thus ended the prosecution's case. If Knowlton's closing argument did no more, it pointed out the complete absurdity of the premise that the murders had been committed by an intruder. That premise, flimsy and baseless as it was, was, or should have been, destroyed by Knowlton's ridicule.

In accordance with Massachusetts law, Chief Justice Mason then addressed the defendant:

"Lizzie Andrew Borden, although you have now been fully heard by counsel, it is your privilege to add any word which you may desire to say in person to this jury."

Lizzie rose slowly, bowed to the Court, and, looking at the twelve men motionlessly seated in the jury box, she responded:

"I am innocent. I leave it to my counsel to speak for me."

These thirteen words were the only words spoken by Lizzie Andrew Borden in the long, unendurably slow-moving, but most spectacular trial in American juridical history.

THE CHARGE

It is, and was in 1893, impermissible for a Massachusetts judge to charge a jury upon the facts of a case, or to express in his charge, even by implication, his own opinion of the evidence or any part of it. In many years of experience in the courts of the Commonwealth I have never heard a Massachusetts judge purposefully do so.

It is axiomatic that it is *not* the function of a trial judge in a jury trial to find the facts in a case, nor to determine where the truth lies, nor to adjudicate the guilt or innocence of a person on trial criminally accused. These are *solely and exclusively* the functions of the trial jury, which must take its instructions *on the law* from the judge and apply the law, as given, to the true facts as they, and they alone, find them to be. To the extent that the judge, in his charge, invades the province of the jury and superimposes, from his authoritative position on the Bench, his opinion of the evidence, to that extent is the jury system emasculated.

It has been strongly and authoritatively stated that Associate Justice Justin Dewey in the Borden case charged the jury upon the facts. Despite his use of rhetorical questions to disguise it, his opinion that the jury should acquit Lizzie shone unmistakably through the words of his instructions. A judicial direction to find Lizzie Borden Not Guilty marked Justice Dewey's charge from beginning to end.

Writing in 1893, Judge Charles G. Davis, a distinguished leader of the Massachusetts Bench and Bar, called Judge Dewey's charge a better and more effective argument upon the facts in favor of Lizzie Borden than that delivered by Lizzie's own counsel, George D. Robinson. Affirming that he was writing for the Massachusetts legal profession in 1893, Davis declared, "It was not the prisoner but the Commonwealth which did not have a fair trial." He accused Judge Dewey of acting not as an impartial judge but as an advocate for Lizzie Borden, by "arguing the case upon the evidence to the jury" and "by teaching the jury to distrust every important item of evidence offered by the prosecution in the case."

Judge Davis carefully pointed out that he did not accuse Judge Dewey of corrupt motives in his judicial action throughout the trial, but he did assert that Judge Dewey was unconsciously overcome by bias and prejudice in favor of Lizzie Borden, and the charge reflected this.

[I do not pretend to know what passed through Judge Dewey's mind on that June day more than eighty years ago, but it must be said that Justice Dewey's charge in the Borden case lacked the objectivity and fairness which is the proud heritage of the Massachusetts courts. In support of this proposition there is appended in the back of this book a verbatim transcript of the charge; artfully phrased though it was, the reader will find that Judge Dewey's question marks do not obscure his message to the jury: the message is there, loud and clear. The following highlights here of the charge, with minimal editorial comment by me, will demonstrate the flavor and thrust of Judge Dewey's instructions to the Borden jury.]

1. As to Lizzie's character:

"I understand the government to concede that the defendant's character has been good; that it has not been merely a negative and neutral one that nobody had heard anything against, but one of positive, of active benevolence in religious and charitable work. The question is whether the defendant, being such as she was, did the acts charged upon her. You are not inquiring into the action of some imaginary being, but into the action of a real person, the defendant, with her character, with her habits, with her education, with her ways of life, as they have been disclosed in the case. Judging of this subject as reasonable men, you are entitled to take into consideration her character such as is admitted or apparent. In some cases it may not be esteemed of great importance. *In other cases it may raise a reasonable doubt of a defendant's guilt even in the face of strongly incriminating circumstances* [italics supplied]."

[Should any weight at all be given to prior membership in church organizations when a jury is considering a crime of such gross brutality provoked by the passion of hate? Chief Justice Lemuel Shaw said (in *Commonwealth v Webster, Massachusetts Reports, 5 Cushing*): "But where it is a question of a great and atrocious crime, it is so unusual, so out of the ordinary course of things, that the evidence of character may be considered as far inferior to what it is in the case of smaller crimes. Against facts strongly proved, character cannot avail."]

2. As to Lizzie's ill will toward Abby, specifically the testimony of Miss Gifford, the dressmaker, relating statements of hostility made to the witness by Lizzie about her stepmother:

"Imputing a motive to the defendant does not prove that she had it. I understand the counsel for the government to claim that the defendant had toward her stepmother a strong feeling of ill will, nearly, if not quite, amounting to hatred. And Miss Gifford's testimony as to a conversation with the defendant in the early spring of 1892 is relied upon largely for that claim . . . . Take Miss Gifford's [testimony] just as she gave it and consider whether or not it will *fairly* amount to the significance attached to it, remembering it is the *language of a young woman* and not of a philosopher or jurist. What according to common observation is the habit of young women in the use of language? Is it not rather the use of *intense* expression? Whether or not they *do not* use words which, strictly taken, go far beyond their real meaning."

[Where does Miss Gifford's testimony manifest irresponsibility?]

3. As to the very important issue of the existence of the note Lizzie claimed Mrs. Borden had received from the mercurial sick friend, delivered by the mercurial messenger:

"Contemplate the possibility of there being another assassin than herself; might it not be a part of the plan or scheme of such a person by such a document or paper to withdraw Mrs. Borden from the house? If he afterwards came in there, came upon her, killed her, might he not have found the letter or note with her? Might he not have a reasonable and natural wish to remove that [note] as one possible link in tracing himself?"

[This judicial exercise of imagination dwarfs even Robinson's fanciful suggestions and completely boggles the mind. Judge Dewey here gave the jury an unknown, invented, mysterious assassin who wrote a note to assure Abby Borden's departure from the house, then went into the house to kill her and to reclaim the billet. The absurdity of this judicial suggestion is immediately apparent and demands comment. Why would the imaginary assassin contrive to have Abby Borden leave her home if it was his design to kill her there? How could he know that when he murdered Mrs. Borden she would have the note in her possession? How would Lizzie Borden have knowledge of the note? Finally, what about the murder of Andrew Borden some time later?]

4. As to Lizzie Borden's numerous inconsistent statements as to her whereabouts and actions at the time of the murder of her father:

"With respect to all verbal admissions [by the defendant] it may be observed that they ought to be received with great caution. The evidence, consisting as it does, in the mere repetition of oral statements, is subject to much imperfection and mistake . . ."

[Words fail me.]

5. As to the all-important testimony of the prosecution's medical experts which firmly established (1) the priority of death of the victims and

the interval of one and one-half hours between the deaths, (2) the gross brutality of the murders, (3) the physical capability of Lizzie Borden to commit the crimes, (4) the uncertainty of blood spurting and spattering, (5) the strong likelihood of the handleless hatchet as the murder weapon, and (6) the presence of a spot of blood externally received on the underskirt of Lizzie's garment:

"Now the Government has called as witnesses some gentlemen of scientific and medical knowledge and experience, who are termed experts and there has been put into the case considerable testimony from them. [This] constitutes a class of evidence *which the law requires you to subject to careful scrutiny* [emphasis supplied]. It is a matter of frequent observation to see experts of good standing expressing conflicting and irreconcilable views upon questions arising at a trial."

[All five medical witnesses, including Lizzie's neighbor and friend, Dr. Bowen, were in complete accord, the one with the other, in all aspects of their testimony. There was no suggestion whatsoever of any conflict in views between the medical witnesses.]

After suggesting to the jury that in the jury room they apply the hatchet-head to the wounds on the skulls, since they could determine these facts as well as the scientific experts could do, Judge Dewey disposed of the most impressive testimony of these distinguished men of science with this extraordinarily debasing language:

"They [the medical experts] sometimes manifest a strong bias or partisan spirit in favor of the party employing them."

[The people of the Commonwealth of Massachusetts, seeking justice, were employing them. One wonders how the Massachusetts Medical Society of 1893 accepted this judicial observation.]

During his discussion Judge Dewey put at issue the fact that Mr. Borden died sometime after his wife. He seems to be the only person in the courtroom, or in fact anywhere, who did not concede that the evidence was conclusive that Andrew Borden died one to two hours after his wife; even Robinson did not dispute this.

6. As to the failure of Lizzie Borden to take the stand in her own defense:

"The defendant may say, 'I have already told to the officers all that I know about this case, and my statements have been put in evidence; whatever is mysterious to others is also mysterious to me. I have no knowledge more than others have. I have never professed to be able to explain how or by whom these homicides were committed.' "

[The reader will note that this is an elaborate and imaginary statement supposed to have been made by Lizzie to the jury. It was invented by Judge Dewey in his charge; he was even, in effect, testifying for her.]

And he continued in this same vein:

"There is another reason why the defendant might not want to testify . . . If she testifies, she becomes a witness with less than the privilege of an ordinary witness. She is subject to cross-examination. She may be asked questions which are legally competent which she is not able to answer, or she may answer truly and it may be argued against her that her answers were untrue and her neglect to answer perverse. Being a party, she is exposed to peculiar danger of having her conduct on the stand and her testimony severely scrutinized and perhaps misjudged . . ."

[Is this not true of every witness in every case? Furthermore, it is of interest to note here that Professor John H. Wigmore expressed his views on Lizzie's failure to take the stand. Writing in the *American Law Review* in 1893, the world-famous Northwestern University Law School professor, author of *Wigmore's Evidence*—perhaps the best-known law text other than Blackstone's *Commentaries*—said of Lizzie Borden:

. . . On the other hand, the conduct of the accused after the killing was such that no conceivable hypothesis, except that of guilt, will explain the inconsistencies and improbabilities that were asserted by her. The statements about the barn visit, and about the discovery of her father's death, are frightfully inconsistent; while the story of the note requires for its truth a combination of circumstances almost inconceivable. We may add to this the inevitable query, Why did the accused not take the witness stand to explain these things? Of course, it was her legal right to remain silent; but the rule against self-incrimination is not one of logic or of relevancy; it is a rule of policy and of fairness, based on broad considerations of average results desirable in the long run. It cannot prevent us as logical beings from drawing our inferences; and if we weigh in this case the confounding inconsistencies and improbabilities of these statements and then place with these the opportunity and the refusal to explain them, we cannot help feeling that she failed to explain them because she could not; and one side of the balance sinks heavily.]

Closing his charge with a discussion of the dress which Lizzie wore on the morning of the murders, here is Judge Dewey's language:

"Taking the evidence of these several witnesses . . . *can you*, gentlemen, *extract* from that testimony such a description of a dress as would enable you from the testimony to identify the dress? . . . [Can you] put their statements together and from these statements say that any given dress was accurately described?"

So ended Justice Dewey's charge to the jury in the murder trial of Lizzie Borden. To put it very kindly, it was unique. Even the free-wheeling dean of the newspaper correspondents present, Joseph Howard—who had been, throughout the trial, virtually canonizing Lizzie—could not quite stomach this charge. His daily dispatch after Judge Dewey's performance was headlined JUDGE'S CHARGE A PLEA FOR THE INNOCENT. His article of Wednesday morning, 21 June, said in part:

> The judge's charge was remarkable. It was a plea for the innocent. Had he [Judge Dewey] been the senior counsel for the defense making the closing plea on behalf of the defendant, he could not have more absolutely pointed out the folly of depending upon the circumstantial evidence alone. With matchless clearness he set up the case of the prosecution point by point and, in the most ingenious manner possible, knocked it down . . . and like the saints he continued to the end throwing bombs of disheartenment into the range of the prosecution and causing smiles of great joy about the lips of Lizzie's friends. I doubt there was ever such a charge before. On the other hand, there never was such a case before. There never was a prosecution so handicapped before.

George D. Robinson's homespun but persuasive argument, capped by Judge Dewey's odd charge, had all but sealed the case for Lizzie Borden. The jurors were ordered to the jury room to commence their deliberations. The exhibits, properly marked and boxed, accompanied the jury. They included the crushed skulls of Andrew Borden and his wife; they also included the handleless hatchet: presumably the jury would undertake the ghoulish task of fitting the cutting edge of the hatchet to the gaping wounds in the eyeless, fleshless, whitened human parts of Andrew J. Borden and Abby Durfee Borden.

THE VERDICT

Lizzie's fate was decided by the first ballot vote of the jury. The boxes of exhibits were never touched; the skulls were undisturbed, the handleless hatchet received not a glance. The jury, out of respect for the feelings of the prosecutors, remained silent and motionless for what they considered a respectable period—one and one-half hours; then the foreman rang the bell signaling that they were ready to report the verdict.

When this bell rang on 23 June 1893, at exactly 4:30 P.M., the milling throng around the courthouse became frenzied. The excitement was as intense as the crushing heat of the early Summer which enveloped the mahogany-paneled courtroom.

Thousands crowded the streets surrounding the small New Bedford courthouse and flooded the pristine platform upon which the four great doric columns rested. Inside the courtroom the perspiring spectators pressed toward the bench with anticipation. At the crash of the bailiff's staff the three solemn-faced, bearded Justices entered and took their places. Every eye was riveted upon the twelve men seated in the jury box as Chief Justice Mason, from his central position on the bench, sternly muttered to the clerk, "Have the jurors rise as their names are called, Mr. Clerk." Each of the twelve jurors stood as the court crier tolled the names from his high-walled box.

From below and in front of the Chief Justice, the Clerk of Courts for Bristol County, Simeon Borden, a relative of the defendant, intoned, "Lizzie Andrew Borden, stand up." She rose. Lizzie had worn a wide-brimmed, feathered hat, pitched well forward on her head with a great plume jutting in an upward direction. The singular impression which the hat created was that of a bird poised for flight, and it contrasted sharply with the utterly unruffled expression of her obicular face.

"Gentlemen of the jury, have you agreed upon a verdict?" inquired Clerk Borden.

Foreman Richards responded for the jury: "We have."

"What say you, Mr. Foreman ——"

But no longer able to restrain himself, and interrupting the clerk, Foreman Richards blurted out the two words which the crowd had been so anxiously waiting to hear: "Not guilty!"

A thunderous cheer arose and swept the courtroom; it was echoed down the corridor and the stairs and then surged from the throats of the people jamming the streets. New Bedford had never seen such a day. The Sheriff, unable to sustain any semblance of order, sat in his courtroom box and wept unabashedly, overcome by emotion and fatigue.

Lizzie Borden, as if she herself was felled by a hatchet, crashed back into her chair, her head rolled somewhat, and she swooned. Only momentarily: she then grasped the rail before her with her two hands, thrust her face between her outstretched arms and burst into tears.

"Take me home," she murmured, "take me home. I want to go to the old place tonight."

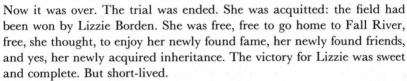

Now it was over. The trial was ended. She was acquitted: the field had been won by Lizzie Borden. She was free, free to go home to Fall River, free, she thought, to enjoy her newly found fame, her newly found friends, and yes, her newly acquired inheritance. The victory for Lizzie was sweet and complete. But short-lived.

On Wednesday, 21 June, the newspapers of the entire nation wallowed in the story. The verdict seemed to be almost universally well received, and in some places hailed as a triumph of justice. Interviews with each of the twelve jurors appeared in every major newspaper; speculation as to Lizzie's happy future was widespread. A Day of Sunshine for Lizzie, Back in Her Old Home, Friends Warmly Welcome Lizzie Home, Church and Charity May Claim Her—so read some of the congratulatory headlines.

More temperate were the reports of the verdict carried by journals in Britain, but carry them they did. Outstanding for succinctness and accuracy was the story in the London *Daily Telegraph* of 22 June, under the heading A Sensational Murder Trial. The story ended:

> . . . In view of these facts Lizzie Borden was arrested one week after the murders, and held for trial. The self-possession of the prisoner was such as to excite universal comment. . . . She refused to say one word either in acknowledgment or denial of the charges brought against her, declined to make any statement, and rested her defence solely upon the inability of the State to prove its case.

Meanwhile in America, Lizzie Borden, whose name was already a household word, had overnight become something of a national heroine. The church organizations and the women's-advancement groups rejoiced; the Fall River police and the prosecutors were again publicly chastised for persecuting Lizzie.

Even Judge Dewey set an unusual precedent which hopefully will never be repeated: he granted an interview to the press. In the Boston *Globe* of Wednesday, 21 June 1893, appears a statement by the trial Judge: "I am perfectly satisfied with the verdict," he is quoted as saying, among other things; "I was satisfied when I made my charge to the jury that the verdict would be not guilty, although one cannot always tell what a jury will do."

Behind the Verdict

AT THE OUTSET of her trial Lizzie Borden was presumed to be innocent. But this presumption of innocence should not have been considered evidence in her favor (although Judge Dewey charged otherwise). It meant only this: the fact that she was in the New Bedford courtroom on trial, and the fact that she had been found "probably guilty" by Judge Blaisdell at the preliminary hearing, and the fact that she had been indicted by a grand jury on 2 december 1892 were not to be considered by the jury as the slightest evidence of her guilt; and further, that she was not to be convicted by the jury on speculative evidence, guesswork or surmise, but only if and when the prosecution had satisfied the requirements of law imposed upon it, as to the burden or quantum or degree of proof required to convict. That is to say, she was to be convicted only if and when the jury had been satisfied of her guilt *beyond a reasonable doubt*, for that is the burden of proof required of the Commonwealth of Massachusetts in the Borden case, and in every criminal case—i.e., to satisfy the jury of the guilt of the accused beyond any reasonable doubt.

"Reasonable doubt" has been defined thus: "It is that state of the case, which, after the entire comparison and consideration of all the evidence, leaves the minds of jurors in that condition that they cannot say that they feel an abiding conviction, to a moral certainty, of the truth of the charge."

Now the words "proof *beyond* a reasonable doubt" do *not* mean proof beyond *all* doubt; nor do they mean proof beyond all possibility of innocence, for if the latter were the standard of proof required, few, if any, criminals would be convicted, and the administration of criminal justice would be rendered impossible.

Proof beyond a reasonable doubt means proof to a moral certainty: not a mathematically accurate certainty, but a moral certainty, the certainty that jurors would use in making determinations of great significance in their own personal affairs. It means this; it does not mean more.

Let us measure the evidence adduced at the Borden trial against this traditional framework of safeguards to protect the rights of the criminally accused, to protect the rights of Lizzie Borden. In the following short analysis of the trial we shall, of course, ignore the evidence offered by the prosecution and rejected by the Court: the prussic-acid purchase, and the incredibly inconsistent statements made under oath by Lizzie at the inquest.

The prosecution's case with regard to pre-determination to kill (motive or state of mind):

Even without the evidence of the attempted purchase of the prussic acid the afternoon before the murders, a true and clear picture of pre-dispostion is painted by Miss Gifford's testimony as discussed earlier; by Miss Russell's testimony with regard to Lizzie's statements made the evening before the murders concerning her pretended fear of impending disaster; by the description of the hostile atmosphere pervading the Borden home; by the long-standing habit of locking and blocking inner doors; by the unnatural dislike Lizzie demonstrated for her stepmother; and by Bridget Sullivan's reluctant statements of the hostility between the daughters of Andrew Borden and their stepmother. Any one of these bits of evidence standing alone might not be enough, but the composite seems absolutely clear.

Exclusive opportunity and capability:

On all the evidence it must be said that Lizzie Borden *and she alone* had the opportunity to commit these crimes. The hypothesis that an intruder intervened appears from the evidence to be absurd. No stranger could have been the assassin; Bridget was not. There can be, on this evidence, only one hypothesis within the realm of reason: Lizzie Borden was the assassin; her physical capabilities and the means of committing the crime (the hatchet, which later was handleless) available to her, were both the subject of compelling medical testimony which was left entirely unrebutted.

Acts revealing consciousness of guilt:

Ignoring Lizzie's statement made at the inquest and barred from evidence by the trial court, from the trial record alone the number and degree of inconsistencies and incongruities in Lizzie's actions and words after the discovery of each murder are staggering, their import definitively incriminating. The pattern of Lizzie's consciousness of guilt which the prosecution demonstrated was overwhelming.

The defense:

Lizzie did not testify, and thus, in effect, the defense was nonexistent:

Robinson's attempt to cast doubt on the prosecution's forceful evidence of guilt failed. It was an impossible task to rebut the terribly incriminating evidence against Lizzie Borden; the prongs of the prosecution's case were too multifold and too sharp. However, Robinson did his best to cloud the evidence. For example, what difference did it make to the central issue whether Mrs. Reagan, the police matron, did or did not make a statement to the press, or did or did not lie or exaggerate about the argument between Lizzie and Emma? At best this had a barely tangential relationship to the question of Lizzie's innocence or guilt, and yet Robinson made it seem of great moment. There really was no effective defense, nor could there be.

The absence of blood on Lizzie's person, and the dress-burning incident:

If the minds of the Borden jurors were set upon searching for doubts, not searching for the truth, they could have found some slight solace in the facts that no blood-soaked garment belonging to Lizzie was produced at the trial and that no one noticed blood upon her person on the morning of the murders. No analysis of the testimony would be complete without a discussion of this, since it appears that the defense relied, if not wholly, at least in major part, upon the premise that if Lizzie had committed these bloody crimes, she herself would have been bloody. Yet any reading of the full testimony totally disproves this proposition.

As to the slaughter of Mrs. Borden, the testimony—expert and nonexpert—the entire sense of the evidence, and all the legal participants including George D. Robinson agreed that Abby D. Borden was killed some appreciable time before Andrew J. Borden. The reader will recall that the entire record clearly established that the *minimum* time interval between the murders was one hour. Thus Lizzie had nearly one full hour alone after she had butchered her stepmother to remove from her person and her clothing any traces of blood which had resulted from the first killing, or indeed to wash and change her outer clothing so that she was able to descend the stairs at 10:35 A.M. with all the traces of blood removed, and confront Bridget and Andrew Borden when he returned home from his morning business.

As to the murder of Andrew Borden, the explanation for the absence of blood on Lizzie's person is equally clear. Anyone who visited the Borden premises on Second Street, as this writer did, and as the jury had done on the view—indeed anyone who studies the ground-floor plan of the Borden residence, an illustration here and an exhibit at the trial—can readily discern that the head of the couch upon which Andrew Borden lay was exactly flush with the door leading into the dining room. Andrew Borden, when he slept that morning of 4 August, slept with his head only inches from the open interior door leading to the dining room. He was within easy range of a well-directed blow, or blows, delivered by Lizzie standing shielded by the door opening, very probably with her feet in the dining room.

A little-known version of the world-famous quatrain, despite its inaccuracy with regard to the number of blows, tells the story in its four lines:

> *Lizzie Borden took an axe*
> *And gave her mother forty whacks.*
> *Then she stood behind the door*
> *And gave her father forty more.*

In addition, there was the thrust of the medical testimony: first that the distribution of blood spurting, if any, was a subject of sheer speculation; and second, that there would be no spurting at all unless an artery was cut, and unless the victim's heart was beating at the time of the actual blow which severed the artery. It is easy to see how Lizzie escaped being badly blood-smeared from spattering, since she stood behind and above her victim as she rained her blows upon him. It has also been suggested that Lizzie had shielded herself with newspaper, or other readily burnable material, which would have accounted for the long roll of completely carbonized paper found in the stove by the police shortly after their arrival on the morning of the murders.

At any rate, it is clear that after the murder of Andrew Borden, Lizzie had an interval of about fifteen minutes to eliminate any traces of blood upon her person, if any there were, and to wash the hatchet in the sink, take it to the cellar and plunge the wet, newly washed hatchet head into the coal ashes after breaking it from the handle. All these matters could have been, and no doubt were, easily done in the time span ending with her call to Bridget, "Come down quick! Father is dead! Somebody came in and killed him!"

Notwithstanding all the above, the absence of blood stains on Lizzie's outer garments becomes academic when one considers the dress-burning incident. This, in my view, is the most incriminating evidence in a veritable mountain of inconsistencies and incongruities which marked Lizzie's proven actions and statements after the murders.

It should be marked and marked well that the dress-burning incident, which is the obvious answer to the fact that no blood-stained outer garment of Lizzie's was produced at the trial, *was admitted by the defense.* It was not denied at any time; even the misguidedly loyal Emma in her testimony admitted that it had taken place. The position adopted by the defense was that the incident had occurred but that it was explainable. The explanations of the dress-burning offered by the defense were so completely contrived as to tax the credulity of the most naïve person in Bristol County, nay, America—if that person were approaching the evidence with an open and lucid mind.

What are the odds against Lizzie Borden, amid the excitement and confusion, the searches and outright suspicion of the days following the murders, singling out the Sunday morning after the murders to tidy up her wardrobe? And what are the odds against Lizzie Borden on that day choosing as a method of tidying up her wardrobe the unheard-of method—unheard of in that frugal family—of burning in the kitchen stove a soiled dress only ten weeks old?

I suppose almost everything in human affairs is possible, but the likelihood of Lizzie Borden choosing that time, that dress and that mode of total and irretrievable destruction to tidy her wardrobe literally defies reason.

The dress-burning as a full explanation of the absence of blood on Lizzie's clothing is one of the paramount pieces of evidence in this case. I have appended Judge Dewey's charge to the jury in its totality. In the one and one-half hour charge, Judge Dewey related the evidence so one captures his view of all the testimony; all the important factual features of this case are discussed—all but one. *In no place in Judge Dewey's charge will the reader find the slightest hint or suggestion of the evidence, or any of it, from Miss Alice Russell, from Emma Borden or from any witness regarding the dress-burning incident.* He treats it as if it never was told.

Can there seriously be any doubt that Lizzie Borden was guilty, proven so beyond a reasonable doubt? I think not, and further, had the evidence of the prussic acid incident, and the inquest statement of the defendant been admitted into evidence, as contemporary professionals in the law thought they should have been, the proof against Lizzie Borden would have approached the legal millennium—*proof beyond all possibility of innocence.*

THE PART OF THE PRESS

The inverse of the concept of pre-trial prejudicial publicity so often complained of by criminal defendants had occurred in the Borden case. Immediately after Lizzie's arrest the press had begun a sustained display of pre-trial publicity which was very *favorable* to the defendant. It is likely that one type of unobjective pre-trial publicity is as effective as the other in misguiding the hand of justice in celebrated murder trials.

In 1893 the press, like the rest of America, was overcome by the overriding reluctance to witness a woman sentenced to death. The press also felt the same surge of utter incredulity that had swept the nation: it, like all America, found it difficult to believe that a woman with Lizzie Borden's background and social position was capable of these horrible crimes. In addition, of course, the strongly voiced conviction by various pressure groups that Lizzie was innocent, unquestionably influenced the press to adopt the position favorable to Lizzie which was so manifest in the contemporary newspapers. For months before the trial Lizzie had been pictured as a frail woman who had been put upon by the police and prosecutors; she was portrayed in the press as a proper subject for public sympathy and public support. This widespread image of Lizzie was calculated to make it difficult, if not impossible, to find twelve prospective jurors in Bristol County who were totally unaffected by the favorable pre-trial publicity she had received.

The only sharp departure from Lizzie's beneficial press treatment was the result of a hoax which victimized the Boston *Globe*. Ironically, the subsequent disclosure of the hoax brought the fortunate defendant great public sympathy and cast upon the prosecution's entire case a cloud of suspicion which was never to lift.

No analysis of the Borden case can give the reader a firm purchase on the circumstances surrounding the verdict without a discussion of the "Trickey-McHenry affair," so-called.

Henry G. Trickey, appropriately named, was a twenty-four-year-old crime reporter for the Boston *Globe*, who, despite his youth had earned a considerable reputation for effectively covering celebrated murder trials and other sensational events. What Trickey lacked in judgment he compensated for with energetic enterprise; he was the prototype of the "news-at-any-cost" reporter romanticized in old motion pictures and in the scenario of *The Front Page*.

Edwin D. McHenry was trickier than Trickey. A free-lance private detective, he made his home in Providence but operated on an interstate basis, seeking employment wherever he could find it.

In 1893 few small cities had trained detectives regularly assigned to the police force, and local police officials often retained private detectives to assist in handling particularly difficult cases. This was unfortunate, since private detectives in the last part of the last century were not an altogether noble lot. Their value lay in their intimacy with the underworld and its

Reporter Henry G. Trickey (*above*)

Private Detective Edwin D. McHenry

BOTH FROM PORTER

members, and they worked through personal contacts among the criminals. At times, for a fee, they arranged for the return of stolen property, non-negotiable securities, or jewelry by using their acquaintanceship with the criminals responsible for the thefts. In short, many private detectives in 1893 and thereabouts were not minions of the law and were deservedly held in less than high repute. McHenry was a shady character at best; a rogue.

On the day of the Borden murders, McHenry was sent for by the Fall River authorities, and the following day Mayor Coughlin and Marshal Hilliard of Fall River employed him to assist the police in handling the Borden case.

Reporter Trickey had met Detective McHenry in connection with the investigations of other sensational crimes which had taken place before the Borden murders. It was natural that their paths should again cross in Fall River, where Trickey was searching for news as McHenry was searching for clues.

After some circuitous scheming and bargaining, the two concocted a plan whereby Trickey was to pay McHenry five hundred dollars for the purchase of all the evidence the prosecution had against Lizzie Borden, the results of two months' of investigation by McHenry's employers, the Fall River police. This was to be an exclusive story for the Boston *Globe*, and McHenry was to provide Trickey with the names and addresses of prospective witnesses for the Commonwealth, as well as the testimony each witness was prepared to give, and all supported by affidavits. In addition, Trickey was to allow McHenry twenty-four hours before the *Globe* published the story so that McHenry would have time to leave the jurisdiction in advance of it becoming known that he had betrayed his employers, the Fall River police.

On 9 October 1892, still two months before Lizzie Borden was to be indicted by a grand jury, Trickey and McHenry had their fateful meeting. Trickey paid McHenry the five hundred dollars and received the detailed story of the prosecution's case from the detective.

Understandably, Trickey was distrustful of McHenry, and he feared that McHenry was negotiating to sell his story to the *Globe*'s arch-rival, the Boston *Herald*. Accordingly, he rushed to Boston late Sunday and convinced his superiors to publish the story without even taking the precaution of checking the most basic of the ream of detailed facts McHenry had sold to him.

The story exploded in the *Globe*'s morning edition of Monday, 10 October 1892. In massive headlines it was announced that LIZZIE HAD A

Secret, Mr. Borden Discovered It, Then a Quarrel, Startling Testimony of Twenty-five New Witnesses.

Column after column, page after page, the *Globe* related McHenry's minutely detailed account of the prosecution's case against Lizzie. So long was the disjointed and rambling tale that little else was printed in the newspaper. It was alleged among many other things that Lizzie was pregnant and that, in certainly one of the most striking sentences ever penned, her father had ordered her to "name the man or leave this house by Saturday"; that Lizzie was seen in the guest room with a hood on her head at the time of the murder of her stepmother; that Andrew Borden had executed a will disinheriting Lizzie and leaving large sums to his wife's family, the Whiteheads, with the amounts of the legacy and the legatees' names given. Interestingly, the ten-year-old Abby Borden Whitehead (now Mrs. Potter) was, according to McHenry's facts, to receive five thousand dollars under the terms of the will. The testimony of each of the "twenty-five new witnesses" was, as it appeared in print, more than incriminating against the defendant Lizzie Borden: it was damning in every detail.

The Monday evening edition of the *Globe* repeated the entire story and accompanied it with several columns devoted to a description rejoicing in the impact the morning edition had had. "All New England Read the Story, Globes Were Bought by the Thousands, Lizzie Borden Appears in New Light, Belief in her Innocence Sadly Shaken—these were the giant column headings as the *Globe* congratulated itself on its sensational exposé of the entire tragedy in Fall River.

By Monday night, however, the bubble burst: telegrams poured into the *Globe* from the Fall River police; from John Vinnicum Morse, whom the story had also implicated, threatening law suit; from scores of Fall River people connected with the case. The witnesses whom the *Globe* quoted were all fictitious, their addresses nonexistent; the rambling, complicated story was completely without foundation in fact; Lizzie's physician heatedly denied the implication of her pregnancy.

And, blow of blows, the Boston *Herald* headlines that evening read A $500 Fake, Assault on Miss Borden's Honor Is Purely a Myth, Statements Given as Evidence Untrue, Public Sympathy Aroused for the Accused; and the *Herald* related how Detective McHenry had an "old score to settle" with the *Globe* and had defrauded Trickey to do so.

Apparently not sure of where to turn, the morning *Globe* of Tuesday, 11 October, carried the following long legend across its front page, all in bold capital letters: DETECTIVE MC HENRY TALKS—HE FURNISHED

THE *GLOBE* WITH THE BORDEN STORY—IT HAS PROVEN WRONG IN SOME PARTICULARS—*GLOBE* SECURES BEST DE- TECTIVE TALENT AVAILABLE TO FIND MURDERER. Then, in smaller print: "The *Globe* interviewed Dr. and Mrs. Bowen and Reverend Mr. Buck on the question of Lizzie Borden's physical condition at the time of the murders, the result of which was the conviction that in this respect at least Mr. McHenry was wrong. The story may be wrong in some other minor particulars, but the weight of evidence favors the main facts to be true."

Finally, totally capitulating, the *Globe* ran in the evening edition of Tuesday, 11 October, a full and sincere apology. In fairness it must be said that the apology, written in editorial style, was carried in the most conspicuous manner, in giant type across the top of the front page. Headed THE LIZZIE BORDEN CASE, the text said:

The *Globe* is, first of all, an honest newspaper. To err is human, and, as newspapers have to be run by men and not by angels, mistakes are inevitable.

The *Globe* feels it a plain duty, as an honest newspaper, to state that it has been grievously misled in the Lizzie Borden case. It published on Monday a communication that it believed to be true evidence. Among all the impositions which newspapers have suffered, this was unparal- leled in its astonishing completeness and irresistible plausibility. Judging from what we have heard, it impressed our readers as strongly as it did the *Globe*. Some of this remarkably ingenious and cunningly contrived story is undoubtedly based on facts, as later developments will show. The *Globe* believes, however, that much of it is false, and never should have been published.

The *Globe*, being thus misled, has innocently added to the terrible burdens of Miss Lizzie Borden. So far as lies in our power to repair the wrong, we are anxious to do so, and hereby tender her our heartfelt apology for the inhuman reflection upon her honor as a woman, and for any injustice the publication of Monday inflicted upon her. And the same sincere apology is hereby tendered to Mr. John V. Morse, and any other persons to whom the publication did an injustice.

The *Globe* comes out in this manner because it believes that honesty is the best policy, and because it believes in doing what is right. We prefer to build up rather than to tear down, to help rather than to injure, to carry sunshine and not sorrow into the homes of New England.

When we make a mistake, whether through our fault or not, we believe that justice to our readers demands that we should fairly and honestly and boldly proclaim the fact in the same conspicuous place in The Globe where the error was committed.

Louis M. Lyons, dean of New England journalists, in his marvelously entertaining book *One Hundred Years of the Boston Globe*, published in 1971, details the story of the Trickey-McHenry affair of 1892 and gives an insight into the newspaper's feelings at that time. He says that "the *Globe* was lucky to escape ruination," but that the Borden lawyers were so busy trying to work out a defense for Lizzie that they had little time for libel suits.

Edwin H. Porter wrote in his *The Fall River Tragedy*, published in 1893, that Trickey feared McHenry would sell his story to the Boston *Herald* before the *Globe* published his "scoop." Porter also wrote that Trickey paid an unnamed policeman one hundred dollars to check the authenticity of McHenry's facts and argued this to his editors to persuade them to publish McHenry's story immediately.

Edwin Porter closed his discussion of the Trickey-McHenry affair with this statement: "This writer [Porter] has been assured by the police that if Mr. Trickey had given the twenty-four hours' notice before publication, the Boston *Globe* would have been spared the trouble of publishing the fake. In justice to the Boston *Globe* it must be said that its editors made the most humble and abject apology for the wrong done Miss Borden by the publication of the lies which Detective McHenry had sold to Mr. Trickey. The apology was made as prominent as the story had been, and the *Globe*'s position, although not an enviable one, appeared to be as graceful as the circumstances would admit."

In an odd sequel to this odd affair, Henry G. Trickey was indicted 2 December 1892 by the same grand jury which indicted Lizzie Borden. He was charged with interference with the proper administration of justice. Informed of the indictment, Trickey fled to Canada to avoid service of process and was killed in Toronto on 4 December 1892 in a train accident.

Thus ended the sensational Trickey-McHenry affair, a journalistic error of mammoth proportions.

One can imagine the impact of this barrage of blunders upon the news-hungry public: enormous sympathy had been generated for the defendant, Lizzie; anything said by or about the prosecution's case was henceforth suspect, and the *Globe*'s large-captioned story that it was retaining the services of the finest detective talent to find the killers not only undermined public confidence in the prosecution, but also, by strong implication—since Lizzie was in jail—said that Lizzie Borden was innocent.

This was for her a giant stroke of good luck. The poor judgment of an overzealous young reporter, combined with the keen rivalry between the Boston *Globe* and the Boston *Herald*, had resulted in an incident which had cascaded to her support the power of both these newspapers, two of the most important dailies in New England.

The full, firm, and sustained support of the Boston *Globe* and the Boston *Herald* was to aid Lizzie up to and through her trial eight months later.

THE DEATH PENALTY

Strangely enough, the very influence which affected the press in their pre-trial handling of the Borden case probably had more impact than any other factor on the minds of the public and thus the minds of the jurors in Lizzie Borden's favor. I am referring to the great reluctance to convict a female defendant of a crime requiring the imposition of the death penalty.

It is true that in 1893, at the time of the Borden trial, there were two degrees of murder defined by law in the Commonwealth of Massachusetts, and it was for the jury to determine the degree within the statutory definitions. Nonetheless, on any reading of the facts of these murders, Lizzie Borden could not possibly have been found guilty of murder in the second degree within the definition of that crime. The Borden jury had one alternative and one alone—send her to her death or set her free. Robinson had recognized this and stressed it time and again in his closing argument.

Research into the subject allows this statement to be made with reasonable certainty of its accuracy: *No female criminal defendant has been executed in the Commonwealth of Massachusetts since the Revolutionary War.* The last female put to death by the state was Bathsheba Spooner, publicly hanged in the courthouse square in Worcester in 1778, and the chilling sequelae to her hanging were to have a deterring effect long felt in Massachusetts. Here in brief is that sad saga:

Like Lizzie Borden, Bathsheba was a member of a well-known and distinguished family. Her father, General Timothy Ruggles, was, by an odd coincidence, Chief Justice of the Court of Common Pleas. The Massachusetts Superior Court is the lineal successor to Chief Justice Ruggles's Court of the Massachusetts Bay Colony.

Because he owed his judicial appointment to the Crown and because he had been a British general in the army of Jeffery Lord Amherst, Ruggles, a confirmed Tory, was forced to flee to Nova Scotia at the outbreak of the Revolution. Before leaving, he arranged a marriage of convenience for his beautiful daughter Bathsheba with Joshua Spooner, an elderly cantankerous merchant of Brookfield, a town near Worcester. The marriage was a great failure and the embittered young wife soon sought surcease from her aging spouse and unhappy state.

Ezra Ross, a seventeen-year-old veteran of the Battle of Bunker Hill, invalided from Washington's army, passed through Brookfield en route home from New York State and met Bathsheba, who undertook to nurse him back to health. Her nursing ministrations, though protracted, were yet so remarkably effective that the end result was glowing health for Ezra and pregnancy for Bathsheba Spooner.

Gauging correctly that her husband might be suspicious of her pregnancy and adopt a dim view of it, Bathsheba joined her lover in a plan to murder Joshua, and engaged, to help her, two freebooting British soldiers who were passing her way.

On 1 March 1778 the task was quickly done, and shortly thereafter Joshua's body, badly beaten, was found head down in his own well. The discovery came too soon to allow the British soldiers to escape, for they had tarried to celebrate in a Worcester tavern, wearing Joshua's clothes and toasting Bathsheba's health with the fee she had paid them. At the time of their arrest they implicated Bathsheba and Ezra, and almost immediately all four confessed, and on 21 April 1778 they were put to trial together.

The trial was remarkable for the speed with which it was carried out: beginning very early, and ending very late, in one day all four were tried by a jury, convicted, and sentenced to hang. After the death sentence was pronounced upon all four defendants, it was protested that to execute Bathsheba would, of course, take the life of her unborn child.

A body of two male midwives and twelve "discreet and lawful matrons" was appointed to examine Bathsheba physically, and they pronounced that her assertion of pregnancy was without foundation. A second examination by a group of five midwives resulted, unhappily for Bathsheba, in a split decision.

The entire matter was resolved by marching the three men to the gallows erected in the square in front of the Worcester courthouse and hanging them. Shortly thereafter Bathsheba was conveyed to the gallows in an elegant carriage, accompanied by the local minister. This delicacy in allowing a suitable interval between the hanging of the three men and the hanging of Bathsheba Spooner, together with the thoughtfulness in allowing Bathsheba to ride to her death in a fine carriage, added a chivalrous touch to the day's events for the howling throng gathered in the square to witness the hangman's skill.

Almost immediately after Bathsheba's swaying body was cut down from the gallows, an autopsy was performed. It revealed the presence of a well-formed, well-nourished five-month fetus.

The self-guilt of the people of Worcester County was not soon erased. No female was ever again executed in that county.

Further, my research has been unable to discover that any female was ever again executed in any county of the Commonwealth of Massachusetts. In the early nineteenth century, however, executions were performed, and records of them were kept, only by the county officers of the fourteen counties of the state; thus it is difficult to assert with finality that no female was hanged during that period. Yet all indications point to the truth of this assertion.

In 1857 a female charged with murdering her husband by arsenic poisoning was tried in Plymouth County. The evidence against her was overwhelming, but the jury resisted conviction and was unable to reach a verdict.

Months later, in 1858, the state legislature enacted the so-called "murder statute" for the first time, distinguishing murder in the first degree and murder in the second degree, defining both and requiring a mandatory sentence of life imprisonment and not the death penalty for persons convicted of murder in the second degree. It had been argued to the legislature that regardless of the evidence, it was impossible to convict female defendants in murder cases because of the mandatory death penalty.

Immediately after the new murder statute was enacted, the Plymouth County female defendant just mentioned was re-tried and, after a discussion of abandonment of purpose to kill and some flimsy evidence of lack of deliberate premeditation, she was convicted by the jury of second degree murder and sentenced to life imprisonment.

Some thirty years later, and only a few years before Lizzie Borden came to trial, Sarah Jane Robinson, accused of six murders, was convicted of first degree murder and sentenced to death. Shortly thereafter, on the sole ground that she was a woman, her sentence was commuted to life imprisonment. Incongruously, militant equal-rights-for-women groups exerted considerable pressure upon the Governor to obtain this commutation.

We should note here that no second-degree escape hatch was open to the prosecution or the jury in the Borden case: among many reasons, there were two separate murders involved, committed with some time interval. The facts of the Borden case simply did not accommodate anything but a first-degree murder conviction.

In 1900 the method of execution in Massachusetts was changed from hanging to electrocution. Since then the electric chair has been used sixty-five times. All sixty-five persons who were put to death by the Commonwealth by electrocution were males. The last was executed in 1947.

It is said that scientific scholars have urged that the reluctance to execute female criminals has its psychological genesis in the evolution of an early misogyny on through to the male attitude which we know as chivalry, and that chivalrous forces extend to protection of the female from all recognizable harm, including the hangman's noose. In the facts of the Borden case with specificity, students of psychology urge that a Guilty verdict would have also been an acknowledgment by the male jury that Lizzie had the mental and physical strength and capacity to commit the gruesome acts, thus negating the universally preconceived image of the weak and helpless female of the nineteenth century.

Whatever the psychological explanation of the Borden verdict may be, the law, if it is a science, is a practical science, and it deals in hard facts. The hard facts are, first, that there is a clearly recognizable pattern of reluctance to convict females of murder when the death penalty is involved, and, second, that Lizzie Borden was guilty of double parricide— and despite the evidence she was acquitted.

One wonders how many persons have escaped punishment for murder solely because the death penalty was the jury's only alternative to acquittal. And one wonders why this compelling, if inverted, argument was not more forcefully advanced by the organized opponents to capital punishment in their long, untiring, and fruitful campaign to re-orient the nation's views on criminal punishment, this re-orientation being reflected in the 1972 Furman opinion of the Supreme Court of the United States, equivocally abolishing capital punishment in the nation.

THE EVIDENTIARY RULINGS

But so far we have spoken only of those impalpable forces which acted on the minds of the public and, more specifically, on the minds of the jurors. Let us now consider the more readily discernible influences on the verdict: the rulings of the Court on evidentiary matters. The two very significant evidentiary rulings which were made by the Court during the trial of

Lizzie Borden were favorable to the defendant. Each of the two rulings was a staggering blow to the prosecution and a great victory for the defense. The first was the exclusion of the incriminating statements made by Lizzie, under oath, at the inquest hearing held by Judge Blaisdell five days after the murders. The second was the exclusion of all evidence pertaining to the attempted purchase of prussic acid made by Lizzie the afternoon before the murders.

The position taken by this writer is that despite these unfavorable rulings of the Court and without the evidence so excluded, Lizzie Borden was proven guilty beyond a reasonable doubt, and the verdict of acquittal therefore was odd. Had the prosecution had the advantage of presenting to the jury the evidence which the Court had by these rulings excluded, a verdict of acquittal would have been completely absurd.

It is important to note that Professor John H. Wigmore, perhaps the greatest authority on the law of evidence America has ever produced, disagreed with the Court's rulings in both instances. Professor Wigmore published in the *American Law Review* in 1893 a lengthy discussion of the Borden case and with particularity he discussed the two significant evidentiary questions which the Court resolved in favor of Lizzie Borden. His conclusion was that in both rulings the Court was mistaken and acted contrary to legal authority and sound reasoning.

Professor Wigmore was not alone in his views either then or now. Judge Charles G. Davis wrote in 1893 that the rulings were received with almost universal surprise by the Massachusetts Bar, and that the rulings were clearly contrary to existing law.

I do not intend to argue at length the fine legal points or support with authority my disagreement with the Court's determinations. This short discussion is intended for the lay reader only. For those interested, later in Appendix III can be found supporting case and text authority.

As to the exclusion of Lizzie Borden's statements made under oath at the inquest:

In analyzing the ruling of the Court which favored Lizzie by excluding from evidence her inconsistent and incongruous statements made at the inquest before Judge Blaisdell, two thoughts must be borne in mind: first, that Lizzie did not testify in her own defense, and, second, that this ruling of the Court was made in 1893 and its validity, or lack of it, must be discussed in the light of the law as it then was. The United States Supreme Court under Chief Justice Warren gave us much law that has had the salutory result of effectively protecting the rights of those criminally accused, but some of the members of the Warren Court were not born in 1893. Even considered in the light of the law as it now exists, it is certain that the Borden Court erred in excluding this evidence.

The real issue before the Court in 1893 was whether the statements made by Lizzie under oath to Judge Blaisdell at the inquest were *voluntarily* made. The Borden Court said that if they were made before her arrest, they were voluntary and admissible, but if the accused was under arrest at the time of giving her testimony to Judge Blaisdell, then the statements made by her were not voluntary and were inadmissible only because she was under arrest.

Nowhere in the long trial were the professional skills of Moody and Robinson placed in sharper contrast. Moody argued the law intelligently, soundly and well. Robinson's argument was bombastic and, as Moody described it in rebuttal, "surrounded with a good many vocal gymnastics and fireworks."

Reading Robinson's argument to the Court, it is impossible not to agree with Moody, who said to the Judges when Robinson was finished, "I could not help being reminded of a remark of a French general on the Charge of the Light Brigade, which I make suitable to the occasion, and I say of his [Robinson's] argument generally—it is magnificent, but it is not law."

Moody continued about Robinson's argument: "I have been trying to find out precisely what the learned counsel means, and as far as I can understand his position, it is that the testimony is inadmissible because it is not. There is not, if I followed his argument correctly, a single case cited anywhere of an exclusion of declarations of this sort."

The Court rendered this opinion, taken from the trial transcript:

> It has been held that statements of the accused as a witness under oath at an inquest before he had been arrested or charged with the crime under investigation, may be voluntary and admissible against him in his subsequent trial, and the mere fact that at the time of his testimony at the inquest he was aware that he was suspected of the crime does not make them otherwise. But we are of opinion both upon principle and authority that if the accused was at the time of such testimony *under arrest, charged with the crime in question, the statements so made are not voluntary and are inadmissible at the trial.*

Of course all confessions, admissions and declarations against interest previously made by any defendant at a criminal trial must be shown to be voluntary. But here the Court held that the mere fact of the defendant's making the declarations against interest when she was under arrest would be sufficient to make the declarations involuntary and therefore inadmissible. This is judge-made law, manufactured for the occasion. It is not the law now; it was not the law in 1893; and so far as I know it was never the law. It is little wonder that professionals in the law in 1893 were "surprised" at the ruling, as Judge Davis put it.

But with all the law which the Warren Court has given us, today admissions—confessions of criminal defendants—are as they always have been: admissible when it is established that they were voluntarily made, before or after arrest. And certainly the mere fact of arrest does not in and of itself destroy voluntariness, as the Court held in the Borden case.

Going even further, the Borden Court then held that although Lizzie Borden had not been served with a warrant when she made her statements at the inquest, she was constructively, or "effectually," in custody. It is hard to determine what this means. One assumes that a person is in custody or is not, and a determination of a state called "effectual arrest" is very puzzling.

Quite naturally this untenable position adopted by the Borden Court in this ruling was the object of widespread criticism. Professor Wigmore in his disagreement with the Court writes that it did not matter whether Lizzie Borden was under arrest or not, since she had already been fully advised of her Constitutional rights against self-incrimination, and to protect those Constitutional rights she was obliged only to respond, "Upon advice of counsel, I decline to answer." It should be recalled here that Attorney Jennings had the opportunity to confer at length with Lizzie Borden just before she gave her testimony at the inquest, five days after the murders, and after Mayor Coughlin had told Lizzie she was suspected.

Vehemently criticizing the Borden Court, Professor Wigmore said:

. . . Is there any lawyer in these United States who has a scintilla of a doubt, not merely that her counsel fully informed the accused of her rights, but that they talked over the expediencies, and that he allowed her go on the stand because he deliberately concluded that it was the best policy for her, by so doing, to avoid all appearance of concealment or guilt? And yet the ruling of the Court allowed them to blow hot and cold,—to go on the stand when there was something to gain and to remain silent when the testimony proved dangerous to use. It would seem that, as a matter of law, the fact that an accused person, whether under arrest or not, has had the benefit of counsel's advice ought to make subsequent statements competent as far as regards the free will of the witness.

As to the prussic-acid evidence:

I recognize that the exclusion of this evidence is, or may to a certain extent be, considered discretionary with the Court. Nonetheless I am completely at a loss to understand the exclusion of the evidence offered to show that on the afternoon before the murders Lizzie Borden attempted to purchase the deadliest of poisons, prussic acid, in order, she said, to mothproof a fur cape—a pretence so thin that even the most naïve would equate it for absurdity with using dynamite to destroy a wasps' nest.

Since the attempted purchase took place only hours before the murders, it could not conceivably have been considered too remote in time to be material to a determination of her state of mind before the crimes. Certainly these actions of Lizzie's manifested a clear intent to kill, or a pre-disposition to kill. Why else would she attempt to purchase the deadly poison? If it was to be purchased for some innocent use and in the unlikely event that she had an innocent purpose (for there is quite obviously no commercial use for prussic acid) should not the jury determine this, or have the opportunity to determine this?

Finally, it is specious to urge that merely because Lizzie ultimately used another deadly weapon, a hatchet, the jury should not be told that hours before the murder she was attempting to buy deadly poison. We are here concerned only with a determination of her state of mind prior to the murders, whether or not she was pre-disposed to kill. That and that alone was the sole purpose of offering the prussic-acid testimony.

The admissibility of this evidence in these circumstances and in this time frame seems so basic to the law of evidence that it is sound common sense and hardly requires the support of legal authority, although there is considerable support, as can be seen in Appendix III.

Both these evidentiary problems, when they arose, had been argued by District Attorney William H. Moody for the prosecution. He presented a formidable array of case authority to support the propositions of law he advanced. His statements of the law demonstrated careful preparation and profound grasp of the problems. The Court rejected his arguments.

Robinson in turn had argued both issues in the manner which characterized his trial technique. As he himself declared, he "relied on good common sense" as a substitute for legal authority—and probably as a substitute for adequate preparation. His arguments were short, yet somewhat rambling. The Court was compliant. Lizzie Borden prevailed.

IMPACT OF THE COURT

The long record of their accomplishments makes it very clear that former Governor George D. Robinson and Superior Court Justice Dewey were honorable men. In the nineteenth century they served the Commonwealth of Massachusetts for many years with dignity and with distinction. This writer would be sorely remiss in not certifying to the truth of that fact.

In 1886 Governor Robinson had appointed Justin Dewey a Justice of the Superior Court for life. The fact of this relationship makes it difficult to understand why these two distinguished men, either or both of them, would allow themselves to be cast in rôles at the Borden trial which could be reasonably expected to be the subject of considerable public comment, if not outright public criticism. Perhaps Judge Dewey had convinced himself that he could preside at the Borden trial with complete impartiality, and he chose to ignore the view that a trial judge should recuse himself if his impartiality can reasonably be questioned. Perhaps the climate in which a trial judge operated in 1893 was different from that of today, for the 1893 news reporters seem to have minimized the juxtaposing of Robinson and Judge Dewey. An examination of the major newspapers discloses few references to the relationship between the two in the accounts of the Borden trial. Most of these comments came as a result of Judge Dewey's charge and in press discussions of the verdict.

Judge Charles G. Davis published in 1893 his critical commentaries on the conduct of the Borden trial. In them he asserts his belief in the incorruptibility of Judge Dewey, but charges him with bias and prejudice in favor of the defendant, and protests that as a result of Judge Dewey's actions the Commonwealth did not receive a fair trial.

Alexander Woollcott, renowned literary critic, wit, author, and "Town Crier" of radio fame, was an ardent student of the Borden case. On the occasion of Lizzie Borden's death in 1927 Woollcott published a short essay about the Borden case in which he blamed "the folly" of the Borden jury on a "biased judge" (Judge Dewey).

Holding, for somewhat longer than did Judge Dewey, the same judicial office which he held in the last century, I find it uncomfortable to criticize his judicial action in the Borden case, and I do not. I do, however, disagree.

Any assertion that there was a hint of collusion in Judge Dewey's conduct at the trial is false and absurd, nor do I charge Judge Dewey with bias or prejudice. But it is here suggested that the appearance of bias or prejudice can, at times, be as damaging to public confidence in the proper administration of justice as would be the actual presence of prejudice or bias.

The contention I make here is that Judge Dewey displayed a lack of objectivity in his charge to the jury. This characteristic is self-evident to the professional in the law and to the non-professional alike, upon even a cursory examination of Judge Dewey's charge. In support of that assertion I have placed a transcription of the charge in its entirety in this book as Appendix II.

I believe that Judge Dewey's charge, in its form, had an effect upon the Borden jury and therefore upon its verdict, for certainly every judge believes that his charge in every case will guide the jury through the sometimes complicated forest of the law. But that it should *not* attempt to sway the jury in its determination of the facts.

It is also my view expressed in these pages that it was an unhappy coincidence that Lizzie Borden, acting through her capable attorneys, Andrew Jennings and Melvin O. Adams, retained former Governor Robinson to try the case for the defense a short time before the trial began. I have been unable to determine whether or not Robinson was selected before the names of the panel of judges chosen to hear the Borden case were made public.

One of the recurring fictions in discussions of the Borden case is that Robinson was an accomplished lawyer and that his adept trial technique won acquittal for Lizzie. I do not view his efforts in this light. In 1893 there were approximately twenty-two hundred lawyers practicing in Massachusetts and certainly some of them, including either the able Jennings or the experienced and able Adams, themselves could have tried the case as successfully as did Robinson, and even more creditably; and probably for a much smaller fee.

It is reliably reported that Lizzie Borden paid Robinson $25,000 for his services at the trial. The enormity of this fee can best be measured when it is considered that the Superior Court judges who presided at the trial received in 1893 an annual salary of five thousand dollars. Apparently Lizzie considered the fee satisfactory and paid it, because it is said that there was considerable post-trial correspondence between Lizzie and her former attorney, which ultimately came into the hands of Governor Robinson's grandson, a distinguished member of the Springfield Bar until his death late in 1973. I inquired of the correspondence, hoping for the opportunity to examine it, but learned from associates of Mr. Robinson that he was then very seriously ill, that he had destroyed much of the correspondence several years ago, and those letters which he had retained he did not wish to make public on the understandable ethical grounds of confidentiality of client-attorney communication—a most creditable position to have adopted, and one that I respect.

How can one evaluate the impact of the Court, its actions, its rulings, its instructions upon the jury and upon the jury verdict? It cannot be done with reasonable accuracy; there are too many imponderables. This fact, however, *is* certain: there *is* an impact, there *is* an influence, and when the Court's actions, rulings and instructions to the jury are done with propriety, with dignity and in accordance with the law, there *should be* an impact, an effect which, combined with an earnest, honest, objective search for the truth by the jury, produces justice.

How did the handling of the Borden case fit this pattern for achieving justice? Can it fairly be said that the Borden case was a shining hour in the long and glorious history of Massachusetts jurisprudence? I think not.

THE MANCHESTER MURDER

Consider the impact on, the shock to, the prospective jurors of Bristol County summonsed to serve on the Borden jury and to report for impaneling 5 June 1893 when on 31 May, five days before they were to report for jury duty, they read in screaming headlines that one Bertha Manchester had been murdered, butchered to death in her Fall River home by an unknown assassin—butchered to death by an unknown assassin *wielding an axe.*

Can anyone deny that this coincidence, coming as it did just before the Borden jury was selected, would crush the prosecution, exult the defense, and persuade the jury? An unknown axe killer was again at work in Fall River—but this time Lizzie Borden was in Taunton Jail.

I have no statistics as to how many axe murders committed by unknown assassins have occurred within the city limits of Fall River in the one-hundred-and-twenty-year history of that community. It would be most surprising if there were any others, yet one did occur exactly five days before the Borden jury was chosen: the so-called Manchester murder.

Stephen Manchester was a taciturn, hard-bitten, penurious and disagreeable eccentric who operated a small dairy farm on the outskirts of the city of Fall River. He was called "Old Steve," not because he was beloved but because he was old. By contrast with his contemporary and fellow townsman, Andrew J. Borden, Borden appeared as the late-nineteenth-century precursor of Dale Carnegie.

Deserted by two wives in quick succession, Manchester's farmhouse was run by his youngest daughter, Bertha. Although only twenty-two, Bertha, by virtue of many years of farm work, was, as the press said, "as strong as any man"; she kept house, worked the farm, and, when her father was delivering milk, she bossed the farmhands. She was hard physically, hard-minded, and, like her father, hard to get along with.

On 31 May 1893 Bertha was found dead in the farmhouse kitchen. Her body was stretched on the floor beside the black iron kitchen stove, her clothing disarranged from a struggle, but she had not been sexually molested.

The Medical Examiner, our acquaintance Dr. William Dolan, performed an autopsy. His report disclosed that the back of Bertha's head and the lower neck region had been savagely hacked by an assassin using an axe. There were, according to the autopsy report, "twenty-three distinct and separate axe wounds on the back of the skull and its base."

The people of Bristol County, already in a great froth of excitement over the impending Borden trial, were plunged into near hysteria. The axe killer was loose again in Fall River; fear and speculation again swept the city. Naturally the press reported every detail of the gruesome crime. The wild scenes of panic and apprehension which followed the Borden murders were replayed. STARTLING PARALLELISMS cried the headline 1 June in the Boston *Globe*: "Many Points of Resemblance Found Between Borden and Manchester Murders."

How Lizzie Borden, sitting in her Taunton Jail cell, must have enjoyed the scene, with the beginning of her trial only hours away! Had she herself written the scenario for this weird coincidence, it could not have worked more to her advantage.

Charles J. Holmes, Lizzie's friend and loyal supporter, filled the newspapers with his lengthy statement on Lizzie's behalf, making "a detailed comparison between the Manchester murder and the Borden murders." The newspapers dwelt upon Holmes's news release of 2 June—and with good reason. No one can fault the press for its handling of the Manchester murder. The newspapers printed only the facts, and the facts surrounding the Manchester murder *were* indeed similar to those surrounding the Borden slayings. Here are the parallels the press pointed out: (1) Both the Borden murders and the Manchester murder took place within the city limits of Fall River; (2) both crimes were committed with savagery and with great and senseless mutilation resulting to the victims; (3) the wounds on Bertha Manchester's skull were in almost the precise location and numbers as the wounds on Abby Borden's skull; (4) there was evidence that the unknown assassin had tarried for a considerable time at the Manchester farmhouse; (5) both crimes indicated audacity on the part of the killer—9:30 A.M., when Bertha Manchester was slain, was normally a busy time at the farm; and (6) as in the Borden case, jewelry in clear view was left undisturbed by Bertha Manchester's assassin.

When he heard the news, Andrew Jennings, Lizzie Borden's Fall River attorney, was in Boston, where he and Robinson and Adams were making last-minute plans for Lizzie's defense. Immediately, Jennings took the train to Fall River, and there he was met at the station by the eager representatives of the press. All had gathered to report the Borden trial; to them the Manchester murder was a news bonus. Smiling happily, Jennings stood jauntily on the station platform. If his client had not had enough favorable publicity, she was getting it then. "Well," quipped Jennings to the newsmen, "are they going to claim that Lizzie Borden did this too?"

Jennings's stinging and sarcastic question was given wide circulation. Did it not with great brevity express what was passing through the minds of the newsmen, the public, and especially the minds of the one hundred forty-five men of Bristol County who had been summonsed as jurors in the case of the *Commonwealth v Lizzie Andrew Borden* ?

Schooled by their experience in the Borden case, the Fall River police had roped off and secured the Manchester farmhouse. Even Old Steve was denied access to his home and forced to sleep in the barn. It was noted in the press, however, that his daughter's murder did not in any way interrupt his daily milk deliveries.

Acting swiftly, on Sunday, 4 June, the day before the Borden trial, the police arrested a suspect in the Manchester murder case. This fact, however, was not published in the newspapers until Monday, 5 June; thus the jury chosen to try Lizzie Borden, being isolated on that day, undoubtedly never knew an arrest had been made in the Manchester case. Even if they did, the results would have been the same, since the newspapers on 5 June carried no statement of any kind made by the suspect; they published only that the suspect's uncle was an alibi witness for him, but left the alibi unexplained.

The person arrested and charged with the Manchester murder was a Portuguese immigrant, Jose Correira, also known as Manuel Correira, a small, fiery, twenty-two-year-old itinerant farm worker. He was one of a long line of transient laborers whom the disagreeable Manchester had hired and fired. Correira argued with Manchester over his severance pay, but there was a language barrier since Manchester spoke no Portuguese and Correira no English, and the frustrated Manchester struck Correira. During his short employment at the farm Bertha had fed the disgruntled employee codfish three times a day, and Correira did not like codfish; he did not like Manchester for discharging him, and, for that matter, he did not like Bertha.

After brooding for a few days, he had revisited the Manchester farm, and he became involved in a struggle with the larger, more powerful Bertha. She lost.

These details were all developed long after the Borden jury was isolated; and indeed much of them many months later, after the trial of Lizzie Borden was ended. Correira was finally sentenced to life imprisonment; he served twenty-six years at Charlestown State Prison until he was pardoned by Governor Eugene Foss on condition that he return to his native Azores.

It is absolutely certain that Jose Correira had no connection whatever with the Borden murders. He did not arrive in the United States from the Azores until April 1893, eight months after the Borden killings had taken place and only two months before he committed the Manchester murder.

Although he neither spoke nor read English, it is possible, if not likely, that he was inspired by Lizzie's handiwork ten months before; at least he may have been influenced by Lizzie's example in his selection of weapon. The Portuguese-speaking community in Fall River, of which he had been a short-term member, was quite as excited about the Borden killings as was the rest of the nation; and although Correira arrived in Fall River months after Andrew Borden and his wife were slaughtered, he most certainly had been told of the crimes. Of course this is quite speculative; but it is not uncommon in the annals of crime that shortly after a sensational and unusual murder, another or several will occur, emulating the first in pattern and method. It is a recognized course for psychotics sometimes to follow.

Whatever caused or provoked Jose Correira to commit his foul murder, Lizzie Borden owed him a great debt for his timeliness. When one considers the extraneous influences which were brought to bear on the minds of the Borden jury to persuade them to reach their odd verdict, the murder of Bertha Manchester, completely unsolved as it was at the time of the Borden trial, must stand high on the list. It towers as an example of the incredible luck of Lizzie Borden.

Is it not reasonable to suggest that the jury considered that the unknown assassin of Bertha Manchester had also killed the Bordens in the same way, and realized that the unknown assassin of Bertha Manchester could *not* have been the jailed Lizzie Borden? Can one deny that the timely occurrence of the Manchester murder was for Lizzie Borden a magnificent stroke of sheer blind luck?

From Acquittal

L ET US CONSIDER the extraordinary spectacle of the days immediately following the verdict of acquittal.

Lizzie Borden, an unpleasant spinster, had, in the most barbarous manner, savagely butchered her elderly father and her docile stepmother. Now—by orchestrating guile, stubbornness, complete unflappability and incredible luck—she had become a heroine, even an idol, to a large segment of the American people. Exactly how Lizzie transformed her image from murderess to martyr, projected herself from pitiless assassin to a pitiful person persecuted by perverse police and prosecutors, we shall never know. Certainly, in this regard, the influences treated in the preceding pages were persuasive when brought to bear upon the minds of the Court and jury. What weight, or what inducive force, any one of these imponderables standing alone had, no reasonable person would attempt to assess. Taken altogether, however, these influences *must* have impelled the unreal verdict of acquittal; the evidence did not.

For two days the nation's press reflected the rejoicing of Lizzie's supporters as they hailed the jury's verdict; congratulatory messages inundated her; exultation reigned; and Lizzie was the focal point of attention. Then the first note of discord was sounded. The thinking public began to recognize the utter irrationality of the situation: if Lizzie did not kill Andrew Borden and his wife—*who did?* Contributing to this discord, the Fall River police pointedly announced that no further efforts would be made to find the killer; the case was closed.

As always with its finger on the public pulse, the press also began to have second thoughts. The first salvo was fired by the Providence *Journal*, which throughout the trial had been fair, if not favorable, to Lizzie. Editorially the *Journal* baldly argued that the verdict was questionable, citing Lizzie's exclusive opportunity to commit the crimes.

In its lead editorial of 21 June the *Journal* challenged: "There is no reason now for Miss Borden's silence; let her speak! Let her spare no effort to bring this horrible case to a more satisfactory conclusion than it now has reached, with so much evidence barred out by the Court, and the presumption of innocence so strenuously insisted upon by the Judge in his charge to the jury."

Two days later the *Journal* struck again, this time with unusual force. Dismissing the chorus of jubilation after the verdict as "led off by a lot of women," the *Journal* attacked "Lizzie's other kind of champion, the Reverend W. Walker Jubb, who obviously thinks that the fact of Miss Borden's attendance at his church should immediately hush all inquiry into her connection with the murders." The editorial ended defiantly, calling upon Lizzie's friends to name the assassin *"if Miss Borden didn't do it* [italics supplied]."

Although the Boston *Globe* at that time had the largest circulation in New England, the Providence *Journal* was the most widely read newspaper in Bristol County. The effect of its clarion call to reason was chilling: There arose a deluge of protest against the verdict that soon cooled pro-Lizzie ardor beyond its own readership. The responsible press swung into line with expressions of dissatisfaction and disenchantment. Intelligent people reflected—first amazed, then suspicious, they were finally convinced that the verdict was contrary to the weight of the evidence.

In a short span of time there had been a phenomenal turnabout. Lizzie Borden had been acquitted by the jury, but now the public was passing judgment. The two clergymen who had flaunted their attentions to Lizzie from the day of the murders to the day of her acquittal became, deservedly, objects of ridicule. Former Governor Robinson felt the sting of rebuke when such an eminent legal authority as Professor Wigmore publicly termed Robinson's argument concerning the missing note "a blot on the conduct of the trial," "decidedly a breech of propriety," and a "false quotation of the testimony." The rulings of the trial Court were attacked as prejudicial, biased and erroneous.

The American public's proclivity to witticize its errors was never more manifest. Lizzie Borden and the jury's verdict were lampooned in every conceivable way, from the world-famous jingle to one-line jokes. Lizzie was called "the self-made heiress," and in time William Roughead, writing what may be the world's greatest understatement, termed her "unfilial."

It must be stressed, however, that all the wit, all the waggery, all the jokes emerged *after* the Borden verdict. Lizzie's trial was not a travesty of justice, because "travesty" implies burlesque, and burlesque implies humor, and there was nothing humorous about the Borden trial. This case was a failure of justice—a defeat of justice. Yet acquitted as she was by the established court system, Lizzie Borden was soon to be convicted by the court of popular opinion.

Little more remains to tell of this sad story. Shortly after the trial Lizzie and Emma moved to "Maplecroft," a stately house located on French Street in the fashionable Hill section of Fall River. Here Lizzie lived for the balance of her life.

Maplecroft—that name is carved into the top stone riser of the front steps—stands today as sedately as it did when its celebrated owner first occupied it. A large house of fourteen rooms, it is decorated throughout with dark wooden beams and paneling. The ceiling in the dining room is linen cloth, an elegant decorating touch at the turn of the century, and even the laundry room in the basement has exquisite dark wood wainscoting, although the barred cellar windows add an eerie note. Perhaps overcompensating for the rudimentary plumbing at 92 Second Street, there are four bathrooms at Maplecroft. A line of fine old maple trees flanks the east and north sides of the premises. Frank M. Silvia, Jr., a prominent Fall River attorney who now owns and occupies Maplecroft, told me that the back porch was designed by Lizzie so she could see and not be seen while she sat watching the birds and squirrels which she fed daily.

For thirty-four years after the trial Lizzie lived in Fall River in near seclusion. The newspaper headline on the day of the verdict that promised "Church and Charity Will Claim Lizzie" was an inaccurate prediction indeed. Her erstwhile clerical friends, the Reverend Messrs. Jubb and Buck, fast lost their enthusiasm to "claim" Lizzie—or in fact have

"Maplecroft" Today

CHARLES CARROLL PHOTOGRAPH

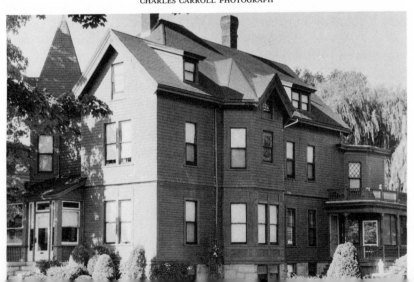

anything to do with her. Her former supporters looked the other way when she passed; she was ostracized by Fall River society. Lizzie was in fact "silenced," in the idiomatic sense of that word. Over the years she was first a source of embarrassment to Fall River; then she became a curiosity. She kept a handsome span of horses and frequently was driven through the city streets by her liveried chauffeur, Ernest Terry. Later a shining limousine replaced the horses, and, as years passed, the aging recluse was seen less often.

In 1904 Emma left the French Street home, and the sisters were never again to meet in life. Emma's reasons for leaving Maplecroft are not at all clear. It is impossible to believe that Emma was at any time ignorant of the identity of the murderer of her father and stepmother. Thus her actions, however reluctant, before and during the trial made her at least a perjuror, perhaps an accessory after the fact of murder; motivated she may have been by some strange sense of loyalty, but nonetheless an accessory she was. It is possible, considering Emma's personality, that a gnawing sense of guilt finally drove her to leave her sister forever. Emma led a completely secluded life in Newmarket, New Hampshire, and died at the age of seventy-three, nine days after Lizzie's death.

It is said that in February of 1897 the Providence firm of Tilden and Thurber, Jewelers, caused a warrant to be issued for Lizzie's arrest, charging her with the shoplifting of two small decorated pieces of porcelain bric-a-brac. Years later this story was amplified by the alleged appearance of a "confession" to the murders, purportedly extracted from Lizzie by the store officials in return for leniency in handling the shoplifting accusation.

Remembering the "robbery" which Andrew Borden had first reported to the police only to reject police investigation shortly thereafter, I am inclined to admit the plausibility of the shoplifting episode, but I do not consider it particularly material to the telling of this story. As to the sequela to the shoplifting and the "confession," so-called, this appears to be a hoax or a fraud or both; at any rate, I consider it unworthy of belief.

From time to time during her life at Maplecroft, Lizzie traveled on pleasure jaunts to Boston, Providence and Washington, D.C. It is said that she had a keen interest in the theatre and at one time was extremely friendly with a well-known actress named Nance O'Neil. This relationship with Miss O'Neil and other entertainers has given rise to stories of wild and protracted parties held by Lizzie at Maplecroft and elsewhere during the period of her incursion into the world of the theatre. I was unable to find any factual evidence of this type of frivolity in Lizzie's life; indeed, it would seem out of character for her. I have therefore concluded that the stories were exaggerated, if not groundless gossip.

Lizzie Borden died at her home in Fall River on 1 June, 1927, almost exactly thirty-four years after her acquittal. Her estate was substantial, and by her will she left a number of small monetary legacies to her servants, cousins, "old school mates" and others. Her friend Helen Leighton and her cousin, Grace H. Howe, were the principal and residual legatees. She bequeathed two thousand dollars to the Animal Rescue League of Washington, D.C., and thirty thousand dollars, together with shares of stock, to the Animal Rescue League of Fall River. Explaining this bequest Lizzie had written, "I have been fond of animals, and their need is great, and there are so few who care for them."

The funeral services were private and quite unremarkable except that a 1927 newspaper noted that a soloist had sung one song for the small gathering at Maplecroft. The name of the song was "My Ain Countree." This seemed to me to be more than coincidental, since the very words MY AIN COUNTREE are conspicuously carved under the mantelpiece in the library at Maplecroft. Feeling that the phrase had a Burnsian ring and remembering that Robert Burns, like Lizzie Borden, had had an unusually strong love for animals, I searched through the myriad of works of the great Scots bard, but with no success. Oddly, the words are from the verses of a lesser-known Scots poet, Allan Cunningham. Cunningham's father had been a neighbor of Burns's in Scotland, but the poet's son was only twelve when Burns died. It appears that although Cunningham was not a protégé of Burns, some consider him Burns's imitator. Here is the rather depressing stanza where the words are found:

> *The green leaf of loyalty's beginning to fall.*
> *The bonnie White Rose it is withering an' all.*
> *But I'll water it with the blood of usurping tyranny,*
> *And green it will grow in* my ain countree.

Is there any significance to this? Is there a message here?

In the first paragraph of her will Lizzie Borden left the sum of five hundred dollars to the City of Fall River, "the income to be derived therefrom to be used for the perpetual care of my father's lot in Oak Grove Cemetery in said Fall River."

The grave site itself is arranged in an unusual manner, and is dominated by a large stone having all family names incised upon it. Lizzie's name appears as Lizbeth Andrews Borden, the thinly disguised pseudonym she adopted in later life, which fact leads one to believe that she herself planned the odd pattern of placement of the individual graves. Each is marked by a small stone, with either initials or first names engraved upon them. Lizzie, or Lizbeth as the stone marker reads, lies beside her sister, Emma. At the foot of these two graves are the graves of A.J.B.—Andrew Jackson Borden—and to its right, S.M.B.—Sarah Morse Borden, Andrew's first wife; to the left of Andrew's grave is the stone marked A.D.B., Abby Durfee Borden; and finally ALICE, Sarah's child who died in infancy, lies beside her mother.

I have been at this gravesite twice: once with Mrs. Abby Potter in 1972 and again more than a year later in the fall of 1973. On both occasions a fresh geranium plant had been recently placed in front of the small stone marked LIZBETH. Either the officials of Fall River have been scrupulously faithful to the testamentary obligation of perpetual care imposed upon them by Lizzie's will, or she has not been forgotten by someone alive today.

So ends the sad saga of the Borden murders and trial. The story reflects credit upon no one. Because from time to time over the years there have been written protestations of Lizzie's innocence, some sensational and some wearisome, I felt that a full and complete analysis of the Borden matter might in some small way help to lay it to rest, might in some modest manner help to end the enduring public obsession with this wretched and deplorable event in our history. It has been my earnest purpose in these pages to lay bare the harsh and true facts surrounding the deaths of Andrew Borden and his wife, Abby, and the unpropitious but irreclaimable trial that followed—to close the book, as it were: to say goodbye to the house of horrors on Second Street in Fall River, and to say goodbye to the mystery of Lizzie Borden.

CHARLES CARROLL PHOTOGRAPH

APPENDIX I:

Testimony of
Lizzie Andrew Borden

[INQUEST]

[The following is a copy of the statement as it was published on the front page of the Providence *Journal* ten months after the inquest. It appears to be a transcription of what was read to Judge Blaisdell at the preliminary hearing, since several times it quotes Mr. Adams interposing objections, and Mr. Adams was not present at the inquest itself.

No responsible person can represent with absolute certainty that the Providence *Journal*'s account of Lizzie's testimony at the secret inquest is either complete or completely in accord with Stenographer White's notes, but a comparison of Lizzie's statement from the *Journal* with that as published by the New Bedford *Standard* reveals that the two vary only in slight detail. In fact, the only significant difference between the two accounts is that the evening *Standard* of New Bedford attributes to Lizzie the statement that her father, preparing for his nap, had "lain down on the sitting room lounge, taken off his shoes and put on his slippers"; this, of course, flies in the face of the fact that at the time of the discovery of his body, Andrew Borden was wearing high congress shoes. However, there are other indications of authenticity, not the least of which is the challenging and defiant manner of the defendant's responses to District Attorney Knowlton's questions, a manner which, from all accounts—including Mrs. Abby Potter's—was notably consistent with Lizzie Borden's personality.]

The following is the testimony of Miss Lizzie Borden at the inquest in August last, which the defense in the trial now progressing at New Bedford will endeavor today to have barred as evidence. The statements were made August 9, 10, and 11 [1892] and were submitted from court stenographer Annie M. White's notes on the fifth day of the preliminary hearing, August 30. At that time District Attorney Knowlton read the testimony as follows:

"Give me your full name."

"Lizzie Andrew Borden."

"You were so christened?"

"I was."

"What is your age?"

"Thirty-two."

"Your mother is not living?"

"She died when I was two years of age."

The remainder of the testimony was as follows:

"My father and stepmother were married twenty-seven years ago. I have no idea how much my father was worth, and have never heard him form an opinion. I know something about what real estate my father owned."

The next question was: "How do you know?" and Mr. Adams promptly objected. He said he did so on the ground of the admissibility of a statement, which was detrimental to her.

Judge Blaisdell said he didn't know that any statement the defendant might make would not be competent. Mr. Jennings agreed in support of his associate. He said any statement that did not bear directly on the issue between the prosecution and the defense was not material. Judge Blaisdell allowed the introduction of the question, and the answer was "two farms in Swansea, the homestead, some property on North Main Street, Borden Block, some land further south, and some he had recently purchased."

"Did you ever deed him any property?"

"He gave us some land, but my father bought it back. Had no other transaction with him. He paid in $5000 cash for this property. Never knew my father made a will, but heard so from Uncle Morse."

"Did you know of anybody that your father had trouble with?"

"There was a man who came there some weeks before, but I do not know who he was. He came to the house one day, and I heard them talk about a store. My father told him he could not have a store. The man said: 'I thought with your liking for money you would let anybody in.' I heard my father order him out of the house. Think he lived out of town, because he said he could go back and talk with father."

"Did your father and anybody else have bad feelings between them?"

"Yes, Hiram C. Harrington. He married my father's only sister."

"Nobody else?"

"I have no reason to suppose that that man had seen my father before that day."

"Did you ever have any trouble with your stepmother?"

"No."

"Within a year?"

"No."

"Within three years?"

"No. About five years ago."

"What was it about?"

"About my stepmother's stepsister, Mrs. George Whitehead."

"Was it a violent expression of feeling?"

"It was simply a difference of opinion."

"Were you always cordial with your stepmother?"

"That depends upon one's idea of cordiality."

"Was it cordial according to your ideas of cordiality?"

"Yes. I did not regard her as my mother, though she came there when I was young. I decline to say whether my relations between her and myself were those of mother and daughter or not. I called her Mrs. Borden, and sometimes mother. I stopped calling her mother after the affair regarding her sister-in-law."

"Why did you leave off calling her mother?"

"Because I wanted to."

"Have you any other answer to give me?"

"No, sir. I always went to my sister. She was older than I was. I don't know but that my father and stepmother were happily united. I never knew of any difficulty between them, and they seemed to be affectionate. The day they were killed I had on a blue dress. I changed it in the afternoon and put on a print dress. Mr. Morse came into our house whenever he wanted to. He has been here once since the river was frozen over. I don't know how often he came to spend the nights, because I had been away so much. I have not been away much during the year. He has been there very little during the past year. I have been away a great deal in the daytime during the last year. I don't think I have been away much at night, except once, when I was in New Bedford. I was abroad in 1890. I first saw Morse Thursday noon. Wednesday evening I was with Miss Russell at 9 o'clock, and I don't know whether the family were in or not. I went direct to my room. I locked the front door when I came in. Was in my room Wednesday, not feeling well all day. Did not go down to supper. Went out that evening and came in and locked the front door. Came down about 9 the next morning. Did not inquire about Mr. Morse that morning. Did not go to Marion at that time, because they could go sooner than I. I had taken the Secretaryship of the Christian Endeavor Society, and had to remain over till the 10th. There had been nobody else around there that week but the man I have spoken of. I did not say that he came a week before, but that week. Mr. Morse slept in the spare room Wednesday night. It was my habit to close my room door when I was in it. That Wednesday afternoon they made so much noise that I closed the door. First saw my father Thursday morning downstairs reading the Providence *Journal*. Saw my mother with a dust cloth in her hand. Maggie [Bridget Sullivan] was putting a cloth into a mop. Don't know whether I ate cookies and tea that morning. Know the coffee pot was on the stove. My father went down town after 9 o'clock. I did not finish the handkerchiefs because the irons were not right. I was in the kitchen reading when he returned. I am not sure that I was in the kitchen when my father returned. I stayed in my room long enough to sew a piece of lace on a garment. That was before he came back. I don't know where Maggie was. I think she let my father in, and that he rang the bell. I understood Maggie to say he said he had forgotten his key. I think I was upstairs when my father came in, and I think I was on the stairs when he entered. I don't know whether Maggie was washing windows or not when my father came in."

At this point the District Attorney had called Miss Borden's attention to her conflicting statements regarding her position when her father came in, and her answer was:

"You have asked me so many questions, I don't know what I have said."

Later, she said she was reading in the kitchen and had gone into the other room for a copy of the Providence *Journal*.

"I last saw my mother when I was downstairs. She was dusting the dining room. She said she had been upstairs and made the bed, and was going upstairs to put on the pillow slips. She had some cotton cloth pillows up there, and she said she was going to work on them. If she had remained downstairs I should have seen her. She would have gone up the back way to go to her room. If she had gone to the kitchen I would have seen her. There is no reason to suppose I would not have seen her when she was downstairs or in her room, except when I went downstairs once for two or three minutes."

"I ask you again what you suppose she was doing from the time you saw her till 11 o'clock."

"I don't know, unless she was making her bed."

"She would have had to pass your room, and you would have seen her, wouldn't you?"

"Yes, unless I was in my room or down cellar. I supposed she had gone away because she told me she was going, and we talked about the dinner. Didn't hear her go or come back. When I first came downstairs, saw Maggie coming in, and my mother asked me how I was feeling. My father was there, still reading. My mother used to go and do the marketing."

"Now I call your attention to the fact you said twice yesterday that you first saw your father after he came in when you were standing on the stairs."

"I did not. I was in the kitchen when he came in, or in one of the three rooms, the dining room, kitchen and sitting room. It would have been difficult for anybody to pass through these rooms unless they passed through while I was in the dining room."

"A portion of the time the girl [Bridget Sullivan] was out of doors, wasn't she?"
"Yes."

Lizzie Borden's testimony continued as follows:

"So far as I know, I was alone in the house the larger part of the time while my father was away. I was eating a pear when my father came in. I had put a stick of wood into the fire to see if I could start it. I did no more ironing after my father came in. I then went in to tell him. I did not put away the ironing board. I don't know what time my father came in. When I went out to the barn I left him on the sofa. The last thing I said was to ask him if he wanted the window left that way. Then I went to the barn to get some lead for a sinker. I went upstairs in the barn. There was a bench there which contained some lead. I unhooked the screen door when I went out. I don't know when Bridget got through washing the windows inside. I knew she washed the windows outside. I knew she didn't wash the kitchen windows, but I didn't know whether she washed the sitting room windows or not. I thought the flats [flatirons] would be hot by the time I got back. I had no fishing apparatus, but there was some at the farm. It is five years since I used the fish line. I don't think there was any sinker on my line. I don't think there were any fish lines suitable for use at the farm."

"What! Did you think you would find sinkers in the barn?"

"My father once told me that there was some lead and nails in the barn."

"How long do you think you occupied in looking for the sinkers?"

"About fifteen or twenty minutes."

"Did you do nothing beside look for sinkers in the twenty minutes?"

"Yes, sir. I ate some pears."

"Would it take you all that time to eat a few pears?"

"I do not do things in a hurry."

"Was Bridget not washing the dining room windows and the sitting room windows?"

"I do not know. I did not see her."

"Did you tell Bridget to wash the windows?"

"No, sir."

"Who did?"

"My mother."

"Did you see Bridget after your mother told her to wash the windows?"

"Yes, sir."

"What was she doing?"

"She had got a long pole and was sticking it in a brush, and she had a pail of water."

"About what time did you go out into the barn?"

"About as near as I can recollect, 10 o'clock."

"What did you go into the barn for?"

"To find some sinkers."

"How many pears did you eat in that twenty minutes?"

"Three."

"Is that all you did?"

"No, I went over to the window and opened it."

"Why did you do that?"

"Because it was too hot."

"I suppose that it is the hottest place on the premises?"

"Yes, sir."

"Could you, while standing looking out of that window, see anybody enter the kitchen?"

"No, sir."

"I thought you said you could see people from the barn?"

"Not after you pass a jog in the barn. It obstructs the view of the back door."

"What kind of lead were you looking for, for sinkers? Hard lead?"

"No, sir. Soft lead."

"Did you expect to find the sinkers already made?"

"Well, no. I thought I might find one with a hole through it."

"Was the lead referred to tea lead or lead that comes in tea chests?"

"I don't know."

"When were you going fishing?"

"Monday."

"The next Monday after the fatal day?"

"Yes, sir."

"Had you lines all ready?"

"No, sir."

"Did you have a line?"

"Yes, sir."

"Where was your line?"

"Down to the farm [Swansea]."

"Do you know whether there were any sinkers on the line you left at the farm?"

"I think there was none on the line."

"Did you have any hooks?"

"No, sir."

"Then you were making all this preparation without either hook or line. Why did you go into the barn after sinkers?"

"Because I was going down town to buy some hooks and line, and thought it would save me from buying them."

"Now, to the barn again. Do you not think I could go into the barn and do the same as you in a few minutes?"

"I do not do things in a hurry."

"Did you then think there were no sinkers at the barn?"

"I thought there were no sinkers anywhere there. I had no idea of using my lines. I thought you understood that I wasn't going to use these lines at the farm, because they hadn't sinkers. I went upstairs to the kind of bench there. I had heard my father say there was lead there. Looked for lead in a box up there. There were nails and perhaps an old door knob. Did not find any lead as thin as tea lead in the box. Did not look anywhere except on the bench. I ate some pears up there. I have now told you everything that took place up in the barn. It was the hottest place in the premises. I suppose I ate my pears when I first went up there. I stood looking out of the window. I was feeling well enough to eat pears, but don't know how to answer the question if I was feeling better than I was in the morning, because I was feeling better that morning. I picked the pears from the ground. I was not in the rear of the barn. I was in the front of it. Don't see how anybody could leave the house then without my seeing them. I pulled over boards to look for the lead. That took me some time. I returned from the barn and put my head in the dining room. I found my father and called to Maggie. I found the fire gone out. I went to the barn because the irons were not hot enough and the fire had gone out. I made no effort to find my mother at all. Sent Maggie for Dr. Bowen. Didn't see or find anything after the murders to tell me my mother had been sewing in the spare room that morning."

"What did your mother say when you saw her?"

"She told me she had had a note and was going out. She said she would get the dinner."

The District Attorney continued to read:

"My mother did not tell when she was coming back. I did not know Mr. Morse was coming to dinner. I don't know whether I was at tea Wednesday night or not. I had no apron on Thursday; that is, I don't think I had. I don't remember surely. I had no occasion to use the axe or hatchet. I knew there was an old axe downstairs and last time I saw it it was on the old chopping block. I don't know whether my father owned a hatchet or not. Assuming a hatchet was found in the cellar I don't know how it got there, and if there was blood on it I have no idea as to how it got there. My father killed some pigeons last May. When I found my father I did not think of Mrs. Borden, for I believed she was out. I remember asking Mrs. Churchill to look for my mother. I left the screen door closed when I left, and it was open when I came from the barn. I can give no idea of the time when my father came home. I went right to the barn. I don't know whether he came to the sitting room at once or not. I don't remember his being in the sitting room or sitting down. I think I was in there when I asked him if there was any mail. I do not think he went upstairs. He had a letter in his hand. I did not help him to lie down and did not touch the sofa. He was taking medicine for some time. Mrs. Borden's father's house was for sale on Fourth Street. My father bought Mrs. Borden's half-sister's [Mrs. Abby Potter's mother's] share, and gave it to her. We thought what he did for her people he ought to do for his own, and then he gave us Grandfather's house. I always thought my stepmother induced him to purchase the interest. I don't know when the windows were last washed before that day. I gave the officer the same skirt I wore that day, and if there was any blood on it, I can give an explanation as to how it got there. I wore tie shoes that day, and black stockings. I was under the pear trees four or five minutes. I came down the front stairs when I came down in the morning. The dress I wore that forenoon was a white and blue stripe of some sort. It is at home in the attic. I did not go to Smith's drug store to buy prussic acid. Did not go to the rooms where mother or father lay after the murders. Went through when I went upstairs that day. I wore the shoes I gave to the officer all day Thursday and Friday."

"I now ask you if you can furnish any other suspicion concerning any person who might have committed the crime?"

"Yes: one night as I was coming home not long ago I saw the shadow of a man on the house at the east end. I thought it was a man because I could not see any skirts. I hurried in the front door. It was about 8:45 o'clock; not later than 9. I saw somebody run around the house last winter. The last time I saw anybody lately was since my sister went to Marion. I told Mr. Jennings, may have told Mr. Hanscom."

"Who suggested the reward offered, you or your sister?"

"I don't know. I may have."

[So ended the Providence *Journal*'s account of Lizzie's inquest testimony read at the probable-cause hearing 25–31 August 1892.]

Charge to the Jury by Dewey, J.

[FROM THE TRIAL TRANSCRIPT]

Mr. Foreman and Gentlemen of the Jury:—You have listened with attention to the evidence in this case, and to the arguments of the defendant's counsel and of the district attorney. It now remains for me, acting in behalf of the Court, to give you such aid towards a proper performance of your duty as I may be able to give within the limits for judicial action prescribed by law; and, to prevent any erroneous impression, it may be well for me to bring to your attention, at the outset, that it is provided by a statute of this State that the Court shall not charge juries with respect to matters of fact, but may state the testimony and the law.

Without attempting to define the exact scope of this statute, it is not to be doubted, in view of expositions made of it by our court of last resort, that it was intended to prevent the judges presiding at the trial from expressing any opinion as to the credibility of witnesses or the strength of evidence, while it does not preclude them from defining the degree of weight which the law attaches to a whole class of testimony, leaving it to the jury to apply the general rule to the circumstances of the case.

I may perhaps illustrate this distinction in the course of my remarks; but, speaking comprehensively, I may now say to you that it will be your duty, in considering and deciding the matters of fact necessary to rendering your verdict, not to allow your judgment to be affected by what you may suppose or believe to be the opinion of the Court upon such matters of fact.

The law places upon the Court the duty and responsibility of furnishing you with a correct statement of such rules and principles of law applicable to the case, as you need to know; and places upon you, and you only, the distinct duty and responsibility of deciding all questions of fact involved in the issue between the Commonwealth and the defendant; and your decision can properly rest only on the law and the evidence given you, together with those matters of common knowledge and experience relating to the ordinary affairs of life, and the common qualities of human nature and motives of action, which are never proved in court, but which, as jurors, you are expected to bring with you to this investigation.

I will here add that nothing in the prior official proceedings in this case, neither the inquest nor the hearing or trial in the District Court at Fall River, nor the action of the Grand Jury in finding the indictment can properly influence your judgment in this case. In connection with those proceedings, by the usual legal formalities, the case is brought before you for inquiry, and it is independent of any official action that has gone before. It is still more plain that neither the defendant's confinement in prison nor her coming here in the custody of an officer, nor the legal restraint under which she manifestly is, raise against her any presumption of guilt. They are a part of that necessary discomfort which under our laws, as they now are, one is called to experience who is regularly charged with a capital crime. The defendant is being tried before you on a written accusation, termed an indictment, which contains two charges or counts; one count by the use of the unusual legal language in substance charges her with the murder of Andrew J. Borden, and the other count charges her with the murder of Abby D. Borden in Fall River in this county on August 4th, 1892. Chapter 202 of the Public Statutes contains these sections, "Murder committed with deliberately premeditated malice aforethought, or in the commission of, or attempt to, commit a crime punishable with death or imprisonment for life, or committed with extreme atrocity or cruelty is murder in the first degree. Murder not appearing to be in the first degree, is murder in the second degree."

"The degree of murder shall be found by the jury"—in connection with rendering their verdict, if they find against the defendant. The government claims that the killing of Mr. and Mrs. Borden, by whomsoever done, was done with premeditated, deliberate malice aforethought within the meaning of the statute and it was murder in the first degree. The statute nowhere defines murder itself, and for such definition we must resort to the common law, and according to that law "murder is the unlawful killing of a human being with malice aforethought." A short explanation may be needed of these elements of murder in the first degree. The term malice as here used means more than personal hatred or ill will. It means any unlawful motive, or it is sometimes said to denote a state of mind manifested by the wrongful act done intentionally without just cause or excuse. The words "malice aforethought" by themselves alone have been settled by our Supreme Court to imply purpose and design in contradistinction to accident or mischance. The words "deliberately premeditated" mean that the wrongful intention to kill must have been formed before the act of killing. The killing must be the result of a plan or purpose to kill unlawfully, formed without reflection and deliberation by the guilty party. The law does not require that this intention, plan or purpose to kill shall have existed for any considerable time before it is carried out. The time may be very short. It is enough if there was a clear intent to kill formed before the act of killing; and so the Government claims that you ought to be satisfied that the killing of Mr. and Mrs. Borden was wrongful and malicious, that is, without just cause or excuse, and that it was deliberately premeditated,—that is, the design to do it was first formed and after that was carried out.

Although most of the evidence may relate to both counts in the indictment, the counts are distinct and will require a separate finding by you.

The second main proposition in the case is that the killing of Mr. and Mrs. Borden was done by the defendant. In considering the evidence with regard to this issue, you will need to have certain legal principles in mind and to use them as guides. One such principle is the presumption of law that the defendant is innocent. This presumption begins with her at the outset of the trial, and continues with her through all its stages until you are compelled by the evidence to divest her of it. As one learned writer has expressed it, "This legal presumption of innocence is to be regarded by the jury in every case as matter of evidence to the benefit of which the party is entitled." This presumption of innocence operating in behalf of the defendant also operates in behalf of all of us, and, as was declared in an important capital trial, it is a presumption founded on that universal beneficence of the law which says that every man does right till the contrary appear.

The law does not undertake to fix or measure the force of this presumption in this case by any formal or arbitrary rule, but leaves it to your just and intelligent judgment. It may vary in different cases, its force being strengthened amongst other things by the character and previous way of life of the defendant. I understand the Government to concede that the defendant's character has been good; that it has not been merely a negative and neutral one that nobody had heard anything against, but one of positive, of active benevolence in religious and charitable work. The question is whether the defendant, being such as she was, did the acts charged upon her. You are not inquiring into the action of some imaginary being but into the action of a real person, the defendant, with her character, with her habits, with her education, with her ways of life, as they have been disclosed in the case. Judging of this subject as reasonable men, you have the right to take into consideration her character such as is admitted or apparent. In some cases it may not be esteemed of much importance. In other cases it may raise a reasonable doubt of a defendant's guilt even in the face of strongly incriminating circumstances. What shall be its effect here rests in your reasonable discretion.

It is competent for the Government to show that the defendant had motives to commit the crime with which she is charged, and evidence has been introduced from which you are asked to find that she had unpleasant relations with her stepmother, the deceased, and also that her father, Andrew Jackson Borden, left an estate of the value of from $250,000 to $300,000, and that so far as is known to the defendant, he died without having made a will. If his wife died before him, it is not disputed that he left the defendant and her sister as his only heirs. It appears that Mr. Borden was 69 years old, and Mrs. Borden more than 60 years of age at the time of their deaths. Taking the facts now as you find them to be established by the evidence, and taking the defendant as you find her to be, and judging according to general experience and observation, was the defendant under a real and actually operating motive to kill her father and his wife? An able writer on the criminal law says:

"In the affairs of life it is seldom a man does anything prompted by one motive alone to accomplish one end." Unless the child be destitute of natural affection, will the desire to come into possession of the inheritance be likely to constitute an active, efficient inducement for the child to take the parent's life?

If you find as a fact that the defendant was under an actually operating motive, pecuniary or any other, to destroy the life of her father and stepmother, then it becomes a matter proper to be considered. For, as one has said: "It may tend to repel the presumption which exists, in addition to the general presumption of innocence, that a person will not commit a crime without reason, inducement or temptation."

It is not necessary for the government to prove motive. It has been said that there can be no adequate motive for murder, but it is a part of the folly and sin of man that he will sometimes act contrary to the highest and strongest motive; by his perversity he will make a weak motive strong and then act upon it.

Imputing a motive to the defendant does not prove that she had it. I understand the counsel for the Government to claim that the defendant had towards her stepmother a strong feeling of ill will, nearly, if not quite, amounting to hatred. And Mrs. Gifford's testimony as to a conversation with the defendant in the early Spring of 1892 is relied upon largely as a basis for that claim, supplemented by whatever evidence there is as to the defendant's conduct towards her stepmother.

Now, gentlemen, in judging wisely of a case you need to keep all parts of it in their natural and proper proportion, and not to put on any particular piece of evidence a greater weight than it will reasonably bear, and not to magnify or intensify or depreciate and belittle any piece of evidence to meet an emergency. I shall say something before I have done on the caution to be used in considering testimony as to conversations. But take Mrs. Gifford's just as she gave it, and consider whether or not it will fairly amount to the significance attached to it, remembering that it is the language of a young woman and not of a philosopher or a jurist. What, according to common observation, is the habit of young women in the use of language? Is it not rather that of intense expression, whether or not they do not often use words which, strictly taken, would go far beyond their real meaning? Would it be a just mode of reasoning to make use of the alleged subsequent murder to put enmity into the words and then use the words, thus charged with hostile meaning, as evidence that the defendant committed the murder?

Again, every portion of the testimony should be estimated in the light of the rest. What you wish, of course, is a true conception,—a true conception of the state of the mind of the defendant towards her stepmother, not years ago, but later and nearer the time of the homicide: and to get such a true conception you must not separate Mrs. Gifford's testimony from all the rest, but consider also the evidence as to how they lived in the family; whether, as Mrs. Raymond, I believe, said, they sewed together on each other's dresses; whether they went to church together, sat together, returned together; in a word, the general tenor of their life. You will particularly recall the testimony of Bridget Sullivan and of the defendant's sister, Emma, bearing on the subject. Weigh carefully all the testimony on the subject in connection with the suggestions of counsel, and then judge whether or not there is clearly proved such a permanent state of mind on the part of the defendant towards her stepmother as to justify you in drawing against her upon that ground inferences unfavorable to her innocence.

Recall the evidence; reflect upon it; compare one part with another, and see whether you, as intelligent and reasonable men, desiring to approach the consideration of this case from a just and true standpoint, would be warranted upon the evidence in taking into your minds the conception and allowing that conception to operate upon all your construction and estimation of the other evidence,—the conception that at and about the time of these murders this defendant had towards her stepmother a feeling that could be properly called hatred. If that is not a just conception warranted by the evidence, then it should not enter and find lodgment in your minds as a controlling idea under the operation of which the evidence in this case is to be judged. Such a conception, if erroneous, may be more serious upon the operations of your mind and more liable to affect improperly your final conclusion than a mistake on any single portion of the evidence.

Because, if it is a wrong conception, unwarranted by the evidence, unjust to the defendant, and you start out in the case with that, it colors and affects all the action of your minds till your verdict is rendered.

Now, gentlemen, the material charge in the first count of the indictment is that, at Fall River, in this county, the defendant killed Mrs. Borden, by striking, cutting, beating, and bruising her on the head with some sharp cutting instrument. In the second count the same charges are made in regard to Mr. Borden. And the Government claims that these acts were done with deliberately premeditated malice aforethought, and so were acts of murder in the first degree.

The law requires that before the defendant can be found guilty upon either count in the indictment, every material allegation in it shall be proved beyond a reasonable doubt.

Now what do the words "beyond reasonable doubt" mean? Some courts do not favor an attempt to define them, thinking that the jury can judge as well without any suggestions. But I am unwilling to omit any further explanation, and I can in no way give you so accurate a description of their meaning, as by reading to you an extract from an opinion of the Court by whose views it is our duty to be governed. The Court says:

"Proof beyond reasonable doubt is not beyond all possible or imaginary doubt, but such proof as precludes every reasonable hypothesis or theory except that which it tends to support. It is proof to a moral certainty, as distinguished from an absolute certainty. As applied to a judicial trial for crime, the two phrases, 'beyond reasonable doubt,' and, 'to a moral certainty,' are synonymous and equivalent. They mean the same thing. Each has been used by eminent judges to explain the other, and each signifies such proof as satisfies the judgment and conscience of the jury as reasonable men, and applying their reason to the evidence before them, that the crime charged has been committed by the defendant, and so satisfies them as to leave no other reasonable conclusion possible. In other words, they must have as clear and strong a conviction in their own minds of the truth of that conclusion to be acted on by them as in matters of the highest importance to themselves."

Now you observe, gentlemen, that the Government submits this case to you upon circumstantial evidence. No witness testifies to seeing the defendant in the act of doing the crime charged, but the Government seeks to establish by proof a body of facts and circumstances from which you are asked to infer or conclude that the defendant killed Mr. and Mrs. Borden.

This is a legal and not unusual way of proving a criminal case, and it is clearly competent for a jury to find a person guilty of murder upon circumstantial evidence alone. Indeed, judges and juries have been somewhat divided in their views as to the comparative strength and value of circumstantial and direct evidence. In direct evidence witnesses testify that they have actual and immediate knowledge of the matter to be proved, so that the main thing to be determined is whether the witnesses are worthy of belief. The chief difficulty with this kind of evidence is that the witnesses may be false or mistaken, while the nature of the case may be such that there are no means of discovering the falsehood or mistake.

In circumstantial evidence the facts relied upon are usually various and testified to by a large number of witnesses, as you have seen in this case. When the evidence comes from several witnesses and different sources, it is thought that there is more difficulty in arranging it so as to escape detection if it is false or founded on mistake. The principle that underlies circumstantial evidence we are constantly acting on in our business, namely, the inferring of one fact from other facts proved.

Sometimes the inference is direct, and almost certain. For instance, the noise of a pistol is heard from a certain room in a hotel. The door is unlocked or otherwise opened. A man is found, just dead, with a bullet hole in his temple. Near him is a revolver with one barrel discharged. In such a case, if no contradictory or controlling facts appeared, we should infer, with a very strong assurance, that the death was caused by the pistol. In other cases the facts from which the conclusion is sought to be drawn are numerous and complicated, and the conclusion not so closely connected with the facts or so easy to draw.

This is illustrated by the case on trial here. You have got to go through a long and careful investigation to ascertain what facts are proved. This is the same process essentially that you go through in dealing with direct evidence. Then after you have determined what specific facts are proved, you have remaining the important duty of deciding whether or not you are justified in drawing, and will draw, from these facts the conclusion of guilt. Here, therefore, is a twofold liability to error, first in deciding upon the evidence what facts are proved, and second in deciding what inference or conclusion shall be drawn from the facts. This is often the critical or turning point in a case resting on circumstantial evidence. The law warrants you in acting firmly and with confidence on such evidence, but does require you to exercise a deliberate and sober judgment and use great caution not to form a hasty or erroneous conclusion. You are allowed to deal with this matter with your minds untramelled by any artificial or arbitrary rule or law. As a great judge has said, "The common law appeals to the plain dictates of common experience and sound judgment." The inference to be drawn from all the facts must be a reasonable and natural one, and, to a moral certainty, a certain one. It is not sufficient that it is probable only. It must be reasonably and morally certain.

In dealing with circumstantial evidence in such a case as this some special considerations need to be borne in mind. One of them is this: inasmuch as the conclusion of guilt, if reached at all, must be inferred or reached from other facts that are proved, every fact which in your judgment is so important and essential that without it the conclusion of guilt could not be reached must itself be proved beyond reasonable doubt, must be proved by the same weight and force of evidence as if it were the main fact in issue. But in seeking to establish a case by circumstantial evidence it may often happen that many facts are given in evidence, not because they are thought to be necessary to the conclusion sought to be proved, but to show that they are not inconsistent with that conclusion, but favorable to it and have some tendency to rebut a contrary presumption.

If any facts of this second class should fail to be proved to your satisfaction, that would not prevent you from drawing the conclusion of guilt from other facts, if they were sufficient to warrant it. In other words, failure to prove a fact essential to the conclusion of guilt, and without which that conclusion would not be reached, is fatal to the Government's case, but failure to prove a helpful but not an essential fact may not be fatal.

Now let me illustrate. Take an essential fact. All would admit that the necessity of establishing the presence of the defendant in the house, when, for instance, her father was killed, is a necessary fact. The Government could not expect that you would find her guilty of the murder of her father by her own hand unless you are satisfied that she was where he was when he was murdered. And if the evidence left you in reasonable doubt as to that fact, so vital, so absolutely essential, the Government must fail of its case, whatever may be the force and significance of other facts, that is, so far as it is claimed that she did the murder with her own hands.

Now, take the instance of a helpful fact. The question of the relation of this handleless hatchet to the murder. It may have an important bearing upon the case, upon your judgment of the relations of the defendant to these crimes, whether the crime was done by that particular hatchet or not, but it cannot be said, and is not claimed by the government that it bears the same essential and necessary relations to the case that the matter of her presence in the house does. It is not claimed by the Government but what that killing might have been done with some other instrument. Take another illustration. I understand the Government to claim substantially that the alleged fact that the defendant made a false statement in regard to her stepmother's having received a note or letter that morning bears an essential relation to the case, bears to it the relation of an essential fact, not merely the relation of a useful fact.

And so the counsel in his opening referring to that matter, charged deliberately upon the defendant that she had told a falsehood in regard to that note. In other words, that she had made statements about it which she knew at the time of making them were untrue, and the learned District Attorney, in his closing argument, adopts and reaffirms that charge against the defendant.

Now what are the grounds on which the Government claims that that charge is false, knowingly false? There are three, as I understand them,—one that the man who wrote it has not been found, second that the party who brought it has not been found and third that no letter has been found, and substantially, if I understand the position correctly, upon those three grounds you are asked to find that an essential fact—a deliberate falsehood on the part of the defendant—has been established.

Now what answer or reply is made to this charge? First, that the defendant had time to think of it; she was not put in a position upon the evidence where she was compelled to make that statement without any opportunity for reflection. If, as the Government claims, she had killed her stepmother some little time before, she had a period in which she could turn over the matter in her mind. She must naturally anticipate, if she knew the facts, that the question at no remote period would be asked where Mrs. Borden was, or if she knew where she was. She might reasonably and naturally expect that the question would arise. Again, it will be urged in her behalf, what motive had she to invent a story like this? What motive? Would it not have answered every purpose to have her say, and would it not have been more natural for her to say simply, that her stepmother had gone out on an errand or to make a call? What motive had she to take upon herself the responsibility of giving utterance to this distinct and independent fact of a letter or note received with which she might be confronted and which she might afterwards find it difficult to explain, if she knew that no such thing was true? Was it a natural thing to say, situated as they were, living as they did, taking the general tenor of their ordinary life, was it a natural thing for her to invent? But it is said no letter was found. Suppose you look at the case for a moment from her standpoint, contemplate the possibility of there being another assassin than herself, might it not be a part of the plan, or scheme, of such a person by such a document or paper to withdraw Mrs. Borden from the house? If he afterwards came in there, came upon her, killed her, might he not have found the letter or note with her, if there was one already in the room? Might he not have a reasonable and natural wish to remove that as one possible link in tracing himself? Taking the suggestions on the one side and the other, judging the matter fairly, not assuming beforehand that the defendant is guilty, does the evidence satisfy you as reasonable men beyond reasonable doubt that these statements of the defendant in regard to that note must necessarily be false? Sometimes able judges and writers in dealing with circumstantial evidence have made use of illustrations. They have compared the indispensable facts to the several links in a chain. If one link of the chain breaks, the chain ceases to serve its purpose as a chain, no matter how strong the remaining links may be. So in the chain of circumstantial evidence, if one essential fact fails to be proved, the connection is broken, a gap arises in the process of proof and it cannot be legally affirmed that the conclusion aimed at is established beyond reasonable doubt.

Sometimes the process of proof by circumstances is compared to a rope cable, and the several facts that may be material but not absolutely essential to the conclusion, are likened to the strands or cords in that cable. Some of the strands or cords may give way and yet the cable may not be broken, but may bear the strain put upon it. So in the process of proof by circumstantial evidence. Important but not absolutely essential facts may fail to be established, and the loss of them, while it may weaken, may not destroy the force of the remaining evidence. But I much doubt whether in ordinary life in reaching a solution and determination of problems that arise, the elements on which our decision depends assume, either in the visible outward world or in our minds, the relation to each other of links in a chain or strands in a cable. Some of the facts may have a real connection with each other so that one may involve or imply the other; and they may thereby have additional weight and importance to us. Another fact may be independent of the rest, may have no connection with them in the real and outward world, the only connection being in our minds, and yet this separate fact may be decisive upon our conclusion. Let me illustrate: Suppose a gentleman already engaged in business is proposing to himself to start some kind of manufacturing business in this city. He inquires into the matter, the cost of his plant, the facilities for transportation, the cost of making the article intended, the probable demand for, and the price of, the goods in the market, and all such other things that a prudent man would consider, and reaches the conclusion with a clear and strong assurance on which he is ready to act, that he will go forward with the enterprise. He then mentions his plan to his family physician. The physician at once says to him: "This new enterprise may promise all that you think of it, but you must not undertake it. You are already carrying all the burden that your strength of body or mind will endure. If you take on another burden there is great danger that it will be disastrous to you." Having confidence in the skill and fidelity of his physician and believing the opinion given to be correct, he at once decides to relinquish the enterprise. Now we see a large body of facts leading to a certain conclusion are controlled by one separate fact opposed to that conclusion. Yet the body of facts and the separate fact have no connection with each other, save in the person's mind. This body of facts had nothing to do with causing his state of health, and his state of health had nothing to do with the body of facts.

Hence it is a rule in the use of circumstantial evidence that as every real fact is connected with every other real fact, so every fact proved must be reasonably consistent with the main fact sought to be proved,—namely in this case, the fact of the defendant's guilt. However numerous may be the facts in the Government's process of proof tending to show defendant's guilt, yet if there is a fact established—whether in that line of proof or outside of it—which cannot be reasonably reconciled with her guilt, then guilt cannot be said to be established. Now gentlemen, you know that I am expressing no opinion as to what is proved. I am only trying to illustrate principles and rules of law and evidence. Referring to the present case let me use this illustration: Suppose you were clearly satisfied upon the testimony that if the defendant committed the homicides she could by no reasonable possibility have done so without receiving upon her person and clothing a considerable amount of blood stain; that when Bridget Sullivan came to her upon call and, not long after, some of the other women, she had no blood stains upon her person or clothing; that she had had no sufficient opportunity either to remove the stain from her clothing, or to change her clothing. If these supposed facts should be found by you to be real facts, you could not say upon the evidence that the defendant's guilt was to a moral certainty proved. So you see that in estimating the force of different facts, or portions of the evidence, it is not enough to consider them as standing apart, for the force which they appear to have when looked at by themselves may be controlled by some other single fact. In order to warrant a conviction on circumstantial evidence it is not necessary for the Government to show that by no possibility was it in the power of any other person than the defendant to commit the crimes; but the evidence must be such as to produce a conviction amounting to a reasonable and moral certainty that the defendant and no one else did commit them. The Government claims that you should be satisfied upon the evidence that the defendant was so situated that she had an opportunity to perpetrate both the crimes charged upon her. Whether this claim is sustained is for your judgment. By itself alone the fact, if shown, that the defendant had the opportunity to commit the crimes would not justify a conviction; but this fact, if established, becomes a matter for your consideration in connection with the other evidence. When was Mrs. Borden killed? At what time was Mr. Borden killed? Did the same person kill both of them? Was the defendant in the house when Mrs. Borden was killed? Was she in the house when Mr. Borden was killed? In this connection you will carefully consider any statements and explanations of the defendant put in evidence by the Government and shown to have been made by the defendant at the time or afterwards, as to where she was when either of them was killed, and all other evidence tending to sustain or disprove the truth and accuracy of these statements. Did other persons, known or unknown, have an equal or a practical and available opportunity to commit these crimes? Is there reason to believe that any such person had any motive to commit them? Is there anything in the way and manner of doing the acts of killing, the weapon used, whatever it was, or the force applied, which is significant as to the sex and strength of the doer of the acts? For instance, the medical experts have testified as to the way in which they think the blows were inflicted on Mrs. Borden, and as to what they think was the position of the assailant. Are these views correct? If so, are they favorable to the contention that a person of the defendant's sex and size was the assailant? Is it reasonable and credible that she could have killed Mrs. Borden at or about the time claimed by the Government, and then with the purpose in her mind to kill her father at a later hour, have gone about her household affairs with no change of manner to excite attention? As you have the right to reason from what you know of the laws and properties of matter, so you have a right to reason and judge from what you know of the laws and property of human nature and action; and if it is suggested that the killing of Mr. Borden was not a part of the original plan, that it was an incident arising afterwards, it will be for you to consider under all circumstances, and upon all the evidence, whether that suggestion seems to you to be reasonable and well founded.

Several witnesses called by the Government have testified to statements said to have been made by the defendant in reply to questions asked, I believe in each instance, as to where she was when her father was killed, and considerable importance is attached by the Government to the language which it is claimed was used by her as showing that she professed not only to have been in the barn, but upstairs in the barn. And the Government further claims it is not worthy of belief that she was in the upper part of the barn, as she says, because of the extreme heat there and because one of the officers testifies that on examination they found no tracks in the dust on the stairs and flooring. Now what statements on the subject the defendant did make and their significance and effect is wholly for you to decide upon the evidence, and there is no rule of law to control your judgment in weighing that evidence. But here, gentlemen, I may repeat to you the language of a thoughtful writer on the law, not as binding upon you, but as containing suggestions useful to be borne in mind in dealing with this class of evidence. He says, "With respect to all verbal admissions it may be observed that they ought to be received with great caution. The evidence, consisting as it does, in the mere repetition of oral statements, is subject to much imperfection and mistake, and the party himself either being misinformed, or not having clearly expressed his own meaning, or the witness having misunderstood him. It frequently happens also that the witness, by unintentionally altering a few of the expressions really used, gives an effect to the statement completely at variance with what the party actually did say. But where the admission is deliberately made and precisely identified, the evidence it affords is often of the most satisfactory nature."

Gentlemen, it will be for you to judge whether that extract which I read, which I say I give to you in the way of suggestion and not as a binding authority, expresses a reasonable principle, a principle that is wise and safe and prudent to be acted upon in such a case as this—whether there is not more danger of misunderstanding, some inaccuracy, some error creeping into evidence when it relates to statements than there is when it relates to acts. Would you not hold that it was a just and reasonable view to take that if a party is to be held responsible in a case like this largely upon statements, that those statements should be most carefully and thoroughly proved?

Now the Government has called as witnesses some gentlemen of scientific and medical knowledge and experience, who are termed experts, and there has been put into the case considerable testimony from them. Now, following a distinction which I have before pointed out, I think I may say to you that expert testimony constitutes a class of evidence which the law requires you to subject to careful scrutiny. It is a matter of frequent observation to see experts of good standing expressing conflicting and irreconcilable views upon questions arising at a trial. They sometimes manifest a strong bias or partisan spirit in favor of the party employing them. They often exhibit a disposition to put forward theories rather than to verify or establish or illustrate the facts. While they are supposed to testify on matters not the subject of common knowledge and experience, and in distinction from ordinary witnesses, are allowed to express their opinion where the ordinary witness could not, yet when the jury passes judgment upon them and their testimony they have no peculiar privileges. The jury has the full right to consider them, their appearance, their candor or want of it, their apparent skill, the reasons they give in support of their view, the nature of any experiments which they have made, the consistency or otherwise of what they say with other proved facts or with the common knowledge and experience of the jury and finally, acting under a due sense of their responsibilities, to give to the testimony of the experts such value and weight as it seems to deserve. It often happens that experts testify to what is in substance a matter of fact rather than of opinion. A surveyor called to prove the distance between two points may express his opinions founded on his observation, or he may say, "I have actually applied my measuring chain and found the distance." So, for instance, Professor Wood may say, "There are in science tests of the presence of blood as fixed and certain as the surveyor's chain is of distance. I have applied those tests to supposed blood stains on a hatchet, and I find no blood"; or "I have applied them to stains on a piece of board furnished, and I find it to be a blood stain." This testimony may be regarded as little a matter of opinion as the testimony of a surveyor. On the other hand, if Professor Wood shall be asked to testify as to the length of time between the deaths of Mr. and Mrs. Borden, from his examination of the contents of the stomachs, his testimony must perhaps be to some extent a matter of opinion, depending possibly on the health and vigor of the two persons and constitutional differences; upon whether they were physically active after eating, or at rest; upon whether one or the other was mentally worried and anxious, or otherwise. Now his knowledge and skill may enable him to form an opinion upon the subject with greater or less correctness; but the question to be dealt with is by its essential nature different from the other. If you should accept his testimony as correct and satisfactory on the first subject, it would not necessarily follow that you should on the second. So as to whether certain wounds in the skull were caused by a particular hatchet head or could have been caused by that hatchet head only, if you have the hatchet head and the skull, you may think you can apply them to each other and judge as well as the expert. I call your attention to the subject in this way to make clear to you, first, that you are not concluded on any subject by the testimony of the experts, and, second, that it is important to apply to their testimony an intelligent and discriminating judgment. So doing, you may find that each person who has appeared as an expert has so testified as to warrant your confidence in his skill and knowledge, in his fairness, and in the correctness of his opinions.

Now, gentlemen, I have been asked by the counsel for the Commonwealth to give you instructions upon another view of this case, a view, so far as I remember, not suggested in the opening, or in the evidence, or hardly in the closing arguments for the Commonwealth. And yet the evidence is of such a nature that it seems to us that as a matter of law, the Government is entitled to have some instructions given you on this point; as a matter of fact, it would be entirely for you to consider whether the claim of the Government upon the matter to which I am going to refer is consistent with the claim which it has urged to you; whether the Government has not put this case to you, practically, upon the idea that the defendant did these acts with her own hands.

But it is a principle of law that a person may be indicted in just the form in which this defendant is indicted, that is, indicted as if she were charged with doing the act herself, and yet she may be convicted upon the evidence which satisfies a jury beyond reasonable doubt that the act was done personally by another party, and that her relation to it was that of being present, aiding, abetting, sustaining, encouraging. If she stood in such a relation as that to the act, the act was done by some other person and she aided him, encouraged him, abetted him, was present somewhere, by virtue of an understanding with him, where she could render him assistance, and for the purpose of rendering assistance, then she would be a principal in the act just as much as the other party who might be acting.

But you notice the essential elements. There must have been an understanding between her and her third party, if there was one, an agreement together for the commission of these crimes. She must have given her assent to it. She must have encouraged it. She must have been in a position where she could render assistance to the perpetrator, with his knowledge, by virtue of an understanding with him, and for the purpose of giving assistance either in the way of watching against some person's coming or furnishing him facilities for escape or in some other manner. The central idea of this proposition is that she must have been present by virtue of an agreement with the actor where she could render assistance of some kind, and for the purpose of rendering assistance. And if there was another party in this crime, and if she is proved beyond reasonable doubt to have sustained the relation to him in committing that crime which I have expressed to you, then she might be held under this indictment, because under such circumstances in the eye of the law, they both being in the sense of the law present, the act of one is the act of both.

Gentlemen, something has been said to you by counsel as to defendant's not testifying. I must speak to you on this subject. The constitution of our State in its Bill of Rights provides that "No subject shall be compelled to accuse or furnish evidence against himself." By the common law, persons on trial have no right to testify in their own defense. We have now a statute in these words, "In the trial of all indictments, complaints, and other proceedings against persons charged with the commission of crimes or offenses, a person so charged shall, at his own request, but not otherwise, be deemed a competent witness; and his neglect or refusal to testify shall not create any presumption against him." You will notice that guarded language of the statute. It recognizes and affirms the common law rule that the defendant in a criminal prosecution is an incompetent witness for himself, but it provides that on one condition only, namely, his own request, he shall be deemed competent. Till that request is made he remains incompetent. In this case the defendant has made no such request, and she stands before you, therefore, as a witness incompetent, and it is clearly your duty to consider this case and form your judgment upon it as if the defendant had no right whatever to testify.

The Supreme Court, speaking of a defendant's rights and protection under the constitution and statutes, uses these words: "Nor can any inference be drawn against him from his failure to testify." Therefore I say to you, and I mean all that my words express, any argument, any implication, any suggestion, any consideration, in your minds, unfavorable to the defendant based on her failure to testify is unwarranted in law.

Nor is the defendant called upon to offer any explanation of her neglect to testify. If she were required to explain, others might think the explanation insufficient. Then she would lose the protection of the statute. It is a matter which the law submits to her own discretion and to that alone. You can see, gentlemen, that there may be cases where this right to testify would be valuable to a defendant. It may be able to afford the jury some further information or give some explanation that would help the defense. In another case where there was no doubt that an offense had been committed by someone, he might have no knowledge as to how or by whom it was done, and could only affirm under oath his innocence, which is already presumed. The defendant may say, "I have already told to the officers all that I know about this case, and my statements have been put in evidence: whatever is mysterious to others is also mysterious to me. I have no knowledge more than others have. I have never professed to be able to explain how or by whom these homicides were committed."

There is another reason why the defendant might not wish to testify. Now she is sacredly guarded by the law from all unfavorable inferences drawn from her silence. If she testifies, she becomes a witness with less than the privileges of an ordinary witness. She is subject to cross-examination. She may be asked questions that are legally competent which she is not able to answer, or she may answer questions truly and yet it may be argued against her that her answers were untrue, and her neglect to answer perverse. Being a party, she is exposed to peculiar danger of having her conduct on the stand and her testimony severely scrutinized and perhaps misjudged, of having her evidence claimed to be of little weight, if favorable to herself, and of great weight so far as any part of it shall admit of an adverse construction. She is left free, therefore, to avoid such risks.

Gentlemen, we have given our attention to particular aspects of this case and of the evidence. Let us look at it broadly.

The Government charges the defendant with the murder of Mr. and Mrs. Borden. The defendant denies the charges. The law puts on the Government the burden of proving beyond reasonable doubt every fact necessary to establish guilt. The defendant is bound to prove nothing. The law presumes she is innocent. The case is said to be mysterious. If so, the defendant cannot be required to clear up the mystery. There is no way, under the law, by which the burden of proof as to any essential matter can be transferred to her. The Government offers evidence. She may rest on the insufficiency of that evidence to prove her guilt, or she may also offer evidence partially to meet or rebut it, or raise a reasonable doubt as to any part of the Government's case.

You are not to deal with the evidence in a captious spirit, but to allow it to produce on your minds its natural and proper effect. You are to think of it and reason upon it in the same way you think and reason on other matters, only remembering the strict proof to which the Government is held by the law.

In such a case as this, or in any case, you cannot be absolutely certain of the correctness of your conclusions. The law does not require you to be so. If, proceeding with due caution and observant of the principles which have been stated, you are convinced beyond reasonable doubt of the defendant's guilt, it will be your plain duty to declare that conviction by your verdict. If the evidence falls short of producing such conviction in your mind, although it may raise a suspicion of guilt, or even a strong probability of guilt, it would be your plain duty to return a verdict of not guilty. If not legally proved to be guilty, the defendant is entitled to a verdict of not guilty. The law contemplates no middle course.

You will be inquired of by the clerk as to each count of the indictment separately and in the same manner. If you find the defendant guilty of murder in the first degree, the Foreman, in reply to the inquiry of the clerk, will say, "Guilty of murder in the first degree," and so as to murder in the second degree, if you find that to be the degree of murder. As to the second count, if the finding is the same, the answer should be the same. If, on the other hand, your finding is "Not guilty," the Foreman should so reply to each inquiry.

Gentlemen, I want to refer at this point briefly to one or two matters, not in a connected way, where it seems proper to me that a brief suggestion should be made. Something was said in the arguments in regard to the defendant's attitude towards the officers, and criticism made of the officers by defendant's counsel, not by her.

Of course there are certain senses in which a party is represented in Court by his counsel or her counsel and bound by their action. But in a matter relating to the personal guilt of the defendant, where evidence is sought to establish that guilt, I do not understand that the law turns the attention of the Jury to any action of the Counsel. The action of the Counsel may affect her in some ways, may affect her legal rights, but the question is: Is she guilty? Has she done anything which, as a matter of evidence, should be reckoned against her?

Now take this question of her relations to the officers. Turn over the evidence, recall so far as you can, every portion of it, and do you recall any portion—it will be for you to determine whether you do or not—do you recall any portion of the evidence where it appears that at any time, any place, under any circumstances she found any fault with the officers for asking her questions or making searches? Something was said in the argument—properly said because the Counsel charged with the duty of presenting the evidence to the Jury in such a light as they honestly think the evidence ought to be considered and weighed,—in regard to statements alleged to have been made by the defendant. The duty of Counsel for the Government is different from that of the Jury and different from that of the Court. Primarily it is,—while they do not seek to do anything wrong or to mislead the Jury or to introduce any untrue evidence—to present to the attention of the Jury those things that make for the side which they are sustaining or seeking to sustain. I said something was said in regard to the statements which there was evidence tending to show the defendant had made in regard to presentiments of some disaster to come upon the household; and as I understand the argument, you were asked to look upon those statements, which were testified to by one of the witnesses, as evidence tending to show that the defendant might have been harboring in her mind purposes of evil with reference to the household—statements made only, I believe, the day before this calamity fell on the household, only the day before the deed was done by the defendant, if she did it.

Now, in considering that evidence, you should not necessarily go off in your view of it upon the suggestion of counsel, but, so far as you deem it important, hold it before your minds, look at it in all its lights and bearings, and see whether it seems to you reasonable and probable that a person meditating the perpetration of a great crime would, the day before, predict to a friend, either in form or in substance, the happening of that disaster. Should any different principle be applied to such a statement made by the defendant with reference to her own family than should be applied to the statement which one man might make to another man and his family?

Suppose some person in New Bedford contemplated the perpetration of a great crime upon the person or family of another citizen in New Bedford, contemplated doing it soon. Would he naturally, probably, predict, a day or two beforehand, that anything of the nature of that crime would occur? Is the reasonable construction to be put upon that conversation that of evil premeditation, dwelt upon, intended, or only of evil fears and apprehensions?

Take this matter of the dress, of which so much has been said, that she had on that morning. Take all the evidence in this case, Bridget Sullivan's, the testimony of these ladies, Dr. Bowen's. Lay aside for the moment the question of the identification of this dress that is presented. Taking the evidence of these several witnesses, considering that evidence carefully, comparing part with part, can you, gentlemen, extract from that testimony such a description of a dress as would enable you from the testimony to identify the dress? Is there such an agreement among these witnesses, to whom no wrong intention is imputed by anybody—is there such an agreement in their accounts and in their memory and recollection, and in the description which they are able to give from the observation that they had in that time of confusion and excitement, that you could put their statements together, and from those statements say that any given dress was accurately described?

Then take, again, the matter of Mrs. Reagan's testimony. It is suggested that there has been no denial of that testimony, or, rather, that the persons who busied themselves about getting the certificate from Mrs. Reagan had no denial of it.

Mr. Knowlton: Not by me, sir. I admit it.

Dewey, J.: Admit what?

Mr. Knowlton: That she did deny it.

Dewey, J.: Mrs. Reagan?

Mr. Knowlton: Yes, sir.

Dewey, J.: Oh, no doubt about that. It is not claimed that Mrs. Reagan does not deny it. But I say it is suggested that the parties who represented the defendant in the matter, and who were seeking to get a certificate from Mrs. Reagan, were proceeding without having received any authority to get the certificate, and without having had any assurance from anybody that the statement was false and one that ought to be denied.

You have heard the statement of Miss Emma about it here; and it would be for you to judge, as reasonable men, whether such men as Mr. Holmes and the clergymen and the other parties who were interesting themselves in that matter, started off attempting to get a certificate from Mrs. Reagan contradicting that report, without first having taken any steps to satisfy themselves that it was a report that ought to be contradicted.

Gentlemen, I know not what views you may take of the case, but it is of the gravest importance that it should be decided. If decided at all it must be decided by a jury. I know of no reason to expect that any other jury could be supplied with more evidence or be better assisted by the efforts of counsel. The case on both sides has been conducted by counsel with great fairness, industry, and ability. You are to confer together; and this implies that each of you, in recollecting and weighing the evidence, may be aided by the memory and judgment of his associates. The law requires that the jury shall be unanimous in their verdict, and it is their duty to agree if they can conscientiously do so. And now, gentlemen, the case is committed into your hands. The tragedy which has given rise to this investigation deeply excited public attention and feeling. The press has administered to this excitement by publishing without moderation rumors and reports of all kinds. This makes it difficult to secure a trial free from prejudice. You have doubtless read, previous to the trial, more or less of the accounts and discussions in the newspapers. Some of you, when you were selected as jurors, said that you had formed impressions about the case, but thought that they would not prevent you from giving a candid judgment upon a full hearing of the testimony. Doubtless you were sincere in that declaration; but in this matter you will need great care and watchfulness, for we are often influenced in forming our judgments by what we have heard or read at some previous time, more than we are conscious of. You must guard so far as possible against all impressions derived from having read in the newspapers accounts relating to the question you have to decide. You cannot consistently with your duty go into any discussion of those accounts or in any way use or refer to them. Your attention should be given to the evidence only, for the discovery of the facts, and any other course would be contrary to your duty.

And, entering on your deliberations with no pride of opinion, with impartial and thoughtful minds, seeking only for the truth, you will lift the case above the range of passion and prejudice and excited feeling, into the clear atmosphere of reason and law. If you shall be able to do this, we can hope that, in some high sense, this trial may be adopted into the order of Providence, and may express in its results somewhat of that justice with which God governs the world.

Memorandum of Law

Memorandum in support of the proposition that evidence offered by the prosecution that Lizzie Borden attempted to purchase deadly poison (prussic acid) the afternoon before the murders should have been admitted by the Borden trial Court.

This circumstantial evidence, excluded by the Borden Court, tended to show a prior design or plan to commit the murders, although by a means different from that eventually used.

"The kinds of conduct which may evidence a design [to kill] are innumerable in their variety. Any act which under the circumstances and according to experience, as naturally interpreted and applied, would indicate a probable design, is relevant and admissible."

Wigmore: Evidence Section 238

"The acquisition or possession of instruments, tools, or other means of doing the act, is admissible as a significant circumstance, the possession [or attempt to procure] signifies a probable design to use: the instruments need not be such as are entirely appropriate, *nor such as were actually put to use.*"

Wigmore: Evidence, Section 238

"Since malice can not usually be directly proved, the evidence thereof being circumstantial, any facts going to establish an inference of its existence are admissible, and *evidence of preparation is always admissible.*"

Warren on Homicide, Section 201

Thus:

"The state in a murder case *may prove the purchase* or possession of firearms, *poison* or drug by the accused, to show preparation for the commission of the crime."

Warren on Homicide, Section 201

Both Warren and Wigmore are in agreement that *the instrument purchased need not be actually used.* For this proposition both cite *Mobley v State, 41 Fla. 621, 26 So. 732.* In this case the murder was committed *by stabbing,* but evidence of the *prior purchase of poison* by the defendant was admitted as indicating a design to kill the deceased. In *State v Saale, 308 Mo. 573, 274 S.W. 393* the Missouri Court stated that it was competent to prove that the accused had a pistol prior to the killing, even though the homicide was not committed with it. See also: *State v Webster, 21 Wash. 63, 57 Pac. 361,* and *People v Cuff, 122 Cal. 589, 55 Pac. 407.*

In *Walsh v People, 88 N.Y. 458* the defendant was tried for the murder of a young girl. It was established that on the morning of the crime the defendant asked a fellow employee about the effect of throwing pepper into a person's eyes and if the person would be blinded. In holding such evidence admissible against the defendant the New York Court held in *Walsh* (1882):

> ". . . *it was for the jury to determine* upon all the competent evidence, tending to show deliberation, whether this element [intent] of the crime of murder existed. The conversation in respect to the pepper tended to show that the prisoner *was meditating the commission of a personal injury upon someone, and it was so proximately related to the other circumstances and to the commission of the crime charged that the jury would be entitled to infer that the prisoner was then meditating injury to the deceased.*"

* * *

Nor did Massachusetts suffer from a paucity of case law on this particular question. In *Commonwealth v Turner, 3 Metcalf 19,* decided in *1841,* the defendant was charged with kidnapping an eight year old Negro boy with the intent to sell him as a slave in Virginia. The Court, exercising its discretion, allowed evidence to be presented to the jury that the defendant attempted to kidnap another Negro boy *one day* prior to the offense charged. In material part the Supreme Judicial Court said:

> "*It is always competent* to resort to evidence of *other transactions* by the defendant whenever it is necessary to establish the guilty knowledge of the party . . . Evidence of other facts than those connected immediately with the act charged *are always admissible, when the intent of the defendant forms a material part of the issue,* and where those facts can be supposed to have any proper tendency to establish that intent."

In 1878, in the case of *Commonwealth v Bradford, 126 Mass. 42,* the Supreme Judicial Court set out the criteria which the Borden Court rejected, or ignored, in the exclusion of the prussic acid evidence.

In this case the defendant was being tried for the burning of a building. The trial judge admitted evidence offered by the prosecution to show that three days earlier the defendant had attempted to burn the same building. In permitting the evidence to go to the jury, the trial judge had instructed, "The only use to which the jury may apply this evidence was to determine the intent of the defendant."

In *Bradford* the Supreme Judicial Court said:

"The evidence was competent on the question of the intent with which the defendant subsequently burned the building . . . The unsuccessful attempt to do the same thing a few days before was evidence that the burning was wilful and intentional. *It was sufficiently near to the time of the commission of the offense* charged to justify the inference that the defendant then had a settled purpose . . . *When a previous act indicates an existing purpose* which, from known rules of human conduct, may fairly be presumed to continue and control the defendant in the doing of the act in question, it is admissible in evidence . . . The limit to its admission is that *it must be sufficiently significant in character*, and *sufficiently near in point of time* to afford a presumption that the element sought to be established existed at the time of the offense charged."

See also *Commonwealth v McCarthy, 119 Mass. 354*, decided in 1876.

Conclusion: Although it may be argued that exclusion of the prussic-acid evidence was discretionary with the Court, it must be said that such a use of discretion, in the circumstances of the Borden case, was an abuse of discretion. Nonetheless, an error that could not be reviewed since the Commonwealth had no right of appeal and since there was an acquittal.

Clearly the Borden Court's exclusion of this evidence, prejudicial as it was to the prosecution, contradicted the text authorities and the case law in Massachusetts and elsewhere, as that law was in 1893 and as it is today.

BIBLIOGRAPHY

American Bar Association Project of Standards for Criminal Justice, *Standards Relating to the Function of the Trial Judge.* American Bar Association, 1972.

American Bar Association Projects of Minimum Standards for Criminal Justice, *Fair Trial and Free Press.* American Bar Association, 1966.

Birkett, The Lord, *The Art of Advocacy.* Harmondsworth, Middlesex, England: Penguin Books Ltd, 1961.

Borden, Lizzie A., The Trial of, 2 Volumes. Official Transcript of the Massachusetts Superior Court, Transcribed by Philip H. Burt, Official Stenographer for the Superior Court: Boston, 1893. (Microtext, Boston Public Library: 1971)

Borden, Lizzie A., Will of. Bristol County Registry of Probate.

Centennial History of Fall River. New York: Atlantic Publishing and Engraving Co., 1877.

Centennial of the Superior Court of the Commonwealth of Massachusetts, 1859–1959. Boston: 1959.

Clarkson, Paul S., *The Goddard Biblio Log.* Volume II, No. 3. Worcester: Clark University, Friends of the Goddard Library, 1972.

Cushing, Luther S., *Reports of Cases Argued and Determined in the Supreme Judicial Court of Massachusetts,* Vol. V. Boston: Little, Brown and Co., 1852.

Chandler, Peleg W., "Bathsheba Spooner," *American Criminal Trials,* 2 Volumes. Boston: 1841, 1842.

Davis, Charles G., *Collection of Articles Concerning the Borden Case.* Boston: 1893.

Dimond, Alan J., *The Superior Court of Massachusetts—Its Origin and Development.* Boston: Little, Brown and Co., 1960.

de Mille, Agnes, *Lizzie Borden: A Dance of Death.* Boston: Atlantic Monthly, Little, Brown and Co., 1968.

Dershowitz, Alan P., and Goldberg, Arthur J., "Declaring the Death Penalty Unconstitutional," *Harvard Law Review*, June, 1970. Cambridge, Mass.

Eliot, Charles W., *The Works of Robert Burns*, Volume VI. New York: Harvard Classics, P. F. Collier & Son Co., 1910.

——*The Works of Allan Cunningham*, Volume 41, Harvard Classics. New York: P. F. Collier & Son Co., 1910.

Essex County Bar Association, *Minutes of Memorial Proceedings for William Henry Moody*. Salem, Mass.: April 26, 1919.

Fall River, City of, *City Directory*. 1892.

——*City Directory*. 1973.

Fowler, Reverend Orin, *History of Fall River*. Fall River: Almy & Milne Press, 1862.

Howe, Mark A. DeWolfe, *Boston: The Place and the People*. New York: The Macmillan Company, 1903.

Kennedy, Edward M. v James A. Boyle, as he is the Justice of the District Court of Dukes County, Commonwealth of Massachusetts, Supreme Judicial Court, Suffolk County, Boston, Mass., Case No. 14421. Boston: Press of George H. Dean Co., 1969.

Lane, Roger, *Policing the City*. Cambridge, Mass.: Harvard University Press, 1967.

Lyons, Louis M., *One Hundred Years of the Boston Globe*. Cambridge, Mass.: Belknap Press of Harvard University, 1971.

Manual for the Use of the General Court, Commonwealth of Massachusetts for 1971–72. Boston: Wright & Potter Printing Co., 1971.

McDade, Thomas M., *The Annals of Murder: A Bibliography of Books and Pamphlets on American Murders from Colonial Times to 1900*. Norman, Okla.: University of Oklahoma Press, 1961.

Morison, Samuel Eliot, *Builders of the Bay Colony*. Boston: Houghton Mifflin Co., 1930.

Mottla, Gabriel V., *Proof of Cases in Massachusetts*. Rochester, N.Y.: Lawyer's Cooperative Publishing Co., 1966. Supplements yearly.

New England Historical and Genealogical Register. Boston: Samuel A. Drake; published quarterly from 1847.

Philipps, Arthur Sherman, *History of Fall River*. Fall River: privately printed, 1946.

Porter, Edwin H., *The Fall River Tragedy*. Fall River: published privately, 1893.

Reno, Conrad, *Memoirs of the Judiciary and the Bar of New England for the*

Nineteenth Century, 2 vols., Leonard A. Jones and Conrad Reno, eds. Boston: The Century Memorial Publishing Co., 1900.

Roughead, William, "To Meet Miss Madeleine Smith: A Gossip on the Wonder Heroine of the 'Fifties," *Mainly Murder*. London: Cassell and Company Ltd., 1937.

————"The Mulbuie Murder," *Malice Domestic*. Garden City, N.Y.: Doubleday, Doran & Company, Inc., 1929.

Smith, Kent B., *Criminal Practice and Procedure*, Massachusetts Practice Volume 30. St. Paul, Minn.: West Publishing Co., 1970.

Sullivan, Robert, *The Disappearance of Dr. Parkman*. Boston: Little, Brown and Co., 1971.

Sutherland, Sidney, "The Mystery of the Puritan Girl," *Liberty Magazine*, Vol. I, No. 6. New York: 1927.

Warren, Oscar Leroy, and Belas, Basil Michael, *Warren on Homicide*, 5 vols. Buffalo, N.Y.: Dennis & Co., Inc. Various editions.

Weld, H. B., *The Borden Family*. Fall River: published privately, 1896.

Wigmore, John H., "The Borden Case," 27 *American Law Review*. 1893.

————*A Treatise on the Anglo-American System of Evidence in Trials at Common Law, Including the Statutes and Judicial Decisions of the United States and Canada*, 10 vols., 3rd ed. Boston: Little, Brown and Co.

Willard, Joseph A., *Collection of Photographs*. Boston: Social Law Library, n.d.

————*Half a Century With Judges and Lawyers*. Boston: Houghton Mifflin Co., 1895.

Windsor, Justin, *Memorial History of Boston*, 4 vols. Boston: James R. Osgood & Co., 1881.

Woollcott, Alexander, "The Theory and Lizzie Borden," *Vanity Fair*, Cleveland Amory and Frederic Bradlee, eds. New York: The Viking Press, 1960.

INDEX